1,000,000 Books

are available to read at

www.ForgottenBooks.com

Read online
Download PDF
Purchase in print

ISBN 978-0-260-85669-2
PIBN 11193152

This book is a reproduction of an important historical work. Forgotten Books uses
state-of-the-art technology to digitally reconstruct the work, preserving the original format
whilst repairing imperfections present in the aged copy. In rare cases, an imperfection in
the original, such as a blemish or missing page, may be replicated in our edition. We do,
however, repair the vast majority of imperfections successfully; any imperfections that
remain are intentionally left to preserve the state of such historical works.

Forgotten Books is a registered trademark of FB &c Ltd.
Copyright © 2018 FB &c Ltd.
FB &c Ltd, Dalton House, 60 Windsor Avenue, London, SW19 2RR.
Company number 08720141. Registered in England and Wales.

For support please visit www.forgottenbooks.com

1 MONTH OF
FREE
READING

at
www.ForgottenBooks.com

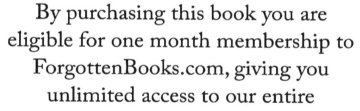

By purchasing this book you are eligible for one month membership to ForgottenBooks.com, giving you unlimited access to our entire collection of over 1,000,000 titles via our web site and mobile apps.

To claim your free month visit:
www.forgottenbooks.com/free1193152

* Offer is valid for 45 days from date of purchase. Terms and conditions apply.

English
Français
Deutsche
Italiano
Español
Português

www.forgottenbooks.com

Mythology Photography **Fiction**
Fishing Christianity **Art** Cooking
Essays Buddhism Freemasonry
Medicine **Biology** Music **Ancient**
Egypt Evolution Carpentry Physics
Dance Geology **Mathematics** Fitness
Shakespeare **Folklore** Yoga Marketing
Confidence Immortality Biographies
Poetry **Psychology** Witchcraft
Electronics Chemistry History **Law**
Accounting **Philosophy** Anthropology
Alchemy Drama Quantum Mechanics
Atheism Sexual Health **Ancient History**
Entrepreneurship Languages Sport
Paleontology Needlework Islam
Metaphysics Investment Archaeology
Parenting Statistics Criminology
Motivational

CONTENTS

The Staff

J. E. Hemby
Ass't Business Mgr.

Tullio A. Pagents
Business Mgr.

Fred J. Horan
University Notes

Henry C. Vail
Editor-in-Chief

Daniel P. Meagher S.J.
Director

Martin A. Murphy
Alumni

Edmund J. Conan
Circulation Mgr.

James E. Neary
Athletics

The Redwood

Entered Dec. 18, 1902, at Santa Clara, Cal., as second-class matter, under Act of Congress of March 3, 1879

| VOL. XIX | SANTA CLARA, CAL., OCTOBER, 1919 | NO. 1 |

The Redwood

EONS have graved their story round my heart
 In mystic records of revolving years,
Whose centuries of circles, like a chart,
 When prone my form lies damp with forest tears,
 Shall pristine age reveal to questing seers;
For I am old as Greece's throne of art
Or Rome's red yoke of war. Sublime my part
 Religious in the scheme of things that are---
My contemplation of the million spheres
 Which fleck yon ether like a spangled sea---
My gratefulness that each celestial star,
 Divinely guided, joins with even a tree
In praise of Him who writeth near and far
 His Authorship of all things else---and me!

CHAS. D. SOUTH

T was just at that period of the day when all manual labor, noticeably lags, and plowmen sleep amid the grass, where they are safe, both from the insects, and the eagle eye of the Spanish overseer, that a slender, well-formed figure, in the elaborate dress of a Mexican caballero sat musingly upon a graceful, glossy Spanish charger, beneath the guardian oak of Rancho Agradable. A refreshing breeze from the mountainside romped past, and cooled his heated brow; and the intermingled perfumes from field and forest and fragrant meadowland sent a thrill of pure delight surging through his breast. His roving gaze followed every scene of thriving activity about the "hacienda" with an air of fervent expectation. His gently mellow eyes rested lovingly upon every manifestation of abounding wealth and contentment. New sources of interest arose on all sides of him and for the moment attracted his unfixed attention. Finally, however, his glances, from uncertain ramblings about the "quinta" turned to an exploration of the sunny yard and broad verandas, until they centered upon a lithe and graceful figure, attired in white, woolen petticoat, and lace "mantilla". A sunset glow was upon her dainty features, and a red rose in a strand of jet-black hair. Beside her lay a great bundle of linen, which she was busily engaged in drying and folding away. These, the young caballero recognized as the altar linens of the Church of Santa Clara de Asis, which she washed for Padre Dominic every month. He quickly scanned the now deserted yard, and perceiving that no one was about, softly called "Maria".

The young Senorita gave no sign, but on a repetition of the name, turned until she faced the caballero. Upon recognizing him, she gave a warning glance toward the "patio" upon her left, and shook her head. Then, seemingly indifferent, she turned about again, and continued as before with the drying of the linens. The young Senor, however, heedless of her expressive warning, impulsively repeated the name. Again the Senorita turned, and casting a quick, darting glance of admonition from her flashing eyes, brought her finger to her ruddy lips, in a reproving plea for silence. He, nevertheless, with that impetuous, turbulent nature of a Spaniard, seemed about to advance into the grounds of the "hacienda", but the maiden, discerning his intentions, coyly fluttered just the lacy end of an altar linen at the fiery lover, and whilst he stood astounded at the unthinkable sacrilege, whisked into the nearest "casa".

After the bewildered young suitor had at last gotten over his astonishment, he gazed long and lingeringly upon the spot in which the fair Senorita had stood. The gaudy sombrero swung from his half-raised hand. His silk-black hair slightly rustled in a gust of wind. With his manly, handsome features, and tall, slight, muscular body poised as if for a portrait upon his glossy steed, he made a handsome picture. A frown of restless petulance darkened his broad, smooth brow, but somehow a lurking smile of exultation seemed to flit about the corners of his delicate, thin-lipped mouth, until his entire countenance lighted up. Suddenly a crimson rose-bud nodding at a tiny window of the central "casa" arrested his attention. Perceiving that it was the Senorita of the Rancho, who signalled to him, he waved his great sombrero toward the casement, and sprang from the plated saddle of his horse. But even as he started for the "casa", the nodding, little rose-bud disappeared. Realizing, then, that to wait about the "hacienda" for the reappearance of the Dona would be hope-

less, he mounted his horse and reluctantly began the ascent of the mountain trail.

* * * *

"Maria!" The gruff Don Juan, that far renowned tyrant of Rancho Agradable summoned his gentle daughter to the "patio", where he reposed upon an ancient lounge, of one of those intricately woven designs so common in older Spanish furnishings.

Maria, all a-flutter, advanced to him and kissed him upon the forehead. "What is it, padre?" She lowered her pretty head, and dared not lift her eyelids, lest she should reveal the modest blush of confusion and embarrassment, which crept over her at this moment.

"Are the linens and the laces for the Mission done at last, daughter?" Senor Castello queried. "I heard you but a moment ago enter the 'casa'."

"No, padre, there are a few more yet to be dried. I came in to speak to Margarita about the evening meal. Have you taken your siesta?"

"Yes, Maria, I have rested well. It is very thoughtful of you to ask. But what caused you to come with such haste into the front room. Surely the evening meal was not as urgent as that. Were you frightened?"

"No, padre, I was not frightened." Maria was becoming more and more confused as the questioning progressed.

"Maria, is it true that you came with such haste into the 'casa' merely to instruct Margarita in regard to supper? It is preposterous!"

"But, padre, what else might it have been?"

Senor Castello cast a fatherly, reproving glance at his disconcerted daughter. "Come, come, Maria! Tell me, at whom did you wave the altar linen of Padre Dominic just before you entered the 'casa'?"

"Ah, padre, I was merely drying the altar linen in the breeze, not waving it!" And she was gone from the veranda as suddenly as she had disappeared from the vision of the gallant caballero that very hour.

But as she rounded the passage, where it turned from the inner garden, to the "sala de recibo", she was startled by a whispered "Maria" in her ear, and turning nervously about, she beheld her congenial madre beside her.

"Oh! it is you, mi querido madre," she cried. "How are you feeling? I hope you have not been working too steadily."

The Senora placed her arms caressingly about the dainty waist, and peered searchingly into Maria's flashing eyes. She was stately, tall, and slightly stern. A spotless, almost youthful, countenance spoke of former energetic beauty, while sympathetic, brownish eyes, and visible lines about the mouth and forehead betokened blooming youth cut short by trials and cares.

"Maria, dear," (Senora Castello's eyes rested affectionately upon her radiant daughter), "I am well, but I am afraid your father is making you ill. Is it not so?"

Maria made no answer.

"Oh, Maria, I can see he is. But daughter, never forget;" (Senora Castello spoke in subdued, yet audible tones), "I am always your friend!" And with this comforting consolation and assurance, she hurried away to the back of the "casa", where Margarita, the clumsy, little Mexican girl from the Mission, was listlessly sweeping.

But, though the gentle Mistress of Rancho Agradable had solaced her lovely daughter in such a low and whispered voice, the tender words had reached Don Juan, reposing on his couch in the shaded "patio", and had provoked a lengthy tirade from this arrogant tyrant.

Senor Castello, to begin with, was one of the exclusive nobility of the coast, who, having fought for the illustrious Portola, in his far-famed conquest of California, and having received this enormous tract of pasture land among the hills in payment for his distinguished services in the conquest, had settled down with his family in the secluded spot, and established the "hacienda". In those bygone days, he had becu a lenient, compliant sort of a master, and an indulgent father, with his seven stalwart sons to manage the Rancho and its lands, and three wonderful daughters to minister unto him in his idle maturity. I suppose he thought it quite enough to have become the owner of the extensive "quinta", without having afterwards to bother about its everlasting cares; and at that time, it is certain, he hardly gave thought or heed to anything outside his immediate sphere and household. It is doubtful whether, even during the bounteous harvest season of the "hacienda", he did more than indolently sit beneath some shading oak tree, and watch the fertile meadows yielding up their sumptuous, mellow bounty, all under the capable direction of his many sons. But his dashing young progenies soon tired of the drudgery of the "hacienda", and really caring not the end of a fig for Don Juan or his pleasant dreams, left him to manage the Rancho as best he was able, and departed for the great, wide world. Likewise had his daughters gone off with their respective husbands, and now the unfortunate old "soldado" was left entirely alone upon his sunny "hacienda" in the hills, except for his wife, and that solitary, blooming Rose o' the Rancho, Dona Maria, his daughter.

It may have been from the experience he had with his other two daughters, that he was loath to trust to the fickleness of the human race, in regard to his remaining offspring, and knowing only too well the lure and attraction that was held by Dona Maria for the stronger sex, he jealously guarded against ambitious young lovers and suitors for her hand, determining to have at least one daughter to brighten

his ripe, old age. And thus it was, that though every caballero or young senor in the valley had at one time or other made her the goal of his affectionate designs, not one of them had had the courage to face the old "soldado".

And so it happened that at the precise moment when a certain lieutenant of the army of the King at Monterey was honorably discharged from his Majesty's service and had come to live in the fertile Valley of Santa Clara, the path toward the affections of the blushing Rose o' the Rancho was clear of all rivals.

This young lieutenant was descended from one of those proud old families, famous in certain parts of Granada and Castile for their early conquests and daring exploits, with seemingly all the names and titles, if not all the virtues of the better of his ancestors inserted between Gaspar and his musical cognomen, Espinosa.

And so it was, too, that old Don Juan, who really supposed that he had at last exterminated all the army of suitors, which had at first besieged his stronghold, became aware of a new and determined competitor for the hand and heart of his daughter. Realizing that the handsome features and manly ways of young Espinosa would shortly captivate the foolish creature, he swore great oaths, and invoked every "demonio" and "diablo" in Hades to bring down curses upon the head of the rash young man who should presume to trifle with an old "soldado" in matters of such import.

* * * *

II

One afternoon, about a week after the foregoing incident had taken place, a lone caballero halted his fiery horse in the center of the roadway, leading to the Mission, and for a few moments rested easily in the saddle. A few rods ahead lay the Mission. Far beyond the little building, Rancho Agradable twinkled down into the Valley, and sent the rider, Don Gaspar, into a series of contemplations and reflections upon the "hacienda" and its inmates. The dominant object of his meditation, of course, was the comely daughter of Senor Castello, and the carrying on of his suit in such a manner as to win her coquettish heart, or better, perhaps, the manner in which to win her obstinate padre. It was with an indescribable thrill that he recalled that sleepy afternoon, when she had waved to him, and afterwards whisked off into the "casa". It would be but a short time, thought he, before he could claim the fair Senorita as his own, and already he saw the chapel bedecked with lilies and golden poppies for the wedding; and out of the very doors of the Mission upon which he had come, himself triumphantly leading his bride away to the marriage festival at the "hacienda".

As he thus silently meditated by the old Mission Cross, he was startled by a song bursting in upon the peaceful air. It came like the trill of a lark in the quiet of a summer's day, but sweeter than the song of the lark, in rich mellow tones, which were like the laughing brook flowing swiftly over the shining pebbles of its bed. Don Gaspar was at first surprised by the wavering notes of the Spanish love ditty, and awakened so suddenly from his reveries, leaned forward, to catch, if possible, the voice of the singer. The rhythmic wavers seemed to come forth from the sacristy door. Suddenly it dawned upon him that the voice was that of Dona Maria, probably preparing the altar for the Sunday services— and alone!

Gladly he put the spurs to his horse, and rounding the corner of the chapel in a great cloud of dust, sprang lightly from the saddle, sombrero in hand, awaiting to greet the Senorita. But apparently she had not heard him galloping up, so he sprang lightly through the doorway into the darkness of the sacristy.

(To be Continued)

A Fact or Two

James B. O'Connor.

THE principles of national self-determination may be paradoxically styled both simple and complex—simple in themselves and prescinding from particular instances; complex if viewed together with the many circumstances which inevitably complicate the affairs of nations. To the citizen of our modern world, no principle is truer than that there can be no just government save with the consent of the governed. Yet that very principle, in its concrete applications, is the stumbling-block in the path of those whose desire seems to be to move forward toward the goal of lasting peace. Why? Simply because the minds of men—of the foremost men—are so often clouded by hate, cupidity, love or fear. The conclusions which, with the necessity of cold logic, follow so sternly from accepted principles are befogged by the miasma that rises from the pool of human passion. For man, as we know, is composed of body and soul, and of these, the body plays not the lesser part. With this fact in mind, it should not surprise us if the ideals held so steadily before us during the days of sacrifice which the great war entailed, fail now of their realization. Then, it was a matter of abstract principle; now comes the conflict of that principle with the greed and avarice of mankind. The grosser element, as usual, seems at first to conquer, but truth is truth, and sometime or other, by some means or other, it must take its rightful place within the scheme of things.

To many, I know, the justice of Ireland's claim to recognition beneath the principle of self-determination is indisputable. However, the enemies of "Dark Rosaleen" still cling to the old falsehoods in their attempt to deceive their fellow-men and so a reiteration of a few ethical truths may not be altogether out of place.

Beyond all sane argument is the fact that there is no legitimate authority to govern except from Almighty God. For He, as the Creator of the world and of man, cannot for a moment cease to be the Master, sovereign and supreme, of them both. Hence, the cardinal issue in any dispute which concerns the validity of one country's claim to rule another is, whether or not the rule of that country is in accordance with the will of the Almighty. Granted this fact—and it is incontrovertible—it follows

as surely as the night the day, that authority exercised in direct violation
of the decrees of God is authority in
name alone, that legislation which over-
steps the limits set by the dictates of
the Natural Law is utterly without obligation as regards those to whom it is
intended to apply. Deny this and you
assert the impossible—namely that an
All-Holy Being could be capable of
sanctioning the forces of its own destruction. In a word, no government
which has not the seal of Divine approval has either the authority or the
right to legislate, nor does there exist
on the part of its subjects any obligation to yield obedience to its behests.
But, one might well ask, how are we
to recognize this Divine approval? In
what ways is it made manifest? The
simplest method is to ascertain whether
or not a government is based upon the
preponderance of might over right, or
upon the free consent of the governed.
If the former, its claims are, beyond
the shadow of a doubt, unjustifiable. If
the latter, it may, in the generality of
instances, be presumed valid and
clothed with the proper authority to demand obedience. It were foolish to
waste words in an endeavor to demonstrate under which of these two cate-
gories England, in her relations with
Ireland, comes. Since the first centuries of invasion, Ireland has never
ceased to utter, by pen and sword, her
protests at the shameful subjection in
which Great Britain has ever sought to
maintain her. In every age have the

children of the Green Isle sacrificed
their very life-blood rather than surrender their priceless birthright of liberty into the hands of the world's bul-
ly. Can we then accuse Ireland's sons
of today of acting counter to their just
rights, when they struggle to break the
chains which bind them in defiance of
the law of God and the law of nations?
Hardly.

But there is another and no less
forceful argument which cannot be
overlooked by anyone willing to give
the cause of Ireland fair consideration.
Legislation enacted in opposition to the
Natural Law is not only not binding,
but, if indefinitely prolonged, is sufficient reason for the forfeiture of a rul-
ers rights, if indeed he have any such.
For Natural Law is but the manifestation of the Eternal Law in man's regard. It is the guiding star of man's
actions, public or private: it is the
norm by which the intrinsic malice or
merit of our deeds must be guaged. It
regulates not only the relations of
equal with equal, but the relations of
ruler with subject. What is right when
judged by its standard is right in the
sight of God—what is wrong when
judged by its standard cannot and will
not merit the approval of Heaven. This
is not Scholastic Apriorism; it is the
necessary and immutable truth. It
must be so. God, Infinite Wisdom personified, in creating man could not do
so without a very fixed and definite
end in view, and toward that end, man,
as a rational being, must rationally

co-operate. This he can do only by making use of the means prescribed him by his Almighty Master. These means are his own actions, directed and co-ordinated by the dictates of the natural Law; and, let me repeat, not only his private actions, but those especially which have any bearing on the well-being of his fellow-men. For man is, by nature, not an isolated but a social being, destined, not to live apart from, but in intimate relation with his neighbor. With respect to others, then, we have certain rights and also, certain obligations. So also the ruler with respect to his subjects. Provided his authority has been justly obtained, he has the right to command what is for the common good, and his subjects have the obligation to obey him. Likewise, he has the obligation to remain, in his decrees, always within the Natural Law; and, should he disregard this law, his subjects have the the right to refuse him their homage. From all this may it not be logically concluded that when a government has for centuries neglected the welfare of a subject people; when its parliament has been but a tyrant and its legislation but the tightening of slavery's chains, the rights and the authority of that government must

necessarily cease? Again, I would not waste words by outlining England's career in Ireland. The world knows the story. Four words would embrace it all—murder, robbery and religious intolerance.

* * * *

In the Book of Kings, the Sacred Historian, after relating David's two-fold sin in murdering Uriah and taking unto himself Uriah's wife, goes on to tell how the prophet Nathan, sent by God, comes into the presence of David to reprehend him for his crime. And Nathan said to him: There were two men in one city, the one rich, and the other poor. The rich man had exceeding many sheep and oxen. But the poor man had nothing at all but one little ewe lamb—and it was unto him as a daughter. And when a certain stranger was come to the rich man, he spared to take of his own sheep and oxen, to make a feast for that stranger —but took the poor man's ewe, and dressed it for the man that was come to him. And David's anger being exceedingly kindled against that man, he said to Nathan: As the Lord liveth the man that hath done this is a child of death. And Nathan said to David: Thou art the man!

Two Pictures

DREAMED a dream of yesterday---
Was it glorious or grand? ---
Only a blood-stained soldier lay
In the mud of No-man's land.

Weirdly in the inky sky,
A watching vulture wheeled.
Its prey---the brave boy left to die
On the ghastly battle-field.

Another picture---Ah! 'Twas fair---
To my conjured vision came;
I saw a hero meet to wear
His country's badge of fame.

About him surged the cheering throng,
But nearer to him pressed
His Mother, her heart a song
For the medals on his breast.

I wonder oft, throughout the day,
Which played the nobler part;
The victor, or the vulture's prey
With shrapnel in his heart.

MARTIN M. MURPHY

With Apologies to Rip

Thomas Crowe.

OR fully two hours I must have battled with the brush and Manzanita, when suddenly I emerged on the edge of a clearing in the center of which stood an old, weather-beaten, dilapidated house of the two-story-and-attic variety. Now I, even as you yourself, have seen a goodly number of houses in my day, but neither of us, I feel sure, has ever had the misfortune of gazing upon a dwelling more forlorn than that one of the wilderness. Ragged, worm-eaten, out-at-the-elbows—I could not wonder at the signs of desolation about it. No one could have tarried long within its walls without experiencing the primitive impulse to betake himself again to the wild, nomadic life of his distant ancestors. Contemplating it, the most hardened "Movie" fan would cease to search for a solution to the world-old enigma, "Why g—I mean boys—leave home." He would have known. From these remarks it may be inferred that the old house did not promise much as a hospice. The inference is eminently correct. Still, it had four walls and I was cold. Please do not say that that sentence lacks unity. The fault is only apparent. There was really a close connection between the existence of those walls and the thermal—or non-thermal —condition of my person. You see, there was a chilly March wind blowing —blowing right through the rents my clothing had received as a result of the struggle I had had with the undergrowth. The walls, however unprepossessing their appearance, might prove a barrier to the breeze. Behold the connection.

So I approached and looked about for some means of entrance. 'Twas in vain. All the doors on the first floor, and the windows too, were locked.. I kicked and pulled and twisted and jerked and—well, yes, I did swear a little, but all to no purpose; there simply was no getting into that house. And all this time, mind you, I continued to be cold. In fact, to be very, very cold. What was I to do? Here it was late afternoon and I had been journeying since sun-up. An attempt to retrace my steps might result in my being frozen. Heavens! Death in that trackless wild! I began to recall stories I had heard of wanderers being frozen in Alaskan snows. Would the same fate be mine? Would some thoughtless youth in years to come take up my

skull and murmur the immortal lines—
"Alas! poor Yorick!" Or perchance
that highly ornamental part of my being would aid the meditations of some
lonely anchoret when he should think
of death.

But hold! I was from fighting stock!
I would not yield to the grim conqueror
without a struggle! Onward I plunged
—pardon me, I should have said onward I intended to plunge. What really happened was, that I plunged downward—straight downward and splash!
into a pool of water. I didn't wait to
recover from my surprise before regaining my feet. A perfect sub-con-
scious reaction brought me into that po-
sitiou in something less than a tenth of
a second. How often I had heard that
water was wet without adverting to the
fact! And how clearly and how vividly I realized that fact now! That particular pool of water, anyhow, was
very, very wet and moreover, very,
very cold. I began feeling about for
some egress and my hands came into
contact with what seemed to be a door.
I pushed, and entered upon darkness—
darkness deep and dire, darkness somewhat akin to that which Moses caused
to descend upon the banks of the Nile.

There followed much groping about
and considerable shin-bruising, to be
rewarded   finally   by   stumbling—I
speak literally—by stumbling upon a
pair of stairs. Cautiously I ascended.
Cautiously I pushed open another door
and found myself on the first floor of
the old building.   Now for a stove!

From room to room I went in search,
but the only thing I found was disappointment. Save for an objectionable
odor, frequent cobwebs and multitud-
inous spiders those rooms contained
nothing.

Up I went to the second story. Alas!
Not to mention Alack! It was the first
story all over again only much worse. I
began to tremble from more than the
cold. Ye gods! Was there no way of
driving the chill from my system?
Once again those visions of a lonely
grave, or bleaching bones—my bones—
arose to torture me. I went to a window and gazed out.   The wind was
howling about the house like a lost soul
and the branches of the trees danced
sadly in accompaniment to that melancholy dirge. Should I again brave the
elements and die nobly, battling to the
last? Or should I stay where I was
and await the—

"Ha!"

I jumped two feet.

"Ha! Ha!"

I jumped three.

"What cheer?"

I glanced up quickly. Framed in a
small square aperture in the ceiling directly above me, was a head. A very
hairy head, the locks like those of some
great hero. From the head two eyes
gazed at me with a questioning expression. Then the lid of one eye solemnly
descended and a hand appeared beck-
oning me to come up. Come up! Did
he think I was going to fly up? Even
as the question formed itself in my

mind a ladder was let down. Well, I always would try anything once, so up I climbed. The sight that greeted me! Ranged round the walls were bottles containing the choicest assortment of liquid joy it had ever been my lot to gasp before. Cognac, chartreuse, beer, wine, whiskey—lord! The stranger smiled. Then reaching under the bed he drew forth a jug of good old mountain dew.

" 'Tis the last in the land, sir,'' he said. ''Drink and warm thyself.''

I obeyed. Never for a moment would I have dreamed of doing otherwise. As I quaffed the fluid mine host watched, at first benevolently, then, as I showed no signs of desisting, apprehensively. Finally, a look of Olympian indignation leaped into his eyes and he tried to pry loose my hands from the death-hold they had acquired on the jug. That look, strangely enough, reminded me of someone—someone prominent in the land of liberty. Who could it be? Ah yes! Certainly. But no! How could it—foolish—but—

* * * *

I awoke on the edge of the clearing. How I ever got there and when, I could not tell. All I know is that I must have slept for a considerable period, for I noticed that the grass in the clearing had grown much higher. Painfully, carefully, I arose. Jee-rusalem! I was stiff. With many a groan I began my slow and agonizing homeward journey.

On reaching civilization I was amazed to learn that I had been absent for an entire month. Down the streets of the old town I moved, in much the same way, I fancy, as did old Rip in years agone. That gentleman though, having slept much longer than I had, was greeted by many more changes than I could expect. But wait! There were the advertisements. Could it be possible, I ruminated, that the quality of the tobacco used in Camel cigarettes was still such as to forbid the distribution of coupons? Did Omar and aroma still blend? Was Dad still the only one on earth who knew why any one should want to smoke Sweet Caps? The sign boards would tell me. I looked. I rubbed my eyes. What face was that, contemplating so serenely the passing multitude? I drew closer to make more sure. Was it possible! There in front of me was a lurid representation of my friend of the old house and underneath the picture was inscribed the legend;— Lost, Strayed, but, we are convinced, not Stolen—One William Jennings Bryan. Finders keepers!

One Summer Day

NE summer day, when the birds were still,
And radiant shone the sun,
I travelled a road
With a heavy load,
Even as you have done.

I climbed a hill, where another hill
Rolled not very far away,
But the thousand cares,
That the whole world bears,
Worried my heart that day.

Then a breeze sprang up, and it played about;
The robins began anew;
And my heart was light,
As the day was bright,
Bearing a song from you.

And now I sing as I stride along
The way down the meadowed slope,
Though the world makes strife,
We have not lost life;
Living, we'll not lose hope.

A. J. STEISS, JR.

14

Cannon Ball.

Emmett Gleeson.

 HOT midsummer day prevailed. Over on the opposite hill a coyote, forgetful of his inheritance of cowardice, through a stronger instinct to satisfy his thirst, braved an approach to a nearby water hole. In the protecting shade of a patch of mesquite lolled two individuals, apparently unaware that the heat waves were taking on a greater degree of intensity, as they danced over the scorched surface of that barren tract. The one, corpulent and excessively flabby; the other tall, lithe and sinewy, grew too preoccupied in their transaction to admit of any recognition of the day's warmth.

"Now Bob!" interposed the burly creature, "Onet an' fer all do ya want thet hoss? Yuh jewed me down to a hundred an' a quarter an' now yuh offer a measly lil ole fifty."

He hesitated a moment and glanced at the other hastily.

"No, by golly!" he continued, "Any time yuh think thet hoss is fer fifty—"

"Fifty's the word, Mac," put in Bob cooly and determinedly.

"Why young feller, thet's the best lookin' cayuse in the country. A hun-dred and a quarter haint nuthin to ast a good jedge fer sich as him. But bein it's you Bob, an bein as we allus wuz good Pals I aint goin to let no few dollars come atween us. Slip me an even hundred and I'll make yuh a present o' thet hoss. Why his daddy wuz a steel-dust and his mammy wuz one o' the—"

The cowboy lazily stretched his six feet of compact muscle, extracted a generous cud of tobacco and fixing his merry blue eyes on MacDonald, interrupted him in his slow Texas drawl.

"Nope Mac," he said, "I reckon ef yuh all won't protect my little fifty, I'd best go look up one o' them Life Insurance agents. Yuh all know that nary a man has ever picked that thar ole banjo for more'n three jumps."

"Aw 'ell, Bob," pleaded MacDonald, "just cause he dumped a few o' these yere shingle men is no reason why YOU can't ride him."

MacDonald waddled to the gate of the corral, laboriously hoisted his five by four foot body to the top bar and glared at Cannon Ball. The horse walked quietly around the corral as if awaiting another victim. For a year the name of this beautiful blue roan had been coupled with broken arms and legs, champion riders and unconquerable horses. Now he paused an instant, tossed his majestic head in the air and looked with almost intelligent but wild eyes at the horse traders.

The cowboy advanced from the protecting shade of the retreat. He picked up his chaps, snapped them on and started with a slightly bow-legged stride towards the horse.

"Drop in when you're up my way Mac," said Bob. "Awful lonesome up there."

The fat, pudgy figure dropped from the gate, half rolled, half walked to where the cowboy was saddling his horse.

"Hold on 'ere Bob!" he put in. "Gimme thet fifty an take the—outlaw with yuh. I hope by crackey, he kills yuh!"

* * * *

Bob grasped the saddle horn in his right hand, Cannon Ball's ear in his left, stepped back a pace and vaulted into the saddle.

Cannon Ball stood perfectly still, his ears thrown back in a menacing attitude and his back humped. Bob stirred uneasily. He was no longer the jesting cowboy with the twinkling eyes. He had become a hard-faced, iron-jawed fighter. Cannon Ball's four feet left the ground at precisely the same instant. Straight into the air he shot, whirled and then dropped over on his back. Bob jumped in time to avoid the impact. Cannon Ball rolled over. Two sharp, cruel Mexican spurs brought spurts of blood jettying from

the horse's shoulders. Up he came once more, dropped his head between his legs and began "wiping 'er up!" He pitched from left to right and from right to left, doubled back, side-winded going high in the air and lighting with crooked, stiff-legged jarring jumps. A rawhide quirt stung long red lashes on his sides. The portion between the horse's shoulder and flank was a spur rowel race track. He bucked with greater speed and the rowels dug the deeper. His red, foam-flecked body turned a half moon in the air. With a terrorized bawl he crashed to a stop.

Bob dismounted, wiping the dust intermingled with perspiration from his face with a big bandana handkerchief. He put his arm around the swan-curved neck; from the agressor the cowboy became the sympathizer.

After the first few days, Cannon Ball began to see in Bob a friend instead of an enemy. Within a year the horse—as much as his irrational instinct would permit—was in love with his master.

MacDonald "dropped in" one day and stared unbelievingly as the cowboy put his horse through a series of tricks. But Cannon Ball would have nothing to do with the fat man. He knew one master and only one.

Mac swore good naturedly and turned to Bob who was rather absentmindedly braiding a rope in his horse's mane.

"Say, young fellow," he said, "them Greasers on this side o' the line are rompin somethin awful. The lower class are joinin' the revolution every day. Jist yestidday one o' them low brows stole a team o' mules from ole Jedge Carmin. Good jedge o' mules that man.''

* * *

Returning one day from a long ride, Bob noticed strange tracks in the thick dust directly in front of his gate. He dismounted, opened the gate and bent carelessly over to examine them. They were not the deep boot tracks of a cowboy nor the broad hob-nails of the miner.

While so occupied, he was oblivious of the crouching, sombreroed form in back of him. A knife flashed. Bob crumpled up in a heap and lay still. A black, sore-covered hand quickly dispossessed the supine form of everything of value. This done, the renegade sprang upon Cannon Ball and rammed into the tender sides of the animal his newly acquired spurs. The horse sprang into the air, whirled and crashed down on his back. There was a sickening crunch, as of flesh, human flesh being ground under the ponderous weight of the enraged animal.

Bob's eyes fluttered open. Cannon Ball was nosing him inquisitively. By a superior effort the cowboy staggered to his feet. Leaning for support on the gate post, he uncinched the saddle and pulled off the bridle. His hand quivered; blood began to well from his mouth and he sank to the ground. With a last long look at the wondering horse above him, his hard weather-beaten features took on a softer hue. His eyes closed and his mouth curved into a boyish, carefree smile.

''Good-bye, old Pal,'' he drawled softly, ''I reckon I won't need yuh all again fer quite a spell.''

On Passing the Twenty-First Year Stone

Peter F. Morrettini.

WHEN one has been hailed by various appellations from early youth to incipient manhood, by his admirers and others, whether in the person of fond parents, indifferent neighbors, ungentlemanly companions or adoring female acquaintances; when one has run the gauntlet of his youthful years with such goading titles as "baby", "child", "boy", "kid", and "young man", and after much chafing and many great expectations finally reaches the bewitching age of a score and one years, then with a mighty, impulsive shrug he throws off all the restraint placed upon him by the arm of the law, and in sweet forgetfulness of a goodly portion of the hitherto inflexible domestic orders, he saunters forth, his head high, his ribs expanding, and for the first time in his young life he proudly, and more or less accurately, designates himself—a man.

What a strange spell there is in that new-found name! What an atmosphere of eminence, physical and mental, clings around the word! What wonderful possibilities might lie hidden in the obscure custodian of that gifted title! Yet the bright sun rises as of old in his course, and as of old, he sets. Millions of people in the same state, thousands in the same locality, hundreds in the same town, and not a few in the immediate vicinity go about their daily duties with never a thought that in their midst there is one who has just crossed the threshold into the independent and predilected class of citizens whom we reverently call men.

Outside the immediate circle of the family, and a few kind relatives and gossiping neighbors, the fact that an "E Pluribus Unus" has attained his majority does not interest anyone; still the "Unus" chiefly concerned IS tremendously interested—in himself, in others, and most of all in his country. Indeed, so interested in himself that one of the first performances of his now responsible life is to hasten to the Hall of Records and enlist in the great army of voters; perhaps, too, with an eye to being one of our future Presidential nominees.

But before going any farther with the antics of such a esoteric youth, let us retreat to a safe distance and then proceed to eye him over for any signs of recent abnormalities. Undoubtedly it is the selfsame hat that pressed his locks a few months previously; in stature there is not the slightest alteration; his habiliment bears the service stripes of prior occupation. But, alas, on further scrutiny it will be noticed that the upper button of his coat is not in its accustomed locality; yea, more, his vest is evidently straining under the increased size and pressure of that part of his anatomy known as the chest. Yet who can blame him for so carrying himself under such world stirring and epoch making events?

After a tumultuous session of congratulating himself, he will naturally raise his vision as well as his mind and begin to contemplate some of his future prospects, possibilities and powers. Of course he is already aware that, as an elector of the elected, he is a political unit worth considering; but, above and beyond all that, he is also cognizant of the fact that he can attempt the unchartered sea of matrimony without the adverse winds of parental restraint or the dragging anchor of the law, and thus for the first time in his life be able to take unto himself, at his own sweet will, a wife—for better or for worse, for richer or for poorer, in sickness and in health, until death shall them part.

Beside all these mere potentialities, in the exuberance of his unsophisticated youth, the thought rushes upon him with overpowering violence that now, being beyond the mandate of his elders and outside the pendulum of the law, he is able to thrust his form past the swinging-doors, across the saliva-marked floor to the bar, and placing his foot upon the rail with a nonchalant air of an accustomed consumer order gruffly "two lagers" from the white-aproned dispenser on the other side. But, alas, 'twas but a thought—the creature of an overwrought mind. "Tempus fugited" and we are on the safe, solemn and salty side of the historical last day of June, 1919.

A frown momentarily clouds the features of our erstwhile enthusiastic aspirant, and lest his simple, unadulterated and spontaneous prose might prove slightly out of the ordinary we are satisfied to let Horace interpret his feelings.

"Euhoe, recenti mens trepidat metu,
Plenoque Bacchi pectore turbidum
Laetatur."

Doubtless, after he has ceased mentally soliloquizing and has returned to his former self, such possibilities will not allure him, nor will any self gratification attract him from the great duties and responsibilities that he has voluntarily assumed as a factor in the government of his country. As a man he is partly responsible for the conduct of that government; as a man he may express his will through the medium of the ballot box; as a man it is his duty to so interest himself in the management of the municipal, state and governmental activities that through his efforts we may be blessed with better officials to execute the multifarious functions of our government; as a man he is one to whom the constitution guarantees a fireside and an altar, his personal liberties and freedom from domestic invasion and tyranny. Yes, every man is a king, and his home is his castle.

It is no wonder then, that, when an American Youth has reached the Yearstone of his Independent manhood, such thoughts—childish, grotesque, serious—should make riot with his brain, that he should contemplate the worthless as well as the worthy and honorable possibilities of the state of man. American Education and American environment have made such a personality possible—have made many such, actual. But today, more than ever, we must be alive to the tremendous duties and obligations that rest upon every American citizen, and, in particular, each American voter.

Today the warning is renewed with ominous forebodings: Eternal vigilance is the price of our liberties. And the unanswered question of the hour is: Whether the American Youth is sufficiently instructed in the hallowed tradition of his country; whether he has imbibed to the full the spirit of those intactible and sacred pages of our constitution and other patristic and venerable documents; whether he sufficiently realizes and appreciates all that they mean now and all that they meant then, when their mighty souls first throbbed upon the soil of this continent; whether he is sufficiently cognizant of his great duties and responsibilities as a man. In other words: Is the American Youth of twenty-one a capable American citizen?

The Redwood

PUBLISHED BY THE STUDENTS OF THE UNIVERSITY OF SANTA CLARA

The object of The Redwood is to gather together what is best in the literary work of the students, to record University doings and to knit closely the hearts of the boys of the present and the past

EDITORIAL STAFF

EDITOR-IN-CHIEF - - - - - - - HENRY C. VEIT
BUSINESS MANAGER - - - - - - TULLIO A. ARGENTI
ASSISTANT BUSINESS MANAGER - - - - - JACOB E. HEINTZ
CIRCULATION MANAGER - - - - - EDMUND. Z. COMAN

ASSOCIATE EDITORS

EXCHANGES - - - - - - - P . F. MORETTINI
ALUMNI - - - - - - - - - MARTIN M. MURRAY
UNIVERSITY NOTES - - - - - - - LOUIS F. BUTY
FRED J. MORAN
ATHLETICS - - - - - - - JAMES E. NEARY

EXECUTIVE BOARD
EDITOR   BUSINESS MANAGER   EDITOR OF REVIEWS

Address all communications to THE REDWOOD, University of Santa Clara, Santa Clara, California.
Terms of subscription, $1.50 a year; single copies 25 cents

EDITORIAL

An Eye Opener

Prescinding from the fact that John Barleycorn came by an early demise and thus precluded what we have above alluded to, nevertheless we can in all sincerity say that this, our first issue, is in every sense of the phrase, an eye opener.

For the most of us a happy vacation has run its course. And for all of us a new year awaits our bidding to be made, accordingly as each shall strive, a brilliant, happy success, or a rank failure. We hope for the former; God forbid the latter. However the vehicle of our progress over the course of ten scholastic months will be of our own choosing. It is for each to recognize which one houses opportunity. Having made the discovery, let him acquaint

21

himself with every requirement he will be expected to meet and thus move rapidly on to the goal ahead of him.

Opportunity is a twin sister to time. Both are fleet of foot and once past can never be recalled. Run abreast of the two and half of the battle is over. We are reminded of the story of the adolescent who was ambitious only in terms of tomorrow. He was going to be all that mortal should be—tomorrow. Well this youth would have been the greatest of workers, but the truth is he died and all that he left when living was done was a mountain of things he intended to do tomorrow. As a very apt answer to this we need merely quote the old adage which goes on to say: "Never put off until tomorrow what you can do today."

The advantages of an early start, particularly along educational endeavor need not here detain us. It is sufficient perhaps, to exhort you to two things, work and sincerity therein. Given these two, naught else than success, prosperity and happiness can ensue. Let's all put shoulder to shoulder and make this year a clarion to resound adown the annals of Santa Clara as being the most successful year on record.

Our Organ It is not a musical instrument we are here referring to; it is the official publication of the Student Body, the Redwood, your book, to be made and supported accordingly as the spirit of your Alma Mater permeates you and incites you in its behalf.

We are not going to preamble you to death by telling you what a really nice book it is, or the prominence it claims in the realm of Collegiate literary organs. But what we do want to acquaint you with is the duty it will ask you to fulfill. The older fellows have oft heard this repeated; the newcomers into our big family will find it new. To remind the one and inform the other, that is our present aim.

On the opposite page you will observe the object of the Redwood. It is to gather together what is best in the literary work of the students, to record University doings and to knit closely the hearts of the boys of the present and the past. Though many of you might say off-hand, "I cannot write," that should deter no one. How frequently are we possessed of latent talents which we never dreamed was part of our make-up. It is only a trial and that oft repeated that should be convincing of whether or not one can write. You have nothing to lose and everything to gain in the mere trying. With this in mind we might suggest that you attempt, in your spare moments, a bit of verse or a short story, or even a short essay on any of the current topics of the day. Who can tell but there may be in our midst another Shakespeare, or an O. Henry or an Andrew Lang!

Permit us one more word in passing, and that in regard to the support of your publication. Our first query is, are you a subscriber, If you are, we thank you; if you have still to hand in your name to the Circulation Manager for a year's subscription, we advise your doing so immediately. Now then, after you have digested its contents, send a copy home to the folks and acquaint them of the inner life pulsating within these hallowed walls of Santa Clara. It is no presumption to say that they will be pleased with it. So fellow students, we of the Redwood extend to you our hearty welcome; we ask your co-operation in the work of bettering your magazine. Lastly we invite your constructive criticism. Censure when occasion calls for it, but let that censure be sincere and of truth, so that we may make stepping stones of our dead selves to rise to higher things.

University Notes

Faculty Changes

The joy of returning to College after the restless days of vacation was considerably lessened this year by the loss—I might say of a corps of Jesuit Fathers who were most successful in guiding our yet unsteady footsteps and who have left memories ever to be cherished by all of us. Father Eline, the real friend of the fellows, has been succeeded by Father Sullivan as Vice-President of the University. Father Hayes from St. Ignatius relieves Father O'Keefe as Dean of the Law School. The members of the House of Philhistorians will miss their zealous Speaker, Father Flynn, who has been sent to Los Angeles. After six years of teaching at Santa Clara, Father E. J. Whelan has left for Spain where he will study Theology. Every minute of his time was spent amongst us doing good for some one, a virtue cold words cannot adequately begin to praise. Fathers Dunne and McGarrigle have also journeyed to Europe to complete their studies. The Preps will long remember their Athletic Moderator, Father McElmeel, who is now stationed in St. Louis. Coming to us as new Professors are Fathers Donovan, Meagher, Kennedy, O'Connell, Egan and Mullen.

Student Body Meeting

The first meeting of the Associated Students was called on August 25th, by President Henry Veit. The purpose of the meeting was to acquaint the new students with their duties as members of the Student Body, and to arouse pep for the coming football season.

President Veit, in his opening remarks dwelt upon the necessity of co-operation along the various lines of student activities. He was followed in his remarks by Student Manager James O'Connor, who pointed out the difficulties which would necessarily arise this year, due to the change from Rugby to American football, and exhorted the students to a whole-hearted support of the team, the coach, and their Alma Mater.

Father J. O'Connell, our new Moderator of Athletics, was then introduced, and in a few words outlined the football situation, assuring the student body that all efforts would be made to secure the best that could be had in the

24

Edmund L. Cowan
Treasurer

Louis F. Buty
Secretary

Thomas F. Whelan
Sergeant at Arms

James R. O'Connor
Student Manager

John O'Connell
Moderator

Henry C. Viet
President

Student Body Officers.

line of athletics, and promising that with its co-operation Santa Clara would this year maintain the high standing in American football which it formerly held in Rugby.

The election of Executive Secretary was next in order, the position being left vacant by the failure of Francis M. Conneally, secretary-elect, to return to college. Louis F. Buty, who had been acting as secretary pro tem. was chosen for the position.

Edwin R. Harter, chief yell leader in '16, who has now returned to Santa Clara after 16 months overseas, was called upon by President Veit for a few remarks. Mr. Harter spoke on the "Santa Clara Spirit", drawing an analogy from the unconquerable spirit of the doughboy "over there". He urged the students to foster and maintain that spirit at all times, whether on the athletic field, or along other lines of endeavor. With the conclusion of Mr. Harter's remarks, the meeting adjourned.

Philaletic Senate

Tuesday evening, September 2nd, saw the Philalethic Senate once more in session, Father Nicholas Bell, S. J., presiding. The evening was chiefly devoted to the election of officers for the coming year, and the proposal of the new names of former Philhistorians, as prospective members of the astute body of Senators. The men selected to carry the honors and glory of the Senate during the forthcoming year have all shone forth in oratorical grandeur, while serving in the House, and possess the qualifications necessary for admittance to the Philalethic body. They are:—T. Bricca, R. O'Neill, J. Henderson, P. Morettini, L. Buty, W. Koch, A. Ferrario, E. Coman, E. Heafey, W. Desmond, T. Kaney, J. Connell, T. Crowe, T. Sturdivant, and L. Trabucco.

From all appearances the Senate will enjoy the most successful year that it has seen for some time. Last year, as is well known, because of the army regime, oratorical attainments were put aside and forgotten almost completely, —lost, as it were, in the military whirlpool of warlike achievements. Now, however, that the sword is sheathed, and the rifle is clothed in a cloak of preservative cosmolene, the Senate is once more prepared to welcome its members, both old and new.

The following were elected to office for the coming year: Vice-President, Henry C. Veit; Secretary, Edwin R. Harter; Corresponding Secretary, Thomas J. Moroney; Treasurer, Thomas E. Whelan; Sergeant-at-Arms, James B. O'Connor; Librarian, W. Ward Sullivan.

House of Philhistorians

The first meeting of the House gave evidence of a brilliant year in debating among the Freshmen and Sophomores of the University. Father Donovan, the new Speaker, assured the members that every opportunity would be offered them to exercise and develop their powers in oratory during the ensuing term. The Freshmen were overwhelmingly the victors in the election for officers. Representative Neary was elected Clerk; Representative Donovan, Corresponding Secretary; the honor of Treasurer was bestowed upon Representative Gleeson and Sergeant-at-Arms was entrusted to Representative Leavey. The political triumph of the evening was the unanimous election of Representative Finnegan to the office of Librarian.

Junior Dramatic Society The Junior Dramatic Society has once more started its regular weekly meetings. At the first of these, held on September 9th, with Father Regan presiding, the following officers for the coming term were elected: Vice-President, John B. O'Brien; Secretary, John K. Lipman; Treasurer, James A. Toner; Sergeant-at-Arms, Raymond E. McCauley.

The following new members were admitted: Francis E. Coles, Jr., J. C. Devine, Gaspero M. Del Mutolo, Karl Koch, S. Martin, W. Makemson, Raymond W. Shelloe, and Frank L. Smith.

This Society is the younger brother of the Senate and the House, and exercises as great a function in prep circles, as do those societies in college. It is in the J. D. S. that embryo Ryland debaters first sprout forth with oratori-

cal vehemence, later to develop into the eloquent leaders of whom Santa Clara feels so proud. Undoubtedly there are many graduates of Santa Clara who now look back upon their first efforts in the J. D. S. and attribute, in no small degree, the success which they may have attained to those ambitious moments.

From the spirit manifested at the initial meeting, it may be predicted that the Society is about to enjoy one of the most successful years of its career.

It is rumored that other "doings", beside mere debating, will be in order this year, but their exact nature we have been unable to determine as yet. Something lofty, perhaps. As is said, "you can never sometimes tell what you least expect the most", so for the present we must patiently sit by, and await further developments.

Senior Society The initial meeting of the Senior Sodality was held on September 8th, under the enthusiastic guidance of Director Fr. Boland. The attendance was most gratifying, as practically the entire collegiate student body was represented. The Senior Sodality, like other student organizations, was temporarily disrupted during the period of the war, but this year will witness its return to the important position which it held in former years. Officers elected for the present semester are: Prefect, Thomas J. Moroney; First Assistant, William

G. Koch; Second Assistant, James E. Neary; Secretary, Frank A. Camarillo; Treasurer, Louis F. Buty; Consultors, Rudolph J. Scholz, William S. Muldoon, John J. Savage, Lawrence Devlin, Thomas M. Kaney, Emmett W. Gleeson, Alfred J. Abrahamsen, Henry C. Veit; Vestry Prefects, Herman C. Dieringer, Frank A. Rethers; Organist, Ernest Delmo Bedolla.

Junior Sodality

Sunday morning, Sept. 7th, the High School students assembled in the chapel to organize and the election of officers resulted as follows: Prefect, John O'Brien; First Assistant, James O'Sullivan; Second Assistant, John Lipman; Treasurer, Lloyd Nolan; Secretary, Francis E. Smith; Sergeant-at-Arms, Austin Regan; Vestry Prefect, Fred Florimont and Albert Duffil; Consultors, Frank L. Smith, James Toner, and Thomas Comyns.

Rally

September 9th was deemed a fitting and proper time at which to hold the first periodic pep installment for the coming football season. Accordingly an impromptu program was arranged and presented in the Auditorium on the evening of the above date.

As a curtain raiser, Ildephonse Hermann Harris, "King of Jazz", made his debut with an original rendition of "Where Has My Lima Bean". Ilde-phouse still retains his good health and reputation, and henceforth should be respected as a duly accredited member of the pick wielders organization.

Following the favorable impression created by Mr. Harris, the Iodine Fusiliers, fresh from a two-night run at the Milpitas Follies, presented their latest success, "Salts Before Breakfast, With Iodine After Meals." Signor Lew Buty appeared in the role of Bro. Iodine, with Capt. Kid McCoy, Abraham Zeke Coman, Michael Patrick Moroney, and Herr Sargent, as the "victim" quartet. Their clever and original songs provided the necessary "kick" for the evening's performance.

Zeke Coman and Bill Desmond, the "Mobile Duo", inflicted themselves upon the benign student body with a repertoire of song hits—and a few misses.

The remainder of the program consisted of boxing bouts, some of which were fast and furious, while others were not so furious. With the paperweight championship of the campus at stake, Jose Farrel, of the Waiter's Union, and Patrick Maximilian Giambastiani, stepped three rounds to a well-earned draw.

In the next bout Pinkie Regan wrested the 135-pound "shimmy" title from Vallejo Kid McCauley. Both boys put up a wonderful defense and displayed admirable "footwork" throughout the three rounds.

Caesar Mannelli and Fat Howell were scheduled for the headline bout of the evening, but owing to failure to make proper connections Howell was unable to appear. Whereupon Bob Sargent, the pride of Iodine Apartments, throwing discretion to the proverbial winds, graciously consented to appease the howling mob, by substituting for Howell. Bob, however, was careful, even in his wildest moments, and Manelli was declared the winner at the end of the third round.

As an extra added feature, a two-round bout between 'Varsity Becker and Kid Mollen completed the bill. Both boys showed a willingness to mix which might have led one to believe that more than reputation was at stake. Their ability to give and take was about equal, hence the judges were unable to give a decision and the bout was declared a draw.

Band and Orchestra　　The enrollment of students this semester brought several musicians of diversified talents, and prospects for the coming year, relative to a worthy band and orchestra, are extremely bright. The "shining lights" include Amaral, Ferrario, Diaz, Florimont, Symons, Brown, Makemson, Brizzolara, Lang, Elbert, Martin, Dieringer, O'Shea, Jansen, Petry, Shelloe, Williamson, Buty, Antonioli, Cassin, Pereira and Moran. Professor Mustol is more than pleased with the first few practices and he promises "pep and class" from both musical organizations.

Sanctuary Society　　Our new Prefect, Father Egan, called a meeting of the society for the election of officers and the following have been selected for the semester: Tobias Bricca, Prefect; Louis Trabucco, Censor; Ferrario, Treasurer; Heafey, Vestry Prefect; Sacristans, Dierenger and O'Sullivan; and Secretary, James B. O'Connor.

Class of '20　　With the addition of several new members, notably Messrs. Harter, Bricca, and Prothero, the Senior Class assembled on August 28th, with all the dignity incumbent upon their honored rank. The purpose of the meeting, as explained by President O'Connor, was the reorganization of the class, and the election of officers for the coming term.

Last year Class '20 existed in two bodies, the Letters class and the Engineers each having their separate organization. However, this has been found unsatisfactory, and a combination of both organizations was effected, with the result that the old spirit which had always characterized the class is now once more in evidence.

The election of officers displayed a unanimity of purpose which bespeaks success in the various undertakings attendant upon the Senior Class. The men honored by office are: Henry C. Veit, President; Tobias Bricca, Vice-President; Herman Dieringer, Secretary;

Thomas J. Moroney, Treasurer; Leopold Di Fiore, Sergeant-at-Arms.

Class of '21 A very spirited meeting of the Junior Class, Monday, Sept. 21st, revived the "pep" characteristic of the boys of '21. A glance at the names of the men who will lead in the activities of that class is significant of untold "doings". "Zeek" Coman, President; John Murphy, Vice-President; Richard McCarthy, Secretary; C. A. Antonioli, Treasurer; Harry Jackson, Sergeant-at-Arms, and D. R. Burke, Athletic Manager.

Class of '22 Due to the return of some of the old fellows the Sophomores have a class that "ye young Freshmen" will not dare annoy. The Chief officials promise the Student Body a few surprises from those of '22, sufficient to perpetuate their fame. "Mopie" Moran is the Prexy; "Luigi" Trabucco, most auspicious Vice-President; the erstwhile philosopher "Pop" Rethers, claims the chair occupied by Secretary; "Tootsie" Argenti, the busiest man on the campus, has consented to act as custodian of the shekels, while "Doc" Kerckhoff is the Sergeant-at-Arms.

Class of '23 On September 3rd, Class '23, the Freshman, first assembled to organize and elect officers for the ensuing year. Mr. "Cactus" Gleeson, a gentleman from Arizona, occupied the chair, with Emmet Daly acting as secretary pro tem. Those elected to office are:— James Neary, President; Daniel Donovan, Vice-President; John Jackson, Secretary; Robert Guthrie, Treasurer; George Noll, Sergeant-at-Arms

President-elect Neary spoke on the necessity of class unity, and offered several suggestions for creating class spirit. These were discussed at length, and plans were decided upon by which Class '23 should make itself felt in interclass affairs.

Louis F. Buty.
Fred J. Moran.

ENGINEERING NOTES

The Engineering Society has resumed its meetings,—and with the same "pep" and "jazz" as characterized the sessions last year. Our first meeting adjourned long after scheduled time, and was a satisfactory indication that the much-to-be-desired spirit of initiative and aggressiveness is present in abundance this year.

Not to save the best till the last we announce that Professor George L. Sullivan is Dean of the College of Engineering. He shows a great interest in the Society's actions; and his support is fully appreciated by the members. Then we have our efficient president, Mr. John J. Savage. Everyone who knows the spirit and personality of Mr. Savage realizes that the affairs of the society are safe in his hands.

And, by the way, have you noticed how the fellows turn to this section of the Redwood, to first read what the Engineers have to say, and what they are doing? We can promise that even more interest will be shown later on; for the Engineers are planning, and when the Engineers plan: results follow. Professor Sullivan, at the last meeting, told the members that a successful engineer must combine his pro-fessional knowledge with his personal ability to persuade, in order that he will be able to influence others and make them work for him. The best time to develop this power is here at College. Realizing this, the Engineers have banded together and aim to show, before this year has been completed, that to be an Engineer is an envied honor. Now a word concerning the end of the Engineering Society. Its purpose is to enable the members to act as a unit along scholarly, practical and social lines. Hence it is that the following committees have been named and given full authority to act along their separate ways:

Program Committee—Mr. Ford, Mr. Reddy; Chairman, Mr. Flannery.

Initiation Committee—Mr. DiFiore, Mr. Heaney, Mr. Manelli; Chairman, Mr. Fowler.

Entertainment Committee—Mr. Bannan, Mr. Berg, Mr. Minnehan; Chairman, Mr. DiFiore.

Publicity Committee—Mr. Koch, Mr. Osterle, Mr. Tuttle; Chairman, Mr. Abrahamsen.

The above gentlemen must have their work approved by the Dean before they act, and are mainly responsible for the success of future exploits.

Congratulations! The dues of the society are now double those of last year. Excelsior!

Almost everyone knows that Howard Nulk is back from France. He seems to have detected quite a bit of tapping and "tipping" across the water.

If anyone is doubtful as to the branch of service in which Roy Fowler received his commission, let him spend an afternoon in the drafting room, and listen to the commands when his pen "springs a leak" in the middle of a stormy drawing.

Bob Sargent successfully re-introduced himself to the Student Body at the rally. Some "heavy", Bob.

All the Engineers are anxiously awaiting the "Smoker" which will be held at Prof. Sullivan's home when the new Engineering Professor arrives. We thank Prof. Sullivan for his kind invitation.

The Juniors seem to have been unable to survey the Alum Rock district last year. For it is rumored that Mr. Savage has taken to the wilds of Alum Rock this year. Look out for the topography, John!

We can't forget the return of our Model man, Mr. Ford; nor of our celebrated rough rider Mr. DiFiore. Tommie and DiFi should be teaming together.

Here's something with which we can conclude: The Engineers are going to have a "jazz" orchestra. Just watch for the names.

—Alfred J. Abrahamsen.

Alumni Banquet

The annual Alumni Banquet took place this year on the evening of May 28th, in the Colonial Room of the St. Francis Hotel in San Francisco. Needless to say, the "pep" and spirit of loyalty to Alma Mater, which has characterized similar reunions in the past was much in evidence among the old boys.

Another gratifying circumstance was the presence of so many old Santa Clarans recently returned from the service where they so nobly upheld the honor of their flag and their Alma Mater.

Father Murphy, the honored guest of the evening, in his first appearance before the Alumni made an eloquent plea for their support. The burden of his speech was as follows: "Santa Clara is still there, but I trust it won't be there still. So when I let it be known to you that I want to get things moving, get behind me!" Judging from the manner in which his remarks were received, Santa Clara will not be "there still" very long.

In addition to the words of Father Murphy, interesting speeches were made by Toastmaster John J. O'Toole, Captain Adolph B. Canelo, James P. Sex, and Norbert Korte, the representative of the class of '19.

After the speechmaking, election of officers took place with the following results: James P. Sex, President; James Bacigalupi, Vice-President; John J. Collins, Treasurer; John J. Jones, Secretary; while Father Boland was retained as Moderator.

With the affairs of the Association in such capable hands prospects for the coming year appear very bright indeed. An especial word of commendation is due here to John J. O'Toole for his lively interest and untiring efforts in behalf of the Alumni, despite his own pressing duties at the bar.

Laymen's Retreat

The series of five gentlemen's retreats given during the past few summer months turned out more successfully than those of preceding years. Father Boland, the Moderator, has expressed himself as highly gratified with the attendance.

A retreat has been aptly defined as "a skillful and effective cure of souls". In the rush of business and professional life it is only too often that spiritual things are forgotten and neglected. Many times a little reflection on religious truths will serve to shape a man's whole career in the proper direction. For this reason the Fathers interested in the movement have seen fit to devote their whole time practically, during the vacation period, toward making these retreats a real benefit to those who attend them. Their efforts thus far have met with ever increasing success. May the good work continue.

'88 It is with genuine sorrow that we report the death of Father Joseph A. Byrne. During his twenty-eight years in the priesthood Father Byrne has set an example of Christian charity and piety seldom surpassed. May he receive the full reward for his labor.

Glad to hear from Panama. The Delaguardia Brothers have substantially remembered the old school by sending up two boys to take the places they vacated way back in the eighties. What a crowd we would have at Santa Clara if every Alumnus did as well.

'92 Father Thomas O'Connell is back from France where he succeeded in covering himself with glory. We are surprised that Tommy has not paid us a visit.

George Green, known in the sporting world as Young Corbett, has been engaged by the University to teach boxing. In his day George achieved a worthy reputation in his chosen profession and for the last few years has been successfully teaching young Olympians how to "sling the mits". With such a capable instructor Santa Clara should turn out some clever boxers.

'94 We record with pleasure that Father James Hayes, an old boy of the Class of '94 is once again in our midst. To Father Hayes' lot has fallen the task of imparting the science of God to the young ideas of his Senior Class.

'13 Constantine Castruccio, of the renowned '13 class is making himself heard in the legal profession down in the city of the chemically pure,—Los Angeles. Cass was about the campus a few weeks ago closing arrangements for a football game between Occidental College and his Alma Mater, to be played in the Southern City.

'13 John Barnard, who was a star football player in his day, is associated with his father in the laundry business at Long Beach.

'15 After his release from the hazardous aviation service, Phil Martin decided to buckle down to the peaceful quiet of farm life. To scientifically equip himself for his chosen vocation, Phil is taking a short course at the Davis Agricultural School. Later he intends to travel back East to the old homestead of his grandparents.

'16 Brother Nick Martin is still well remembered on the campus as one of our ex-Student Body Presidents. He is at present engaged in a law office in the home town —San Diego.

To his many friends on the campus and among the Faculty the news of the death of William Stewart Cannon came as a severe shock. Bill's quiet humor and genial good nature, coupled with his studious disposition, had endeared him in a very intimate way to his teachers and fellow students alike. Besides holding down the enviable position of Cadet Major when the R. O. T. C. was first instituted, Bill had the honor of being one of the two Santa Clara men to obtain the coveted Degree of Juris Doctor from their Alma Mater.

The circumstances of his death were unusually touching. After fighting its way through the battles of St. Mihiel, Chateau Thierry and the Marne, Bill's regiment was ordered home. After several days out he was stricken with appendicitis and forced to submit to an operation. When the troop ship neared land and the soldiers on deck sent up a roar of welcome as the Statue of Liberty hove in sight, Bill lay below, on his deathbed. Still young, always successful and with every prospect of reaping the rewards to which his glorious service record entitled him, Bill had everything to live for. God's Providence, however willed the Supreme Sacrifice and Bill's unquestioning Catholic faith responded with heroic submission.

In a letter written to his mother from France during the dark days when his life was in constant peril, Bill wrote that it was his wish, should worst come to worst, that a plaque be cast in his memory and placed near the altar where in his earlier years he had so often served Mass. In accordance with this request the Faculty has secured a bronze plaque which will shortly be erected in the chapel together with similar memorials for the eight other Santa Clara boys who died in the service of their country.

To the afflicted friends and relatives of William Stewart Cannon, the Redwood extends its sincerest condolences. Requiescat in pace.

George Nicholson was another of the old boys who paid us a visit on his return from France. George was always known as a brilliant scholar and a hard man to beat in a debate. Besides winning many literary distinctions "Nick" was twice Graduate Manager of Athletics. He is now practising law in San Jose.

Marshall Garlinger is at present employed with the Bethlehem Ship Building Corporation in San Francisco, as an expert on steam turbines, his duty being to inspect the power plant of each new ship turned out. He has purchased a home in the city, where he intends to make his permanent residence. The Redwood owes to Marshall an apology for a mistake made in one of its issues of last year. We were so occupied in our congratulations upon the new arrival in his household that inadvertently we chose to append to the name Delorma, girl, instead of boy. However we were misled by the oddity of the name.

Elmer Jensen, another Collegian of the '16 Class was recently discharged from the Navy, where he served as a commissioned officer.

Roy Emerson, of the '16 Civil Engineers, is connected with the Board of Fire Underwriters in San Francisco. Roy made a great name for himself in the army, having attained the rank of Captain before his discharge.

———

'17 Eugene Charles was on the campus several days ago shaking hands with his old friends. He reports that he is holding down a position as Engineer on the same board as Roy Emerson, whose office adjoins his. "Red" was another Santa Claran who made a success of the Army Game, as he was commissioned a First Lieutenant soon after his enlistment.

———

'18 It is reported that Cyril Coyle, our former stalwart Organist, has opened law offices in Sacramento. Cyril should prove a valuable addition to the legal profession in the Capitol City.

Hilding Johnson was last heard from in New York. Hilding attended the Officers' Training Camp at Camp Fremont, but unlike many of his class mates who were with him there, he was fortunate enough to get across. We soon expect to see Hilding among our Post-Graduates.

J. Charles Murphy, sometimes known as the poet laureate of the '18 Class, has entered the Sacred Heart Novitiate at Los Gatos. Last summer, when Charlie found his army discharge papers securely tucked in his pocket at Camp Lewis, he immediately pulled stakes for Alaska, where he spent several days in sight seeing. On his return home he displayed a fine collection of moccasins, bearskins and rugs in lieu of the German scalps and helmets he had promised his friends.

———

'19 Brian Gagan is a Post-Graduate in Law at the Georgetown University.

Clarence Canelo, also of the Class of '19, is registered in the Medical Department of the University of St. Louis.

Ex '20 John O'Neill was down with Jimmy Fitzpatrick, '15, during the summer months, visiting the scene of his former brilliant Rugby exploits.

"Fat" Howell and Joe Taber are studying medicine at the University of St. Louis.

We were pleased to hear that Capelle Damrell has been commissioned a Second Lieutenant in the regular Army. He was in France for over eighteen months where he saw continuous service.

Frank Hovely surely slipped one over on us recently when he dropped in with his bride of three months. The "nunc" Mrs. Hovely was the "quondam" Myrtle Dolan, daughter of Mr. and Mrs. John Dolan, prominent society people of Brawley. Frank was a popular man on the campus and the Redwood takes this occasion to extend the congratulations of the Student Body to the happy couple. May their wedded life be a happy and prosperous one.

what does concern us and what should be the concern of every member of Santa Clara's Alumni Association is the matter of its support. If you have still the interest of the old school at heart and if you are a loyal Santa Claran you will send in your subscription to yours as well as our Magazine. It is dependent upon the undivided support of the Alumni and will attain to success only in proportion to the efforts you extend towards its maintenance.

Just a word then in passing. In the first place be sure you have sent in your name for a year's subscription. It will be money well spent. Again, let us hear from you all frequently. Acquaint us with facts concerning yourselves so that we can do the Alumni justice and write up their department in a manner worth while. Keep the spirit of the old Santa Clara blended with that of the new and thus weld around her sons, both graduates and undergraduates, a chain of fidelity and good fellowship.

Concerning "Redwood" We might be ruled out of order for this insertion, but we have every grounds to presume that such will not be the case. A word concerning the Redwood as regards each and every Alumnus will not go amiss. It would be entirely unnecessary for us to acquaint you with the purposes for which the Redwood was established. But

St. Ignatius Drive Many Santa Clara Alumni took a prominent part in the recent St. Ignatius drive for a million dollars. Although this amount was not realized, the total was a handsome sum and will go a good part of the way toward paying off the heavy debt.

—Martin M. Murphy.

EXCHANGES

A Foreword Leaving the recollections of vacation days to melt away into the mellow mists of the memory, and summoning all our native resolutions for the final lap of our collegiate course, we enter upon the task of again Prussianizing the destinies of this department with a view of expressing our candid opinion upon the various literary productions that shall make their appearance upon the dusty desk of the Exchange.

Our course of the past, perhaps, may have been somewhat uncharitable; our judgments, too, may have appeared somewhat hasty and dogmatic—the fault of a youth entrusted with the dangerous duties of a critic; still, time and circumstances have given color to the unripe fruitions that have played such havoc of late, and, it is hoped, will make the task of 'Xchange man pleasant and profitable and replete with cherished memories that shall extend across the continent in fettered bonds of friendship. But we are reminded by the ancient poet:

"Injurioso ne pede proruas stantum columnem"

for, as he explains in his own peculiar way,

"Nihil est ab omni parte beatum."

Therefore, we are resolved that, whatever fortunes the literary tossed atmosphere of our sanctum may be heir to, we shall not, either by hasty criticism or imagined mental disorder, mar the stately columns of the honest efforts of our literary acquaintances.

The Martian It was with regret that we were forced to temporize the perusal of this "Harp of the North" on the very threshold of vacation; but, whatever circumstances on us imposed, friendship would not allow us to part so unceremoniously, and consequently on our arrival we make haste to take up the interesting pages of this visitor. There is a strange attractive something in the quaint Spanish lore that makes such a subject as "Isabella' always interesting. It is to be remarked, however, that the history of Spanish greatness has always struck a responsive chord in the heart of our Western civilization.

Another essay, with a striking and

37

forceful allusion, is "Ireland"; but, as to this topic, there is no further need of comment: it is on the lips of the world to-day.

The stories "Mutt", "The Turning" and "Perseverance" slightly tend towards mediocrity.

But whatever may be said about the stories, the literary standard of the Martian more than upholds itself by the excellence of the verse "The Fallen Pine". It is seldom that we find in any college magazine verse exhibiting such a high order of imaginative skill and artistic temperament. For its beautiful simile and suggestive thought this bit of poetry deserves our highest commendation. To conclude, it is with regret that we could not enjoy more of such excellent literary efforts.

The Springhillian
From the romantic South, in the region of Mobile, comes our friend with a pleasing array of college literature, which, on account of our annual departure from school, we were unable to review before the end of the term. But although we were forced to set it aside for the nonce, yet it only added to the interest and pleasure with which we perused its pages.

The impressions that we received on reading the opening verse "Easter Spray" were not lessened as we proceeded. Its beautiful imagery and choice of words almost tempted us to quote it at large. "A Chanson of Spring", another peace-time lyric with a melody all its own, led us into another happy mood. But at this moment we can still hear the martial air of the exquisite verse "Chateau Thierry". It has struck a tone, sympathetic as well as heroic, that we cannot quite forget.

In the realm of esays we have singled out the one written by J. Kopecky as the most entertaining and instructive; only, we are inclined to think that it is slightly over-burdened with quotation. Still the appreciative tone in which the author writes, and his able presentation of the charms of Catholic authoresses convert us at once into ardent admirers of their genius. Something with an old world tinge, and an historical setting is "A Memory of old Versailles". Forgotten characters always do interest us, even when almost lost in the shuffle of world events.

Duty compels us, not without regret, however, to record that the standard of the short story is not quite up to the par with other college magazines. The best in this issue is "Stratagems and Spoils". We followed with avidity every line of this stirring detective story, and would like to see more like it in the messenger of the South.

One word about the editorials: "Our New Coach" we consider as hardly proper in such a place, as the editorial sanctum should be rather exclusive. However, that is merely our own opinion.

Taken in all, the Easter number of the Springhillian is a well-balanced issue, and, needless to say, we are glad to continue on the same good terms of friendship and admiration.

The Borromean

When we first became interested in this golden-lettered issue some preternatural voice whispered in our ears the words "Anticipation is greater than realization"; but, with a sense of satisfaction and appreciation for the efforts of our friends, we have since come to the indisputable conclusion that it must have been someone other than our guardian Angel: for it was a literary treat, seldom enjoyed, to read the charming and stirring stories and aptly written verses in the pages of this Southern laureate. Therefore, we take issue with the ancient and unknown proverb-monger, and say "Realization is greater than anticipation".

As to the stories, we must confess that we are like the little girl who was at a loss which to choose between a plate of ice cream and a piece of cake. They are all of such a degree of excellence that to over-portion our praise to one rather than another would, strictly speaking, be slightly unfair. But even at the pain of being unfair, we must say that for intense love and heroism we honor "Of the Gallant 18th"; for unselfishness and a remarkable delineation of character we choose "The Face in a Ring of Gold"; for gripping action and a well-developed plot our meed of praise is for "When Cupid Used a German Code"; while for a delightful succession of romantic incidents we favor "A Question of Secrecy". Still, to oppose the tide, we noticed the absence of anything but war stories, which, however enjoyable they may be, lead us to desire a change of scenery.

As for the essays, we were able to locate only one, "The Champion of a Champion Cause"; but whatever was lacking in quantity was more than compensated for by excellent diction and forceful exposition on the character of the greatest of them all, "the grey man of Christ".

The same difficulty that we met with in the stories again encumbered us in the realm of poetry. "Pace Resuscitata" is a fine example of college verse. "The Tribute of a Rose" and "In a Village Graveyard" both express appropriate thoughts in good poetical imagery. We remarked, however, the custom, still prevalent in some college magazines, of filling in the space at the bottom of a page with ditties which possess very little if any literary value. It appears to us that it would be preferable to omit them entirely as the issue would not suffer in the least by their inconspicuous absence.

Again the good sense of the South manifests itself in its stirring, patriotic and statesmanlike editorials which breathe the unmistakable spirit of intense devotion to God and country. To conclude, our companionship with the Borromean is delightfully entertaining, and, as a suggestion, we would like to welcome it to our midst as a monthly production.

DOMINICAN COLLEGE YEAR BOOK.

"Beyond the sunlit waters,
  The mountains dry and brown
 · A valley lies, encircled
  By an eucalypti crown."

What must be the charms of the place that has sent us such a pleasing bit of literature all done in soothing mellow leaves, and bound with an appropriate cover? The Dominican College Year Book maintains, if, indeed, it does not surpass, the standard of previous years in the remarkable collection of excellent verses, good stories and enlightening essays. We especially noted the superior quality of the verses by Miss Nancy Pattison, who undoubtedly has fallen heir to the Lesbian lyre; and, as an excuse for our familiarity, we were tempted to quote some enchanting lines from "Spring in San Rafael." The beautiful imagery and peculiar sense of technique exhibited in her verses give promise of a bright future. But our praise is also directed elsewhere. For a good exposition and appreciation of the charms of our great poets, we have selected "Joyce Kilmer" and "The Dream of Gerontius" as presenting not only a thorough knowledge of the exquisite beauties of their poetry, but also, what is better, a clear insight of the noble character of these literary geniuses. As lovers of Horace we appreciate the excellent verse translations, which are uncommonly true to the original thought and mood.

There is in the cream-colored pages of this book a certain harmonious blending of verse, essay and story that untiringly leads us to admire it the more. So it is a distinction quite enviable to be able to exchange with such a well-wrought literary production as the messenger from the fairyland across the bay; and, needless to say, its presence is always welcomed in our midst, here in this kindred mission atmosphere. And while waiting for its coming, though its visits are long delayed, we freely confess our sympathy with the thought that—

"There my heart is held imprisoned
 By a fragrant green-tipped spell,
Calling, calling, calling,
 That it's Spring in San Rafael."

Athletic Officials

Robert F. Harmon
Coach

John O'Connell, S.J.
Moderator

James B. O'Connor
Student Manager

Alfred A. Ferrario
Captain

Our dear old pal Rugby, has taken the long, long trail. We have welcomed a stranger into our midst, and his title reads, American Football. There may be a few of us who have had the pleasure of playing this popular sport, but for the benefit of those who are new at the game, we may say that Santa Clara is indeed fortunate in securing such a capable introducer as Robert Emmett Harmon A. B., LL.B.

A good man is hard to find, so they say, but a good coach is still more difficult to locate. If ever you wish to glance at a man who knows the arts and sciences of American football from Alpha to Omega, just stroll down to our field any afternoon, for here is why we put our faith in Bob Harmon.

In the years from 1899 to 1904 he was a student at Illinois College at Jacksonville, Ill. During his first two years at this institution he was a Prep, but nevertheless he held down a position on the varsity, and at the end of his last year there he left the record of playing on every position of that team. The years 1905 and 1906 found him at Denver University. During his first year there he was given a tackle position on the All Rocky Mountain eleven, while in his second term he played on that same team as a guard. During the year 1907 Creighton University lost but one game. Bob alternated at full and half back on that team. From 1908 to 1910 he coached All Hallows College at Salt Lake City, turning out the best elevens that had ever represented that school. In 1911 the speedy Loyola University team of Chicago was tutored by him, and in 1912 the Butte, Montana, High School established a record under the coaching of Mr. Harmon. During 1913 and 1914 Gonzaga University turned out teams that the Northwest was proud of. Though there was, in the first year, a dearth of material, Harmon was quite successful, and only once during the second year did Gonzaga taste defeat, at the hands, namely, of the University of Montana. In 1915

41

Davis Farm changed from Rugby to the American game. In 1916 they lost but one game. St. Mary's, the Olympic Club, the University of Nevada, and the University of Utah were defeated, while the Freshman team of the University of California was played to a tie in one game, but finally won the second by a score of 3-0. After this successful career at Davis Farm, Harmon returned to Illinois and led them through the years of 1917 and 1918.

Out on the new gridiron can be seen daily a squad of players practicing as they have never practiced before, training as only those under the careful guidance of Coach Harmon train, and gradually evolving into an eleven of which we hope the past and present students of Santa Clara may well feel proud. They are: Captain Alfredo Ferrario, Los Angeles; Burke Curley, Berkeley; Larry Devlin, Los Angeles; Harry Jackson, Los Angeles; George Noll, Centerville; Dan Donovan, San Luis Obispo; Paul Reddy, Medford, Ore.; Porter Kerckhoff, Covina, Calif.; Caesar Manelli, San Francisco; Edwin Heafy, Oakland; Rudy Scholz, Medford, Ore.; James Neary, Spokane; Thomas Whelan, San Francisco; John Muldoon, Berkeley; Bill Muldoon, Berkeley; Tom Levy, Arcata, Calif.; John Jackson, Seattle; Tom Bannon, San Francisco; Dan Phelan, Berros; Emmett Daly, Butte, Montana; Louis Buty, Seattle; Tom Crowe, Tulare; Emmett Gleeson, Gleeson, Ariz.; Ernest Badolla, Gonzales; Roy Baker, Long Beach; Norbert Korte, Seattle; Eddie Amaral, Milpitas; John Lewis, Hollister; Edward Harter, San Jose; Ken Burg, Marysville; Alfred Abrahamsen, San Francisco; Lester Perasso, San Francisco; James Needles, Seattle; Demetrio Diaz, Lugo, Spain; Fred Moran, San Francisco; Michael Pecarovich, Seattle; Albert Brown, Colusa; William Shannon, San Jose; Martin Murphy, Milpitas; Leo DiFiori, San Jose; Raymond Schall, Long Beach; Bill Flynn, Los Angeles; and John Cronin, Los Angeles.

It has been said by the skeptical that the better a man is in Rugby the worse he shall be in American. Those who have followed Santa Clara's history in Rugby will undoubtedly recognize the names of a few of our past Rugby stars in our present squad. It is certain that when the whistle is blown and the red and white charge down the field in their first game, that lineup will contain a number of Rugby stars. They will be in that battle not because they know Rugby, but for the obvious reason that they understand American Football and are in a perfect physical condition to play it.

Behind our squad stands our new Moderator of Athletics, Fr. John O'Connell, S. J., our Student Manager, James O'Connor, our Faculty, and a student body wherein the good old Santa Clara pep is paramount.

During the games we are to play this season two familiar faces will be seen in the position of yell leaders. Wilkie

Mahoney, the long-armed individual from San Luis Obispo, who giggles through his nose, and Ed Harter of San Jose, who knows the ways of Santa Clara from hard experience, will lead the husky larynxed youths whose voices will carry high into the thin ether whether the eleven carrying the pig-skin for the red and white is facing victory or defeat.

As yet, our schedule is incomplete, but suffice it to say, whether we play the best team or the worst, and whether we win or lose, our opponents shall always remember that they have participated in an American Football game.

—J. E. Neary.

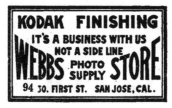

KODAK FINISHING
IT'S A BUSINESS WITH US
NOT A SIDE LINE
WEBBS PHOTO SUPPLY STORE
94 SO. FIRST ST. SAN JOSE, CAL.

BEST SHOES MADE!

Buy New One's and Rebuild the
Old Ones like New

L. SANCHEZ

982 Franklin St.   Santa Clara

If It's Made of Paper
We Have It !

The San Jose Paper Co.

Phone San Jose 200
161-181 W. SANTA CLARA ST.

LOUIS CHABRE & JEAN MILLET, Props.   Phone San Jose 4763

PARISIAN BAKERY

FRENCH AND AMERICAN BREAD

PIES AND CAKES

Pain de Luxe, French Rolls, Parisian, Richelieu, Rolls Fendu, Vienna Rolls, Etc.

Automobiles deliver to all parts of city   251 W. San Fernando St., San Jose

---

A. G. COL CO.

Wholesale Commission Merchants

Tele hone San Jose 309

CONTENTS

Santa Clara Varsity
1919

Cochrane
End

Mueller
Halfback

O'Connor
Student Mgr.

Roe
Asst.

Scholz
*

Jackson
Halfback

Scholz
Co

The Redwood

Entered Dec. 18, 1902, at Santa Clara, Cal., as second-class matter, under Act of Congress of March 3, 1879

VOL. XIX   SANTA CLARA, CAL., NOVEMBER, 1919   NO. 2

In Memoriam

JOSEPH M. NERI, S. J.
Born January 16th, 1836; Died November 17th, 1919

NOT earth's vain pomp, O Saintly Priest, nor fame
Captive thy soul could chain. Up to the high
Eternal throne o'er rugged Calvary
Thy lofty spirit marched. O chast'ning flame
Thrice---sanctified that urged thee in His name
Thy sinless self for sin to crucify---
E'en as thy master, living but to die
For man. O Loved of God! What puissant claim
Thus drew thee? What stirred thy noble heart
To lighten darkened worlds? What presence did inspire
Thy valiant going, Xavier-like, apart
From all thou hadst most dear? What strong desire
Compelled thee hearken to His word---"Depart,
"My son! Go forth and set the world on fire!"

Caveat Emptor

(Let the Buyer Take Care.)

Henry C. Veit.

R. JOHN HOLBROOK, JR., star quarterback of the Clarenta football team was really more perturbed than his thoughtful mien portrayed. His indifferent posture as he lazily lolled in the afternoon sunshine on the steps of the Elite Cottage, suggested the gloom that had come over him. He toyed with his rule book as if undecided whether or not to open it. An undergraduate might have been led to believe that his glum attitude was caused by the recent bawling out received from the Coach. The latter had admonished Holbrook vehemently to forget about furs and frills and confine himself solely to football. To forget the former and devote more thought to the latter was really his present aim, however it was not the burning advice of the Coach that prompted him to action. He was violently engaged in falling out of love for a different reason.

There was a time, only a few short months ago when Holbrook had considered himself heart-whole and care-free, then Julie Baldwin happened along and upset his confidence in himself. Because she had always induced him on many occasions, to buy tickets for dances and socials and church fairs and what-nots, from her, he had grown to always connect her name with ticket selling. He had not been particularly mindful of the legal phrase wherein the buyer is cautioned to take care. Rather had he permitted his heart free scope, with the result that its strings had become enmeshed in an intricate affair, which he traced from that memorable night at the Country Club when he had first danced with Miss Julie, then a tete-a-tete on the dimly lit veranda overlooking the hushed city, when he had made violent love to her. He had a pleasant recollection of his subsequent call at her pretty little home, the night at the movies, the party at Miss Newcome's and ever so many other little incidents that caused him pleasure in retrospection. He had about arrived at that juncture, he thought, when the psychological moment was at hand for man to propose and woman to properly dispose.

Then a string of circumstances arose that caused him to think all womankind too fickle. To be sure there was another man in the case. He had con-

46

cluded there were many. One by one he summoned them for trial in his mind's court and one by one he acquitted them until one Harry Quick, an aspiring—supercilious, he thought— young author took the stand. He found unanimity for conviction. There he rested his case for further evidence.

Miss Julie Baldwin was not the type of heroine the vast majority of young writers choose to eulogize or turn into a beautiful goddess by a facile pen. She had none of the flowing tresses that shone golden in the sunlight like a delicately spun web; neither had she those incomparable, soft-hued, soulful eyes that seem inseparable from attractiveness. She had none of those things grown bromidic by constant repetition throughout the pages of innumerable volumes. Miss Julie was a very ordinary person made extraordinary in the possession of unusual qualities. Holbrook had found in her, good breeding, a sunny disposition and a beaming personality that seemingly had grown in its magnetism as the days of his acquaintanceship had been told. He had admitted long since being in love with her and so being, grew aware of the usual attendant little jealousies.

Holbrook thought Quick too ready to proffer attentions to Miss Julie. He recalled with what avidity the youthful author purchased Julie's tickets at first approach. He disliked such insidiousness, especially as coming from Quick. He was minded how Quick was wont to glow and unconsciously to straighten his tie at mere mention of her name. Repeatedly he had wished to bowl him over, but condescension or something else stayed his impulse.

What annoyed Holbrook most of all was the fact that Julie appeared to manifest no disregard for Quick. Jack's finer sense should have stood him in good stead. Good breeding dictated at least a recognition of these attentions on Julie's part when no infringement of propriety obtained. Unconsciously Holbrook was passing through that stage of misapprehension experienced by everyone tutoring under Dan Cupid.

Holbrook read a few of the rules and permitted his mind, alternately to wander to Julie. He had sent her a little note inviting her to come to the rally, less than a week away, and at the same time, realizing her joy in watching anything athletic, had taken pains to inclose two tickets for the coming Big Game. Her failure to respond annoyed him. She had hitherto been punctual. The mere thought of the possibility that Quick might have bid to be blessed with her company at the big rally, before his own little missive made the reservation, galled him. He confided to himself the wish that his presence with the team that night would not be a necessity. But the Coach had expressed his will and it was inexorable.

A sudden awakening to the realization that practise was but minutes away, disturbed his reverie. He set to that day's work-out with greater determination.

Miss Julie Baldwin had sought the quiet of her room after a troublesome day at the office. The boss had seemed decidedly out of spirit. He had been grouchy. Everyone seemed put out over something and she had seemed to sense a catching of the contagion. The roseate hue of her room had been consoling.

She observed a letter upon the table, however the jangling phone stayed her from acquainting herself of its contents.

"Hello!" she found herself speaking into the phone.

"How do you do," she returned. "Why no.—Yes, I'd love to—You'll call about 7:30?"

It was really the first time Quick had caused her real pleasure. But in her frame of mind anyone could have instilled a spark of joy into her. She reached for the letter. It provoked a surprised "Oh" from her. She was determined to seek a release from her promise to Quick, but on second thought she refrained.

Miss Julie found herself in a very peculiar circumstance. She had long ago decided that she was in love with young Holbrook and seemed at the same time conscious that she had let him guess her fondness. She looked upon Quick merely as a very affable young fellow with not enough seriousness in his make-up to cause her palpitating organ any unusual alarm.

Too, she had awakened to the realization that an old family tradition was about to step in and play havoc with her affair with Holbrook unless she could strike a compromise somehow with this ancestral superstition. She recalled from her fireside memories the admonishment of Granny Jones. She had never thought herself to be really superstitious, yet Miss Julie found it hard to evade this inexorable grip.

"Never accept, the first proposal," Granny had admonished, "it is sure to end in unhappiness, if you do."

Thus tossed between love and the fear of impending unhappiness if she disregarded the old family tradition, Julie had been at a loss to know what to do. She had since hit upon a definite plan.

"Poor Jack will be thinking all-sorts of things," she consoled, "but I must go to the rally with Harry."

II

The huge siren was shrieking its announcement of the coming event. Already numberless machines had lined the driveways. People flocked to the campus to witness the annual conflagration, wherein Drake's effigy, surmounting the huge pyre, was an omen of the defeat that was to be administered to Clarenta's rival in the morrow's contest. The thunderous applause from the serpentining undergraduates, as the flames leaped high above the fifty-foot heap, awed the populace. They watched, gripped by the spirit that made Clarenta's name and fame reach far afield into the domain of rival institutions. It was a manifestation of that spirit that augured well to Holbrook, who with his team mates viewed the spectacle from the speaker's platform, a stand draped with the red and white of Clarenta's colors.

The surging crowd gathered close. The populace, with the students caught up the yells with one accord. The drum yell, the locomotive and other cheers carried far out into the still night as a single acclaim from thousands of throats, to the fearless manly fellows about to defend the laurels of the old institution.

"Wonderful," intoned Quick into Julie's ringing ear.

She nodded approval, with a deal of apparent interest in the youth about to address the multitude. Calm and quiet fell upon the crowd.

A clear resonant voice introduced, Captain Holbrook. Pandemonium broke loose in the subsequent cheer.

Julie observed his gay eyes and fine forehead. She glowed as none other, at the masterful exhortation to loyal backing, spirited rooting and fight as it fell from the lips of Holbrook. She stood on tip-toe to better her view.

Holbrook had stopped abruptly. He riveted his gaze upon her, then upon Quick. An applause broke forth from the crowd. Julie felt herself redden to the shoulder blades. She felt guilty. She longed to explain and set at ease that quizzical countenance. She regretted she had not informed him beforehand.

He hastened on to his conclusion. Ju-

lie thought him wanting a few degrees in the intensity of his earlier enthusiasm. She resolved she would seek him out after the rally and essay an explanation. She hoped he would listen.

The last stragglers hovered about the still glowing embers of the consumed pyre. Julie felt lonesome. She seemed oblivious of the presence of Quick beside her. Holbrook was nowhere to be found. She wanted true companionship.

Julie thought she heard Harry whisper something about moon and stars and romance. She found herself nodding approval, however ignorant of what he had really said.

A late, mellow autumn moon smiled in the heavens, a golden orb in a blanket of sparkling stars, betraying glimpses of some bright, peaceful haven beyond. Quick felt a touch of the romantic surmounting him as they sauntered toward the Baldwin home.

Julie for the first time caught the significance of his words.

"Can't you see, Julie, I love you?" he was saying.

She felt a peculiar twang. She began to realize she had been nodding just the opposite of her true mind. She withdrew from his closeness, abashed.

"You first made me happy, by selling me tickets, Julie," he continued. "They brought me to love you. Won't you let me try to make you happy forever?" he insisted.

She only shook her head negatively.

"You can always be a friend if you want," was all she said.

Harry grew uneasy. He sensed a feeling that he had intruded.

"I have tickets for tomorrow's game. Would you care to go," he volunteered.

"Thank you, but I'm supplied already."

The chrysanthemums, bordering the gravel approach to Julie's home could have told you she felt lightsome as she tripped to her room; gay because the old family tradition still remained unshattered. The same nodding flowers could have told you Quick was putting himself the question, why he had not exercised a little more caution in his purchase of tickets. He regretted the truth of Caveat Emptor.

Julie found a tinge of sorrow discoloring her happiness. She sorrowed over Jack's displeasure and longed to make amends.

"I'll have to call up Ramona," she said, "the dear old soul can help me out."

Julie found in Ramona—of Castilian antecedents—a confidant, worldly wise and prudent.

"Hello, Ramona dear," she was saying over the phone, "this is Julie. I want you to go up to the game with me tomorrow. Jack sent me tickets. Yes I do. I had a perfectly killing experience this evening. But you'll come, won't you. Yes. All right. Bye, bye."

III

Jack Holbrook had returned to his rooms immediately after the rally. He was not exactly surprised over the sight of Julie with Quick. He had surmised as much when she failed to answer his note, however he conceded being a little annoyed by her action. He was rather confident now that woman was made, just to be a flighty creature, with no definite aim, but fluttering about from flower to flower, like a butterfly, sipping of ever changing sweets. Holbrook again thought himself in the class of the heart-whole and care-free.

The day of the Big Game dawned bright and clear. It gave early evidences of a splendid afternoon. Holbrook however had become too absorbed in rehearsing his plays for the coming struggle. He thought of little else, not even the benignity of nature. He grew nervous and wished for the commencement of the fray. It came sooner than he realized, in spite of its seeming slowness.

The stands were filled to the topmost circle. Everywhere was a bustle. The spectators were restless, now and then turning toward the northern entrance to the stadium, to catch a first glimpse of the rival elevens trotting out upon the field. The opposing rooting sections presented a uniform display of nervous, closely crammed human atoms. Yell leaders from the two institutions were giving out final instructions through a huge megaphone eleventh hour reminders of the various stunts to be used.

A mighty cheer arose from thousands of throats, finely attuned, as the teams filed through the doorway and jogged down the turf, fine, robust, sinewy fellows, displaying little of that nervousness usually attendant upon all such encounters. A storm of confetti snowed down over the Drake yell section. It looked for all the world like a miniature blizzard. Now settled, the distinct outline of a huge block D was exposed to view. A like scene was taking place in Clarenta's section of loyal rooters; a red C in a background of white. Echoes of defiance reverberated across field in a rhythmic tune. And above it all, though scarcely audible, sounded the shrill blast of the referee's whistle. The football classic of the season was on.

Julie, nestled by the side of Ramona, was quite the most tickled piece of humanity in all that vast crowd. She manifested her glee by an exuberant display of enthusiasm. She clapped a pair of tiny hands and shouted herself hoarse with each advance of the ball into Drake's territory. She little realized she was repeatedly calling to Jack, exhorting him to a better display of his prowess. Whether it benefitted the cause of Clarenta or not, she did not take time to determine. He was proving an able general and the Red and White was plunging through to its objective by goodly gains. Ramona could have told Julie, that never before had she seen her so enthused over an athletic contest.

Between halves, with the struggle still in a deadlock, Julie was telling Ramona, although in a very hoarse voice that persisted in wandering off in a ludicrous pitch, just how killing her experience was with Quick, the night before.

"He must have thought me in love with him," she intoned. "He told me when I sold him tickets, I'd made him love me. Queer, wasn't it?"

She did not permit Ramona an answer. All the latter could do was nod approval, before Julie rambled on once more.

"Tell me, Romy, do I always sell tickets? Jack told me he always linked my name with ticket selling. That reminds me; I have a number to dispose of for the entertainment."

A moment for a breathing spell ensued.

"I hope," she continued, "he isn't terribly angry with me for last night's ——" but the resumed play carried her thoughts back again, immediately to the game.

A thunderous cheer broke loose from Clarenta rooters, as the Red and White drew first blood.

Julie lost sight of the man, in the heap, who had actually scored the first try for Clarenta. She thought it was Jack. One by one the players arose from on top of the man with the ball. He who had carried it over, lay still. A blast of the whistle signaled time out. A youth, lugging a water pail and a first aid satchel dashed to where the supine form lay. Presently Holbrook was carried from the field unconscious.

While a cheer broke forth from Clarenta's rooters for Captain Holbrook, Julie permitted herself a few brief moments of planning. Had she reflected longer she might not have determined in the manner she did, but she acceded to first impulse.

Ramona caught something about: "I'm going. Meet you at the Garage. Wait for me." And with that, Julie started for the exit.

She overtook the cortege at a halted machine just outside the entrance. She gathered up bits of a fragmentary conversation: "Kick in the head! Emergency Hospital," as the machine darted away.

Julie pondered a moment, then hailed a passing street car. At a florist's she dismounted and ordered a bouquet of roses sent to Mr. Jack Holbrook, Jr., Emergency Hospital.

"Please," she requested of the affable attendant, "include a card with this written upon it: 'You played a magnificent game. Hope you have a rapid recovery,' and sign it, Constance Murray."

Her next determination was to go to the hospital. She was refused admittance to his room.

"He'll be all right, Miss," consoled the elderly nurse. "The doctor says it was merely a stunning blow on the head and he will be out in a day or so."

When Jack Holbrook regained consciousness late that same evening his first question was—who had won the game? When he learned that it had ended in a tie, he felt depressed. He had convinced himself long before the happening of his injury, that Clarenta would surely be the winner. Now he was anxious to learn why a tie score had resulted.

His nurse had an abhorrence of this American way of making undertakers happy. She disapproved of this open exposure to inevitable serious hurt. Holbrook could get little satisfaction from her.

"Some flowers for you," said the nurse presenting him with the bouquet.

Holbrook wondered at sight of the card. He could not quite recall ever having met Miss Constance Murray. However, deeming that fact, really to be unimportant he dismissed further useless worry over it. He thought her possibly to be some society belle, caught up by the love for this sport, and one with an exceedingly kind heart to send such flowers to a perfect stranger.

IV

True to the doctor's prediction, Holbrook was back again on the campus, late in the evening of the day following the Big Game. The coach advised a complete relaxation. He suggested to every member of the team to accept Miss Constance Murray's invitation to the big masquerade two days hence. Holbrook thought indifferently of the matter, but acquiesced, upon further persuasion. He believed his apathy toward the affair to be due to his lost faith in the constancy of the weaker sex. He likewise thought that he had forgotten entirely, Miss Julie Baldwin. More out of appreciation to Miss Murray for her lovely flowers did he choose to present himself at the masqued function.

It proved to be an elaborate affair, with any number of new fads in costume, very much in evidence.

"I want to thank you, Miss Murray," he was saying shortly after his introduction, "for the nice bunch of roses you sent me in the hospital."

He didn't seem to realize she was praising him for his splendid work in the game. Her words seemed meaningless. It was certain he had not heard her saying how much she really enjoyed that game. What Holbrook found a little more absorbing interest in was the fact that she resembled Julie so much. He thought he could recognize certain of Julie's characteristics, even in back of Miss Murray's masque.

He did not know why, but unconsciously he began gazing about, in the expectation of being able to recognize Quick and Julie. Quick had always seemed so attentive to her, so he felt certain of his presence, although as yet he had not discovered any resemblance. Once he thought he had found Quick in a queerly composed costume. He was not sure, although he felt certain the dress was just what Quick would wear.

The orchestra struck up a sprightly

air. Holbrook had not decided to dance but the catchy tune caught his feet in an inclination to one step.

"May I have this dance, Miss Murray?"

"Certainly, you may, Mr. Holbrook."

They circled in and about the laughing, happy crowd. He was aware that his partner had a dress of some shimmering satiny stuff.

Before realizing it the dance had ended when it seemed just begun. Perhaps it was the costume display that had absorbed his interest. He had not spoken a word and he felt he should. The moonlight flooding the veranda in a fantastic design as it filtered through the trellis above, suggested to him to propose a little talk out there.

The night was decidedly Californian, with its balmy air, its golden moon above, in a meadowland of stars. Holbrook heard Miss Murray comment on its beauty. He too sensed the romantic touch.

"I was just simply wild over that game," she said, accepting a proffered seat beside him, in a secluded little nook overlooking the spacious gardens. "I was so afraid I wouldn't get tickets, but a very dear, kind friend sent me some. They seemed so difficult to get."

Holbrook answered in the affirmative. For the first time he began to wonder if Julie had been present at the game.

"That reminds me, Mr. Holbrook," she continued, "I want to sell you a ticket to a benefit entertainment. Won't you buy one for the worthy cause?"

He turned to her inquisitively. He thought he saw a smile flit across her delicate features and wished her masque was removed. .

"Well, really, Miss Murray, I can't refuse you, although I should."

"But why should you hesitate?"

Her query was but part of her natural feminine curiosity.

"Oh! That's a long story," he returned.

"But I'd love to hear it."

"I was once very much caught up with a fine young lady," he narrated, "just because she always sold me tickets. The fact is before I fully realized it I was in love with her."

Julie really thrilled at this confession. A woman always likes to be told she is loved.

"Perhaps I should have been a little more cautious," he continued.

"Why!"

"Well if I had, I might not have been so terribly peeved when I learned she seemed to be fickle."

Julie winced inwardly. The accusation hurt.

"Perhaps she wasn't fickle at all. Maybe she had good cause for her action."

Julie was defending her sex in general, and herself in particular, at the same time thinking how nicely the family tradition had been met with. She really felt a bit sorry for Quick, nevertheless she only thought him a mere friend.

"Perhaps I had better not sell you a ticket then, Mr. Holbrook! You might again—"

"Oh! That's perfectly all right," he assured her, fully confident in himself, "I'd be pleased to buy one from you." .

But Julie, for reasons all her own, tactfully changed the subject to the Grand March. She thought it about time for its commencement. They returned to the Ball Room. Already the masqueraders were forming for the famous old march. Holbrook and Julie fell in line toward the rear.

Jack Holbrook was quite the most surprised being in ages when he turned to his companion as she removed her masque. Speech temporarily left him. He could only stare, undetermined just how to take the situation.

"Please don't look at me that way, Jack," pleaded Julie. "I don't want you to be angry. I want to explain to you. Let's go back out upon the veranda and see if we two can't laugh once more together."

He consented. He couldn't resist her plea. She looked too lovely in her dainty costume.

"Why didn't you answer my note?" he queried.

Then she related the incident.

"But you should have answered anyway," he chided sincerely.

"Please, Jack, let's not quarrel."

The next few minutes he was being informed of the old family tradition, how it had been carried out with Quick as the unfortunate—Holbrook thought otherwise however concerning the young author.

Holbrook was simultaneously listening to Julie and recalling what he had said about her fickleness, just a short while ago.

"Miss Julie," he whispered.

"Yes."

"I want you to forgive me for the uncharitable things I said about you. I was misled."

They caught the plaintive sobbing of a waltz floating out to them on the veranda.

"Before we go in for this dance, Miss Julie, will you sell me one of those tickets?"

"But I thought you were going to be cautious," she teased.

"Why should I now?"

They stood there a moment in silence. Out of the night somewhere ahead of them a whip-poor-will was calling a last good-night to its mate.

Holbrook turned to Julie.

"When my senior year is finished," he intoned softly, "I want you to sell me a life ticket to your heart."

Julie shook her head affirmatively.

Speech of Coach Harmon

We are on the eve of the Big Game. Perhaps many of you are even now putting yourselves the question. "Well, who is going to win?" In answer to that question, I can rightly say: I don't know. But of this much I feel absolutely certain. When we leave the field tomorrow afternoon, after the final whistle has been sounded, Stanford is going to know full well that she has been in a real football game.

To what degree of gridiron grooming these lads have attained, only the morrow's game can decide. Nevertheless I feel every confidence that not a single man who will have played upon the Stanford field against the Cardinal will not but do his utmost, by every possible fair means to assist in carrying home the laurels of victory to Santa Clara.

The wonderful old Santa Clara spirit which I know will be very much in evidence in tomorrow's encouraging indeed. It the Red and White. Pos more of an incentive to a stimulus to quick, ra than is the loyal backing dred rooters, cheering through every minute play. Santa Clara has n spirit throughout the s will not fail tomorrow.

Unfortunately our st will not start the game. slow up some most valu that should not disheart When the whistle soun fray is on, the team will never for a moment to l tensity, until the last n when, we hope, the tall; favor.

ROBERT EMMET.
Coac

The Red and White

I.

O the breeze, inspiring banner! Thou, today, art fitting theme---
Thou whose folds are all resplendent with the sun of glory's beam!
    Yonder purple hills know well
    Santa Clara's ancient yell,
When the White and Crimson standard floats in triumph o'er
    the team!
    And the flame of bright tradition
    Warms the blood of new ambition---
For the annals of the Campus glow with conquests of the team!
    From of old, the golden vale
    Knows the echo-rousing tale :---
      "Victory!
          "Rah, rah, rah! The Team."

II.

When our big corporeal engines, with the fires of life agleam,
Roar adown the struggling greensward, all athrob with virile steam,
    The responsive hills around
    Catch the meaning of the sound
As the foemen reel and stagger from the onrush of the team!
    O, the townsman never wonders
    At the crash of vocal thunders
Which announce another victim to the prowess of the team !---
    He has heard it oft before!
    It's the same old tale once more :---
      "Victory!
          "Rah, rah, rah! The Team."

III.

Red and White, forever onward in the van of Progress stream!
Red and White, the urge of heroes, Honor's sign, Excelsior's dream!
    Field or forum, be our fight
    For thy fame, old Red and White---
For thy fame without a blemish,---while thy warriors of the team
    Wreathe thee ever with their glory---
    Make thee soul of song and story---
While the sons of Santa Clara hail the triumphs of the team,
    And the oft-repeated tale
    Rolls again to hill and vale :---
      "Victory!
          "Rah, rah, rah! The Team."

CHARLES D. SOUTH

The Quitter

Frank Maloney.

UARTER-BACK SAL-
TER received the kick
and tucking the pig-
skin under his arm he
began to swerve and
dodge up the gridiron
towards his opponents' goal.

"Stop him! Stop him!" shouted the
Brandon rooters.

"Go it, Salter! Go it!" screamed
the supporters of St. Ridges.

And Salter went. Twisting, squirm-
ing, fighting like a demon every inch
of the way, on, on, he sped, the white
yard-lines flying away from beneath his
feet. The stands were wild with excitement—the bedlam of sirens, cheers
and yells grew louder and louder till
it became one deafening roar. Then it
suddenly ceased. Salter was out in the
open with a clear field for a touchdown
save for the presence ahead of him of
one man. That one was Clancy, the
wickedest tackler on the Brandon
team. The bleacherites held their breath
in the fascination of the moment. If
Salter should elude him it would mean
victory. Narrower and narrower grew
the space between the two men—the
one crouching and watchful, the other
erect and running with might and main.
Then Clancy left his feet in a powerful
lunge and Salter momentarily paused.

He was going to swerve. No! He had
stopped dead in his tracks and was
borne to the ground without a show of
resistance. The crowd fell back, stupe-
fied. What had happened? Even as
the question formed itself in their
minds the pistol shot announced the
end of the game—the end of the game
and the first victory that Brandon had
gained over St. Ridges in nine years.

The St. Ridges rooters filed out of
the stands in ominous silence. They
were dazed—they could not understand
it. Salter—their star, their idol—had
shown a yellow streak. A St. Ridges
player, yellow. A wearer of the Blue
and Grey a coward! It was too much.

In the club-house too, the players
moved about as though in a dream.
They had fully expected Coach Andrews to dismiss Salter from the squad
instantly, and instead they had observed during his few remarks whenever
his glance met that of Salter, a peculiar
and somewhat sad expression in his eye.
They realized that there was some understanding between the two men, but
in what it consisted they did not know.
But they did know one thing, and that
was that Salter had lost the game. Of
that they were certain and as they
thought it over and played the game
again in their minds, detail after detail,

58

up to the very moment of disaster, their anger grew gradually to white heat. Finally, Butch Conway, the giant captain of the team, could control himself no longer. Rising, he strode across the room to where the little quarter was changing.

"Well," he asked, his tone vibrant with sarcasm, "how does our little hero feel after the game? Was he much hurt by his fall?"

"Not so much that he can't stuff dirty remarks back down the throats of would-be foot-ball players."

Conway's smoldering rage needed just that much to make it break out into flame. "You d———d yellow little cur!" he cried, and all his two hundred and twenty pounds went into the blow he aimed at Salter's jaw. Quick as a flash the quarter-back ducked and then came to the surface with a pair of slashing upper-cuts that almost sent the big fellow to the floor. Hastily the remaining players intervened and after a time succeeded in quieting Conway. Soon after they departed, leaving Salter alone with his own bitter thoughts. The unhappy lad stood for a moment gazing after them; then, with a vicious kick, he sent his equipment into a corner and made his way to his room.

There he found that his troubles had but begun. As soon as he entered, his room-mate who was already within, without so much as glancing his way, stood up, put on his coat and departed. From that time on, sleeping hours excepted, the two were never in the room

together, nor did they ever exchange a single word. On the campus and during the practice it was the same story. At Salter's approach, little groups of students would suddenly disperse as if they feared contamination from his presence. Those, even, who had once called themselves his friends now studiously avoided him; while former enemies took advantage of the popular sentiment to make his life unbearable by open slights and insults. He was ostracised—an outcast in his college world. But he was determined to last it out—to prove to them that, no matter what else they might say of him, he was not a coward.

Of all forms of persecution, however, the most wearing on a man's moral courage is that which consists of endless petty meannesses. Consequently, the coach who was aware of the strain which Salter was under, was not surprised, when one evening the latter called and announced his intention of leaving the school.

"You see, Mr. Andrews," he concluded, "how miserable the whole thing must make me. I hate to be a baby, but I'm detested here. The fellows avoid me; the men on the team cut me openly. They say I'm yellow and a coward. And all because of that—" here he stopped and something suspiciously like a sob caught at his throat. For a long time the coach made no reply. Then rising he approached Salter and placing his hand on the lad's shoulder, asked:

"Jack, are you a quitter?"

Salter's eyes flashed as he answered.

"You know, sir, that I am not."

"Do you know what a quitter is."

"Well, sir, I suppose it's a fellow who begins something, and then gives it up because he thinks it's going to be hard on him."

"Exactly, Jack," replied the coach. "Exactly. Now, you have begun something; you have begun to hold your head high and to put up a fight against the unjust treatment the fellows have dealt out to yon. I know the fight seems hard, but, my boy, don't quit."

"I guess you're right at that, coach," said Salter, smiling rather ruefully. "Gee! I sure would have booted it, if I hadn't come and talked things over with you. Later on, I guess, I'd never forgive myself were I to leave now. I think I'll stay."

"Good, Jack! That's the spirit. Somehow or other, if you stick with it, this whole affair will come out alright. Good-night, my boy."

"Good-night, sir."

As he closed the door and walked down the steps, Salter made up his mind that he would, if necessary, bid defiance to the Student Body for the entire year. The determination expressed itself in the grim smile, the proud carriage, the fearless look with which he met the glances of a little band of students gathered together on the street corner.

"Holy smoke!" ejaculated one of the latter after he had passed. "What's biting the Chrome Kid tonight? He's walking on the world."

"Must be trying to drown his sorrows," said another. "If Andrews catches him at that he'll give him the bounce, sure. If he had any sense he'd have done it already. That kid has about as much scrap as a captured German.

"He hasn't been drinking, Al," put in a third, "if he had, I would have smelt it. We were so close that our overcoats touched. He must have gotten some good news some other way. Wonder what it was?"

"Maybe someone tipped him off that the rules committee is going to abolish tackling and pick the All-American out of the yellowest men in the country."

"Oh, come on, Al! Give the kid a chance. Salter's done enough nervy things on the field to show he's not as bad as all that. Anyway, he stood right up when big Butch started on him that day in the quarters. Maybe there's another side to his story."

"Yes, maybe! Maybe lots o' things! Maybe the Allies would have won the war if the Americans hadn't gone into it. Maybe!"

"Well, just as you like. For my part, I'm going to wait a little while and see."

The words of the second speaker represented the attitude of the students during the rest of the season and right up to the "Big Game", which took place some weeks after the incident related above. On the evening preceding the great day an out-door rally on a large scale was held. A huge bonfire was lighted; songs and yells echoed and re-echoed; boxing matches, fast and furious, were staged. Captain Conway was called on for a speech, but in the manner of foot-ball captains from time immemorial, his words were few, albeit they were full of meaning. Then the coach was called on and silence fell upon the audience, for they knew that Andrews could do two things very well —coach a team and give a speech. He spoke of the team and of its work during the season; he dwelt upon the spirit of the school which, though sometimes defeated had "never been conquered." Finally he announced the line-up for the morrow's contest:

"Hickey and Matthews, ends; Conway and Finnegan, tackles; Casey and Lethaby, guards; Ryan, center; Murray and Roach, halves; McDonald, full, and—"

They were all attention to hear who would play quarter—Salter, the "Quitter", or Holt.

"—Quarter, Jimmy Holt."

Cheers burst from the assembled students; cheers for the team collectively; cheers for the players individually; cheers for the substitutes; and even, in the exuberance of their good feeling, a cheer for Salter.

The next day seemed made by the very gods for foot-ball. The air was crisp and cool with just enough of the bite and tang of Winter in it to make the blood leap along the veins and lend

a deeper tint of red to healthy cheeks. The stands of the St. Ridges stadium were a riot of color. Pennants, ribbons, streamers of all sorts fluttered and danced in the light breeze. On one side reigned the Blue and Grey of old St. Ridges; on the other, the Crimson of St. Charles.

At precisely half-past two, the St. Charles team, amid the shouts of their supporters, trotted onto the field. A minute later, the St. Ridges team appeared and just then a cloud of confetti hid their portion of the stands from view. The strains of "Dear St. Ridges" burst forth from a thousand throats and when the confetti had blown away, a perfect S. R. in blue against a background of grey had been formed, while the right hand of every student moved back and forth, keeping time with the music.

Then the whistle sounded for the kick-off. There was a thud of leather against leather and the ball, propelled by the powerful foot of Duffy of St. Charles sailed far into St. Ridges territory. It was caught by Murray, who ran it back forty yards. Without the loss of a second Holt shouted his signals and Roach plunged through for eight yards. He was followed by McDonald, who went for six and a first down. Then Holt started his tackles, Conway and Finnegan, on a parade for the goal. Three yards, six yards, five yards, two yards —slowly but steadily, St. Charles was pushed back until the oval rested on the twenty-yard line. Suddenly the St. Ridges men opened up into a large spread. It was done so rapidly that before St. Charles could shift into a suitable defense, the ball had been snapped back and forward-passed quickly to Murray, who went over for a touchdown. Conway kicked the goal and the score stood seven to nothing.

It seemed that that one touchdown was all that was needed to bring the Crimson gridders to their senses. From then on, a battle was fought that will live in the annals of both institutions for many a year. Until the close of the half the two teams see-sawed back and forth in the middle of the field, the ball now in the possession of one side, now in that of the other.

When the second half opened, a couple of new men were in the St. Charles line-up. It was evident that the changes had strengthened the team. Inch by inch, step by step, the Crimson phalanx advanced, using all the while straight foot-ball. With their heels planted deep in the chalk of their own goal line, the line-men of St. Ridges held for two downs, but on the third, the pigskin was across by what seemed a fraction of an inch. The goal was easy and the score was tied.

When the ball was put into play again, however, St. Charles was made to realize that it was not for nothing that the Blue and Grey warrors had been dubbed "The Fighting Irish". Though unable to gain consistently themselves the "Micks" put up a stub-born, stone-wall defense and when the final intermission arrived the ball was in neutral territory. At the opening of the fourth quarter both teams resorted to punting tactics with St. Ridges gaining a slight advantage. With five more minutes left to play, St. Ridges at last managed to gain possession of the ball on their opponents' thirty-five yard line. The first section of the signals was shouted. There was a pause; then Conway stepped back ten yards. The stands grew silent. He was going to try a place-kick. No! It was a drop! Back from the center to Conway went the ball. The Crimson line-men crashed in, stopped, then broke through—but they were too late. The oval had left the toe of Conway and sailing high into the air dropped straight and true between the cross-bars. A shout of joy arose from the St. Ridges rooters, but died down instantly as the trainer scampered across the turf and knelt beside a prostrate form. When he arose he was supporting the limp form of Holt. A groan went up from the stands. There was but one man to take Holt's place and that one was Salter. Salter, the quitter—Salter, the man who had disgraced his school. As Holt was helped off the field they gave him a rousing cheer—but when Salter trotted on they were silent. Salter noticed the difference, and it burned him to the very soul. Watchful, wary in his position of safety, still he could not keep the thought of the hostility of his fellow-students from his mind. In his heart there surged a great longing to prove to them that they had been unjust and bitter in their treatment of him. That established, and then they might regard him as they felt disposed. Suddenly a Crimson half-back shot far out around the end for a gain of twenty yards, being captured by Hickey close to the side-line. The teams fell into position once again and the St. Charles quarter began:

"Eight! Four! Thirteen!—"
. "Signal."

The St. Charles line-men turned and glared at the quarter. He, as if in doubt, stepped to the rear and started a whispered consultation with the backs. The St. Ridges players, battered and weary, relaxed their positions, eager to take advantage of the lull for a moment's rest. Instantly the ball was snapped back. St. Charles turned, sped out to the center of the field, formed a square about the quarter who held the ball, and started for the goal line. The hearts of the St. Ridges rooters dropped to their boots. There was only Salter between St. Charles and victory. Salter, the quitter! Salter who was yellow and afraid. But in the latter's breast there was a fierce joy. At last the opportunity he longed for had arrived. With head down he rushed that charging mass, left his feet and dived straight at their legs. When the pile was disentangled he was clinging like death to the man who held the ball! Just as the stands broke out into a mad

cry of joy, the timer's pistol announced the end of the game.

* * * * *

In the dining-room of St. Ridges that night a crowd of tired but happy students was listening to a speech of the coach. He had praised the team and the players amid cheers and yells, but when he came to Salter the vast hall grew still as a tomb.

"You will probably remember," he said, "that in one of the early season games, Salter, after dodging and fighting his way till but one man stood between him and a score, stopped and let that man tackle him without even a show of resistance. To you it appeared that Salter was afraid—and he was. But it was not the fear of cowardice. Three years ago I was refereeing a high school game in the center of state. Salter was playing in that game and toward the end of the third quarter, it so happened that he got away into a clear field with only the safety ahead of him. The two men came together in as fierce a collision as I have ever seen. Both went to the ground, one—the safety—completely unconscious. They took him to the hospital and that night—he died."

The coach sat down and the cheer-leader leaped to his feet:

"Boys," he cried, "a big sky-rocket for Salter, the grittiest, nerviest player that ever fought for the Blue and Grey."

Speech of Captain Ferrario

Those who have gone before me in this evening's display of oratory, have touched upon practically everything.

We, the members of the team fully appreciate the gigantic task before us. We have resolved, to a man, that tomorrow afternoon on the Cardinal field, the Stanford team is going to meet with an opposition, the likes of which she has yet to be able to compare with another of like formidableness this season.

That we are going to lose is too unlikely. We shouldn't for a moment be entertaining such an idea. But that we are going to bring home the laurels to old Alma Mater, to the glorious Red and White is quite another matter. If fight and courage are to be the deciding factors then ours is already the victory. Nothing less than that seems forthcoming, with so many loyal rooters backing us up on the field of battle tomorrow afternoon with our old enemy, Stanford.

"FAT" FERRARIO,
Captain of Varsity Football Team.

Ad Finem

IN rhythmic line or sculptor's bronze,
  We seek undying fame;
With patient toil we tread Life's trails,
  Each one with separate aim.

This day we have a quest in view,
  More splendid than the sun;
Each quest attained, in brighter light
  There shines a greater one.

Until, when hopes are lost in hopes,
  That vagrant thoughts can lend,
Our works converge in one Design---
  Our Love, ambition's End!

                                  A. J. STEISS, JR.

What Eyes Saw Not

James R. Enright.

EORGE had finished his buckwheat cakes and syrup and after a leisurely perusal of his morning paper, stepped out of his home and onto the street. A peculiar glow filled him; the curious thrill that permeates one in expectancy of a good time. He was at a loss to account for it however, as he had no particular destination. He was merely taking his customary morning walk down the nearly deserted street. Could it be a premonition?

His train of thought was suddenly interrupted by a machine that had turned the corner swiftly and was rapidly bearing down upon him as he essayed to cross the street.

It never swerved to avoid a collision with him. Had it not been for his quick run he would have been run over. George shook his fist at the retreating machine, muttering curses against autos in general and careless drivers in particular, who thought it little worth their while to turn out for crossing pedestrians. This driver had seemed particularly cold-blooded. He had not even turned to right or left, but kept his course as if nothing were the matter!

George reached the sidewalk and proceeded, advancing towards a half-grown pup. He had often stopped to caress him or give him a piece of meat.

The pup was lazily curled in front of his master's door-step. As George advanced, he arose and staring intently at George's feet, began to tremble as if in a fit, the hackles bristling on his neck.

"What's the matter, Carlo?" said George in the affected language one uses towards pups and all young things in general, as he stooped to pet the animal.

A surprising change took place in the dog. As George's hand touched him, he crouched, trembling violently. With slavering jaws and a terrible howl of fear, he turned and ran yelping to the back gate where he crouched low with gasping whines of terror!

George straightened. Surely something must be wrong with the animal, he thought as he continued on his walk.

Something was not altogether right with George. There seemed to be a vague uneasiness possessing him, a sense of something radically wrong about him. Try as he might, he could not account for it. It seemed with him always—following him. He shook himself but could not lose that strange feeling. As he crossed the shadow of a telegraph pole, a thought struck him. He stopped short, staring at the sidewalk around him. Gradually a look of mingled fear and astonishment overspread his features. He advanced a few more paces. A cry of unbelieving amazement escaped his trembling lips. He had no shadow!

There was no doubt about it, no more than there was of his not being asleep. Everything was too real to be a dream. How could he account for it, then? He shook his head, puzzled, but proceeded on.

As he walked, he reasoned that if he had no shadow, the sun must shine through him—he must be invisible, despite the fact that he could see himself! Little wonder that dog acted that way. Perhaps that auto driver wasn't such a bad fellow after all!

Someone was coming in his direction. He resolved to give it a test. The fellow, a young man of about twenty-eight, gave no indication of noticing George, but kept on. George followed, his rubber soles making no noise, and touched him on the shoulder. He turned and stared right through George without apparently noticing him in the least. As the fellow muttered under his breath: "I could have sworn someone tapped me on the shoulder," George strolled along convinced.

A spirit of deviltry seized him—a thousand and one possibilities flashed through his mind. He chuckled to himself as he silently paced along.

An open bakery nearby tempted him with its fresh odors. Although not particularly hungry, he entered the place and saw a buxom, blue-aproned woman seated behind the counter with her spectacles far down on her wrinkled nose.

There was a large tray of hot cross buns on the counter marked "3 for 10c". George slapped down a dime, picked up three of them and walked out while the said buxom, blue-aproned old woman watched with saucerlike eyes, three of her choicest buns, pay for themselves and calmly float out of the open door!

George, deep in thought walked through the park, munching the buns as he went along. Three awe-stricken youngsters watched in amazement. A few moments later, three awe-stricken youngsters were telling their respective parents a more or less garbled account of three buns that sailed slowly through the park as they ate themselves!

Thoughtless of the commotion he had aroused, George proceeded towards the principal street, Broadway, as unconsciously one directs his steps while thinking deeply. It was only after bumping into a fellow, who gave a howl of surprise and fear and broke long distance records for running, that he checked himself. It was too late. He was in between two crowds. If they ever touched him—well anything might happen, but surely not what would do George the least bit of good! He could not go out into the street, because he surely would get run over. He had to stick to the gutter.

With all his precaution he could not help bumping into a few people. The varied effects of screaming, fainting and running caused a general commotion. The people crowded all around to see the excitement. George became desperate and plunged through regardless.

Immediately cries of: "something touched me!" "Did you feel it? I did!" and minglings of prayers, curses and shrieks of "Help!" arose from the paralyzed crowd, which galvanized into precipitate motion. George found himself alone again. He ran into a store for protection and bumped into a thin, side-whiskered man of the species, "hen-peeked," who promptly dropped his bundles and proceeded to faint with neatness and dispatch. Frantically George jumped the counter to avoid the on-rush of clerks and other would-be assistants of the "injured" man. He landed squarely upon a remarkably strong-lunged cat that demonstrated its vocal powers in a decidedly roof-raising manner. In despair George raced down the aisle and out the back door, coming into an alley and across into a bakery shop where he overturned a big fat chef, overloaded with steaming hot bread. Kicking the tumbling loaves out of his frantic course, he plunged through the bakery, out of the front door, thereby causing several people to swear off drinking for life.

This street was not so crowded. George drew several gasping breaths and slowed down, dodging the pedestrians as a matter of course. Truly, he thought, being invisible had its disadvantages!

Slowly he walked, and at length, two well-dressed individuals with the stamp of Wall Street spreading all over them, overtook George. The street was nearly deserted, nevertheless these two were talking under their breath. George caught a word and then with growing amazement listened.

"So you say there is no danger of it falling?" said one.

"None at all," responded the other, "according to my agents, Richmond Consolidated will advance up to 135, and at the word, the bottom will drop out. I wouldn't be surprised if it fell to 40 per share. That will drive out most of the holders and we will be able to do what we want with it!"

Richmond Consolidated was what George earned his bread with! Now, unless he could tell his agent, he would be ruined at four o'clock! He could not go there invisible, much less walk through the crowded streets! George cursed; nothing could be done to—the telephone!

He fairly ran to the exchange station, two blocks up. After depositing a coin there seemed an interminable wait and then Central asked, "Number, please?"

"Franklin 8071!" George shouted, and a moment later he heard the familiar voice of his secretary.

"Quick!" he fairly screamed to him. "Buy all the Richmond Consolidated you can lay your hands on, and sell out before it reaches top notch, 135. The bottom's dropping out!"

He heard an exclamation, an uncertain, "allright," and the receiver clicked up, leaving George perspiring and—satisfied.

He bent his steps home and managed to get in the back door without being seen by anyone. He passed through a dark pantry and gave a low exclamation of surprise. His whole body was luminous! A strange feeling possessed him. More by accident than by real thought he came across the buckwheat flour. It also was shining with a clear, penetrating radiance! What was it?

He ran to the phone and called up the best doctor in the city—he could afford to now—and explained what was the matter with him. At first the doctor was cold and impatient, and then unbelieving, but finally, with a trace of excitement in his voice, he said, "I'll be right up."

Soon a powerful motor car sprang to the curb and the doctor advanced up the stairs and opened the door without ringing.

"This way," said George, touching him on the shoulder. The doctor was too curious and professional to be startled, but he felt George's hands, arms and face. Then, with a curious look on his be-whiskered face, he darkened the room. Then and there he saw George shining in the dark.

"What is it, Doc?" asked George. But the Doctor was too intent with a gold leaf electroscope, to answer. Suddenly he stood up.

"I have it," he said, "you have about twelve thousand dollars worth of radium in you!"

George was petrified. The Doctor explained how his body was in a state of ionization caused by a subtle radio-carbide compound and the light passed through him, being conducted by the ions. Only the ultra-violet was not affected, but was sent back. Thus his own eyes in ionization, perceived the ultra-violet. He could see everyone else in their true habiliments, while he remained invisible.

George couldn't quite recall just what the doctor had prescribed to counteract the ionizing of the radium. It was a stupendous word. He thought little of it however.

Next day he was realizing an appreciable sum of money from the radium extracted from the buckwheat flour. He stretched and yawned.

"Not so bad," he said to himself. "With what I cleaned up on Richmond Consolidated I think I'll take a long vacation."

The Romance of Rancho Agradable

(Continued)

A. J. Steiss, Jr.

The lady of his love stood in one corner, enveloped in shadows, folding some rare, old laces into a spacious drawer, when she was startled by his sudden entry. Her pretty head was brought quickly round, and the half-folded lace dropped from her hand.

Gaspar returned it to her.

"Oh, Senor," she cried, heaving a sigh of relief, as she recognized him, "it is you! I was afraid it was an Indian. I am so glad it is you!"

"Are you glad, I am honored."

Dona Maria blushed profusely and hung her head. "Yes, Senor, I am glad it is not an Indian, that is all. You flatter yourself, I think." Maria gazed bewitchingly upon him.

"But you are glad I am here? Surely you must be." He smiled wickedly. "You waved to me only last Saturday, when you saw me at your gate."

"Ah, do not be too sure, Senor. I was but drying the altar linen, not waving at you. You are really quick to see your advantage, I must admit!" And she gave way to rippling laughter.

"But you wish me to remain?" Gaspar had become very humble and subservient.

"If you will help me with my work."

"Ah, nothing would please me

more." Gaspar was shedding his embroidered coat.

"But, Senor, do not take off your jacket. I don't wish you to do such hard work: merely to put away those vestments in the drawer. I shall go outside to gather flowers for the altar."

"But will the Senorita not allow me to accompany her? I can help her in that way too."

"Ah, but you said you would help me with my work. You would not be helping me; you would do nothing but talk foolish nonsense, I am sure."

"Let me try?"

"No. If you wish to please me, put away those vestments."

Gaspar shrugged his shoulders. "Just as you say. I suppose I shall have to do it. But why?"

"Enough! Do not bother me. When I come back, I must see those vestments put carefully away."

She vanished through the portal, and Gaspar began to arrange the robes in a drawer. They were beautiful things, the product of innumerable threads of gold and white and red, interwoven into the most curious patterns of flowers in gold lace. There were scarlet ones, like the blushing berries, that bloom on the hillside in the summer-

70

time; and green ones like the meadowlands in spring. There were white
ones like the clouds that pass about
on high, and some were of the somber
color of leaves in the autumn time.
Some spiced of newness, lately brought
on ships around the Horn, while others
emitted the musty odor of the cedar
chest, and long confinement in damp
and dusty rooms. Carefully and slowly
Don Gaspar laid them away, lest any
harm from moth or wear might reach
them.

With this duty finally accomplished
he gazed out the door toward the garden, whence Maria had departed in
search of flowers. Up the path toward the Mission she tripped, her arms
full of nodding blossoms, roses, poppies,
bluebells, and lilies, until her tossing
head could scarce be seen through the
tangle.

"Ah, Senor," she cried, brushing a
wave of hair from her forehead, and ad-
justing the flowers, so, that her mis-
chievous, dark eyes could see before
her, "you have finished, I see! You
are a quick worker, I thought I would
find you napping."

Gaspar sprang forward to receive
part of her burden. "Yes, Senorita, I
have at last finished. I hope I may
help you arrange the flowers in the
chapel; that is, if you don't wish me to
wash the sacristy floor!"

Dona Maria laughed. "No, I shall
let you help me with the flowers. Carry them onto the altar for me, please."

They had entered the chapel, and

now they stood upon the altar steps,
upon which they had laid their armfuls
of flowers. Before the altar, the wavering lamp burned dimly, throwing but
scanty rays into the gloom of the interior of the church. The patterns upon the ceiling were rendered soft and
indistinguishable in the darkness of the
building; and the pale, cold statues
seemed to have receded into their
niches in the wall, their austere features also rendered soft and kindly by
the mellow light. Upon the whitened
altar, many jugs and vessels were arranged, wherein Maria began to deposit
the flowers she had gathered.

Now with all due credit to young
Don Gaspare, of course, it is very safe
to say that when the gallant caballero
had so willingly and fervently offered
his aid to his lady love, it was not so
much that he enjoyed the labor of the
undertaking, but that it gained for him
her desired company. Certain it is,
anyway, that during all the period,
when Maria was busying herself about
the altar, Don Gaspar did no more
than, with a pretense of activity, gaze
upon her wonderful charms from the
middle aisle. The sight of the lovely
Dona amid the flowers near the altar,
seemed to add to her natural attractiveness; and never had the transported
Senor seen her to look more beautiful.
It seemed as if the late train of events
had been leading to this happy climax,
that the Fates had decreed that the
peerless daughter of Castello should be
found alone in the Mission sacristy on

this Saturday afternoon in August, and Gaspar's resolve was taken.

The adorning of the chapel had become almost completed before Dona Maria realized that her gallant young helper had not been doing more than devotedly watching her, and like all, coy, young damsels, who are modestly aware of their own good.looks, blushed most profusely.

Then a whisper from Maria disturbed the caballero's dreams: "Senor, I really thought you were going to help me with the decorating. And here, it is almost finished, and for the whole time you've been idly sleeping, I'll wager, on the bench."

"Senorita, pardon me. But do not accuse me of sleeping. I busied myself with things of far greater importance than that, you may be sure!"

"Ah, it may be so, Senor," she adroitly responded, "I should not have disturbed you at your prayers, but there are you, and here is work, and I think I am responsible for both."

Don Gaspar stepped forward. "May I not still help you, Senorita? I can at least sweep the floor while you finish with the flowers, and I think you can regard that as sufficient."

"If you would, Senor. And when you have completed that, we shall have finished, at least I shall. Let us hasten."

In a short time, the decorating having been satisfactorily disposed of, the two figures, the stalwart youth, and gentle Senorita, emerged through the heavy portals of the Mission, and strolled leisurely away toward the "hacienda" of the Castellos.

Now what took place at this juncture, when the dusk was falling, I do not intend to relate. I am not versed in the art of proposing, nor am I interested in such preliminary affairs. However, I can assure you that Don Gaspar was eloquent, and that an understanding was finally arrived at between him and his fair Maria. Also I can be perfectly certain of the fact that the impending obstacle to their future happiness and delight, Senor Castello, was taken seriously into consideration, with divers and sundry proposals of reconciliation and abandonment, which caused no little worry to the lovers. At a safe distance from the "hacienda" they parted, and soon "El Capitan", with his youthful rider, was galloping into the starlit dusk.

III

"What is it, Pedro?" Don Juan strode forth from beneath an oak tree, to receive a message from his Mexican "trabajador".

The servant handed him a sealed parchment. "From Monterey, Senor. It is on official beesness, I teenk."

Senor Castello impatiently broke the seal, and cursorily scanning the proffered missive, dismissed old Pedro with:

"Make ready a mule and baggage, for tomorrow I must cross the mountains. I shall take Mateo with me."

* * * *

And so it was that on the Monday following that eventful Saturday of which we have spoken in the preceding Chapter, the proud Don Juan Castello, with sombrero secured by a leathern string, and bestriding a tractable, unenergetic, sleepy old donkey, started out from the Rancho's yard in the early morning, and disappeared round a bend in the tortuous mountain road. And of course, as was natural, the whole household of Rancho Agradable assembled to see him off, and to idle about for an hour or two after his departure. In a wisteria-trellised arbor in the "patio" two silent figures, a stalwart man, and dainty Senorita, saw him leave and disappear into the windings of the mountain-side, and then fell to conversing there among the flowers on themes far too sentimental to be here recorded.

Now, if one has ever made the trip across the Coast Range Mountains by the Monterey trail, on a torrid day in summer, one well recalls the feelings he experienced in making the troublesome journey. Also one can realize only too well the thoughts of Senor Castello on being summoned to the Presidio at Monterey; and not having ridden a donkey for a goodly space of time, the state of his wearied frame as well as mind, when he finally, some days later, trotted out of the forest, into the little settlement of Monterey. The donkey, which he rode, had hung its head, and even disdained to wag his ears in recog-

nition of their having at last arrived at their destination.

Just as they were about to enter the Presidio grounds, an aged Indian emerged from behind a pepper tree, and handed Castello a letter.

Senor Castello glanced at it, and his face flushed crimson. With a Spaniard, the silent rage is the direful one; and Senor Castello was unstintingly indulging in that now. He scowled and cursed inwardly and crossed himself. Then, without a word or a sign to reveal the contents of the momentous letter, he dug the spurs into his donkey's flank, and started back again over the mountains—toward Rancho Agradable!

IV

A cloud of dust rising up along the profile of a hillside, and seeming to gather speed as it travelled downwards, toward the Valley of Santa Clara, attracted the attention of the good Padre Dominic, basking peacefully in the sunlight before the Castello homestead. In a short while, out of the misty cloud, two figures emerged; one, Mateo upon a little burro; the other, the infuriated tyrant of the Rancho, riding just as hard as his unfortunate donkey could go.

At the gateway he sprang stiffly from the saddle, and started for the "casa", muttering dire "sapristis" and "carambas" and "diablos" upon the world in general, and upon mankind, in particular, until he waxed truly profane. He was somewhat taken a-back by the sight of the ample Padre planted in his pathway, and as he refused to remove himself from this position, vented his choicest morsels upon that holy person. Then, in a wild dash for the "casa", he endeavored to thrust aside the troublesome impediment. But the good Padre gripped him firmly, a hand upon each shoulder, his calm, brown eyes gazing into the other's excited ones, and held him there. Now of course, the overwrought Senor had not lost all respect for the clergy, as would seem by his terrible tirades, but truth to tell, I think it was more the size of the good Padre Dominic, than the dignity of his office, that caused the wrathful Senor to be finally halted in his vengeful march.

But so it was, anyway, that after about five short minutes the two men walked silently up to the whitewashed homestead of Castello; the one, with bent and dejected manner; the other, his arm laid in brotherly fashion upon the old Senor's now sunken shoulders.

And so it was, too, that after the good Padre Dominic had at last finished the recitation of the train of events leading up to his daughter's late marriage, and had completely and conclusively laid all the blame upon the side of the old Senor, Dona Maria, her youthful "esposo" and congenial madre following after her, emerged from on⟨ rooms of the "casa", and the⟨ neath the blooming wisteria and roses of the veranda of the of Don Juan Castello, on the enda" near the Mission Santa effected a reconcilation, and bro⟨ a happy ending the little Rom Rancho Agradable.

* * * *

It might be well to here note happy, young couple lived in pe contentment for many years wards, upon their now satisfied "hacienda", whose name ha been changed to Villa Maria; a having many children, and all ⟨ ing the good qualities and famil inspired by their padre's innnu inherited titles, and their ⟨ beauty, they have become one leading families of the Valley o Clara, with descendants scatter⟨ one end of this wide state to th Some say, that if one will sto⟨ the venerable, old Mission of Clara de Asis now, and go with ⟨ padres, whither they shall lea may, perhaps, show you the la linen which Dona Maria wave⟨ blooming lover, and the ve which the lover put away that evening, and even the veil that norita wore at her wedding.

The Redwood

PUBLISHED BY THE STUDENTS OF THE UNIVERSITY OF SANTA CLARA

The object of The Redwood is to gather together what is best in the literary work of the students, to record University doings and to knit closely the hearts of the boys of the present and the past

EDITORIAL STAFF

EDITOR-IN-CHIEF	HENRY C VEIT
BUSINESS MANAGER	TULLIO A. ARGENTI
ASSISTANT BUSINESS MANAGER	JACOB E. HEINTZ
CIRCULATION MANAGER	EDMUND. Z. COMAN

ASSOCIATE EDITORS

EXCHANGES	P . F. MORETTINI
ALUMNI	MARTIN M. MURPHY
UNIVERSITY NOTES	LOUIS F. BUTY
	FRED J. MORAN
ATHLETICS	JAMES E. NEARY

EXECUTIVE BOARD

EDITOR	BUSINESS MANAGER	EDITOR OF REVIEWS

Address all communications to THE REDWOOD, University of Santa Clara, Santa Clara, California.
Terms of subscription, $1.50 a year; single copies 25 cents

EDITORIAL

**Our
General**

All gratitude to the man who has made our crack football team and peppery football season possible! Father O'Connell came to us this year greatly handicapped inasmuch as he had a totally new and different order of things to handle. But he is every inch a man and so he manfully climbed his mountain of difficulty. That we have our men so well equipped; so carefully fed; so thoroughly looked after; so contented; is due in greatest part to Father O'Connell. He has set for us all an ideal and he has constantly and persistently worked towards it. Indeed we feel fortunate to have such a loyal person as Father O'Connell rule our destinies in athletics. Every team we played this year was struck by the fine, clean, well-disciplined men on our squad. In fact Stanford maintained that they were the best they had run up against; and they likewise felt they were lucky to get the breaks in our never-to-be-forgotten contest. Nobody could have handled our situation this year and have handled it more successfully than our "little General" Father O'Connell.

Football Number

Every human institution is subject to constant change. The athletic institution of our own Santa Clara is no exception to the rule. Some say we were driven to it—an inevitable conclusion from existant facts, else remain alone in the football realm. Others not quite so willing to surrender their personal convictions as to the superiority of the two games, American and Rugby football, to follow in the paths of the majority, have decided that the English game, being weighed in the balance was found wanting, while the American style of play, being more characteristic of the American youth and more adaptable to his daily desires, was given precedence. Therefore its present revival after a demise of some dozen years or more.

That, however, is not our present concern. For us it is enough to realize that after mature deliberation we have relegated to oblivion the English game of rugby and adopted in its stead the American way of making undertakers happy. So be it. It is not for us to question the reason why; ours it is to be up and doing for all that is in us, rooting and helping in any way, however small the team whose victories are our victories, whose defeats are our defeats..

That brings us now to the point in question, the FOOTBALL NUMBER. We have thought so much of our team that we have given to them a whole issue of the Redwood, to do with as they please. But such is not a thing entirely new. Past years have recorded their football numbers; future years will likewise be written of as having donated a special issue to the grand old game.

So, fellow students, we offer to you as a keepsake, this number permeated by a football atmosphere, and accompany it with the desire that in after years when you will have passed beyond the portals of Alma Mater, you may look upon its pages and recall many a pleasant rally, many an exciting game, many a spirited activity, of this, Santa Clara's first year of the American science of the pigskin.

College Spirit

We casually put ourselves the question the other day: What is the meaning of college spirit? We had heard of it oft before and naturally we began to ponder. First of all we found it to be a subtle something, part and parcel of every university's life. It proved to be nothing more than a pulse, a determinant of that which makes any institution the place it is. With it the student combats his difficulties, the organization, its problems, the lesser university, its mightier opponent and not infrequently is the outcome, victory. It moves men to action, encourages individuals to attempt the apparently impossible and imbues all those encountering it, with a determination and fiery enthusiasm that knows no abatement.

Such is the heritage of all universities, enhanced or mitigated by exterior circumstances. Some attribute little to its influence; others consider it most important to their progress. Santa Clara acknowledges it to be in the vanguard of her every endeavor. With her it is her whole life. With it she has blazed her way to triumph on the athletic field, in the intellectual world and upon the field of battle. In no instance, where one of her sons is found can it be said there is wanting one iota of steadfastness and loyalty of purpose to the goal set out to be attained.

College spirit admits of no narrowness. It harbours only the broad, ambitious type; courageous, self-reliant men, possessed with endurance and unlimited energy. The goal of success may at first sight prove unapproachable, unattainable. Yet it is only by arduous work that the summit can be reached. Life retains much of its ancient roughness, yet college spirit, acquired in undergraduate days is an effective lotion to assuage the hurts sustained in bumping over its course. It is the one sure means to success. Acquire it by all odds here, where opportunities untold present themselves.

An Ideal

What is so rare as an Ideal realized? Few if any can truthfully say that their dreams come true. Only in part do they work out. Never fully. But notwithstanding, it is no idle fancy to permit one's thoughts to ramble on through a maze of dreams, up to the heights where dwells an ideal. The fault obtains only when we dream and make dreams our master. To have ideals is noble. They exhort men to best endeavor, even though unattainable in themselves. Surely one can never regret having tried.

Human beings are all more or less dreamers in a certain sense. The quiet of our own little sanctum brought us to the realization that after all we were only human. We had a dream of an ideal Santa Claran.

He may have been a Hercules, or even an Apollo. Such was immaterial. But what did matter was the fact that he was a man. Not in name merely, but in principle and thought and in action. He was not a snob, nor a cheat, nor a tramp. Too high minded to do anything which might detract from good fellowship with his companions, he abhorred the idea of snobbishness. To cheat in examinations meant for him the likelihood of cheating in business, in politics or in any other of his deal-

ings in after life. The insignificant
gain in so doing deterred him that the
greater evil therefrom might be avoided. He courted nothing, regardless of
the effort, that might mould itself into
a habit and involve him in disgrace,
once his life's profession had started
its course.

When physique permitted he engaged
in athletics. But not a tramp in the
sport realm. He was a student as well
as an athlete. The tramp degrades ath-

letics and t
and a bette
The idea
a debater, a
ed, level-he
truth and (
he is loyal-
and his sch
fer humilia
dishonor or

Let us se
that ideal.

University Notes

Rally

The evening of October 11th, the eve of our debut into the realms of American football, was deemed a fitting and proper occasion for our second pep installment. Moreover, a long established custom of former years would not have permitted the season to open without a rally to precede the first game. Accordingly a program, designed to bring forth whatever little enthusiasm which did not of its own, accord itself, was arranged and presented in the Auditorium.

Henry Veit, substituting for printed programs, announced the first number as the Whangdoodle Quartet, Purveyors of Harmony, and across the footlights flitted Messrs. "Dumpy" Diaz, "Mopey" Moran, Bill Desmond, and "Phat" Ferrario. After getting away to a bad start on "The Pail of the Amber West", or something, they finally settled down to some pretty fair warbling. At any rate, the audience was considerate, so their efforts were appreciated.

Professor Rolling Stone No Moss II, ably assisted by Abdul Numuhd Vergara, out-Alexandered Alexander in twenty minutes of telepathy, sleight-of-hand, and card tricks combined. Mike Pecarovich, as Prof. No Moss II, held the audience in a convulsive state of expectancy, and showed that besides playing football and the 'cello, he was quite adept at the art in which Thespes shined. Ad Vergara always did have a "phoney" reputation, and consequently his commendable impersonation of Abdul Numuhd was not a surprise to his friends.

Next on the bill came Ragomaniacs—"Turk" Bedolla on the piano, "Zeek" Coman with the banjo, and Bill Desmond on the drums. They dispensed jazz as it should be dispensed, rather affecting the pedal extremities in that peculiar way. 'Nuff sed.

The rally proper followed. Henry Veit, President of the Student Body, spoke on the Santa Clara spirit—its presence not only at college, but also in after life. Student Manager O'Connor and Capt. Ferrario expressed the sentiments of the football squad with a few well chosen words.

James P. Sex, President of the Alumni Association, with his accustomed eloquence, reviewed the success of Santa

Clara on the field in the past, and predicted that the old fighting spirit would insure the success of the future.

Amidst the wild acclaims of the students, Coach Harmon, the man who guides Santa Clara's football destinies, was called upon for a short talk. Although not predicting a victory for the morrow's game, Coach Harmon expressed his confidence that the men who would represent Santa Clara on the field would fight—in the clean spirit of sport—and that, he said, was what he would look to most. American football, he informed his audience, is not a game which can be learned within the short space of one or two months, and, although a victory is to be desired, it is the future which must be provided for. He predicted that within a year, Santa Clara would be firmly entrenched in a foremost position on the football map of the Pacific Coast.

Following the talk by Coach Harmon, the college yells were given under the direction of Yell Leader Ed Harter, and his assistants, Bill Desmond and "Pop" Rethers. The rally closed with the singing of the College Anthem by the entire Student Body accompanied by the band.

Student Body

On Saturday, September 27th, the Student Body assembled in the Auditorium for the second regular meeting of the scholastic year. Following the reading of the minutes of the preceding meeting, a report of the financial condition of the Associated Students was submitted by Treasurer Coman, and accepted on a motion by Mr. McCoy.

President Henry Veit read part of the constitution, thoroughly explaining the more important articles, and followed with some timely remarks on cooperation and the spirit which should characterize student activities.

Student Manager James O'Connor brought before the Student Body the necessity of lending their support in making the Columbus Day game with the Olympic Club a success, remarking that the day scholars were lagging in this respect. His talk was very brief, but nevertheless emphatic.

No further business of importance came up before this meeting.

The third regular meeting of the Student Body was held on November 6th, two days before the annual Stanford game. The purpose of the meeting, as outlined by President Veit, was to stir up pep for the Big Game.

A realization of what the Stanford game means to Santa Clara, financially and otherwise was offered by Student Manager O'Connor. The question of awarding football blocks was opened by Mr. Harter, and considerable discussion ensued, resulting in a motion by Mr. Diaz that the constitution, as it now stands, awarding blocks for participation in any part of the Stanford game, be allowed to stand as it is. The motion was carried by an unanimous vote of the Student Body.

This disposed of a very important question, inasmuch as the change from Rugby to American football also brought with it a change in conditions, which might affect the awarding of blocks. As the schedule this year only calls for two intercollegiate games, the Student Body evidently deemed a change at this time unadvisable.

Senate

Having passed beyond the stage of reorganization, the new members elected this year having taken their seats and been welcomed to membership, the Senate has once again settled down to real business, and is every week holding forth in the most sprited debates that have been heard in its halls for many a semester. A new plan has been brought into being this year, wherein, besides the regular speakers, any member may be called upon to rise and give a short argument upon the question under discussion, so that everyone is at all times alive as to what is taking place, and must be well informed upon the current questions of the day, which are the subjects of Senate debates.

The first debate was on the ratification of the Peace Treaty without amendment, which took in main the shape of an argumentation of the League of Nations. So heated did the discussion become that two whole sessions were devoted to it, practically every member having a rather lengthy argument to make. The affirmative was upheld by Senator Harter and Senator Sullivan, the negative by Senators Veit and O'Connor.

In a later debate the question as to whether the formation of a separate political party would be to the better interests of this country was discussed. Senators Jaeger and Morettini argued for the affirmative, but were defeated by Senator McCoy and Senator Heafy who upheld the negative.

Something of an innovation was instituted this year by an entertainment and "feed" tendered the old members by the new members, as an appreciation of their having been elected to the Senate. A very pleasant evening was enjoyed, and throughout the year entertainments of a similar nature will be had, as a diversion from the regular course of the meetings.

Bonfire Rally

Although the change from Rugby to American football has taken with it considerable of the glamour attaching to the "Big Game", nevertheless the meeting with Stanford continues to remain a big game. In the past the event had always been preceded by a great outdoor rally, the feature of which was the huge bonfire. The efforts of Stanford to burn down the precious pyre have made tradition which still lingers on the campus.

This year the occasion was observed in the accustomed manner. Promptly at 8:30 o'clock, on the eve of November 8th, before a gathering of several thousand friends of Santa Clara, the torch was applied to the pile, amidst the yells and serpentining of the students. As the fire died down, the program was presented on the platform erected for the occasion in front of Senior Hall.

Speeches were made by Henry Veit, President of the Student Body, Rev. Father Murphy, President of the University, and Mr. Dion Holm, of San Francisco, a distinguished alumnus of Santa Clara.

Then followed two boxing bouts. Demartini and Johnny Barrett, 95-pounders, stepped 4 rounds to a draw. "Kid" Giambastiani vs. Karl Koch, at 115 pounds, furnished more joy for lovers of the manly art.

By courtesy of the Leo Feist Publishing Company, Mr. and Mrs. Dennis Sheerin rendered a selection of the latest song hits, which were keenly appreciated by the audience. Mr. Sheerin's rendition of "I'm Irish", was filled with noticeable enthusiasm.

Captain Ferrario, Manager O'Connor and Coach Harmon, spoke on the morrow's game, the trend of their remarks being summed up with "Santa Clara spirit" and "fight".

Kid Alfredo, from Chihuahua, and Battling Romero from the City of the Angels, proved an interesting pair on the program, doing four rounds of real, honest-to-goodness scrapping. The science of the defensive art was sadly ov-

erlooked in their anxious efforts to do some real damage, much to the delight of the crowd.

A new jazz organization was impressed into service for the occasion, delivering several snappy selections. "Chink" Rethers dictated to the ivories, Harris picked a banjo, Daly syncopated on the violin, while Elbert jazzed a trombone.

The headline attraction of the evening, at least for those devoted to fistic endeavor, was the three-round bout between Jack Hartford, and Billy Hurley of Crockett. Both boys have considerable reputations along this line, and the bout brought out some fast and clever work.

The rally closed with the singing of the College Anthem by the Student Body.

The House

The last regular meeting of the House of Philhistorians was held on November 4, 1919. Rep. Conners was the essayist of the meeting and held the attention of the House members while he read a very erudite paper. The debate for the evening was: Resolved: That the President should not lift the ban on war-time prohibition at the time of the demobilization of the army. Its grave importance was impressed upon the House members from the start and it proved to be one of the most successful debates of the semester thus far. Representatives Lewis and Jackson argued for the negative side, while Representatives M. Boyle and Copeland upheld the affirmative. A heated debate ensued, after which the House discussed it freely, having a large majority in favor of the negative viewpoint of the question. After conceding the victory to Representatives M. Boyle and Copeland the House adjourned.

Marshal Foch's Sword In accordance with the other Jesuit Colleges throughout the United States, Santa Clara contributed generously to the fund collected for the engraved sword to be given to Marshal Foch upon his coming to America, by the students of the many schools conducted by the Society of Jesus.

Nor shall our name be last among them. Santa Clara has easily raised the maximum quota and enjoys the distinction with other larger institutions of being a top notcher in this matter of subscription. Marshal Foch being a Jesuit College graduate, from France, the Student Body donated liberally to the token of esteem for the man who made possible our present day peace.

"America" Father Tierney, S. J., of New York, was indeed more than pleased with the goodly number of subscriptions received from Santa Clara, for his Catholic Weekly, "America". Practically every member in the Student Body sent in his name for affixment to the subscription lists. Containing as it does all the important topics of the day, it is sure to be of much material aid to the students in helping them to prepare their weekly and much dreaded compositions. With such a digest of everything important the country over, the class teachers will not be having to weigh the worth of many essayed alibis when the youth appears for class on blue Monday without the assigned work. Father Tierney's publication contains any number of ideas especially suited to College students.

J. D. S. From the Prep department and its Junior Dramatic Society comes word of the wonderful success this deliberative body has achieved thus far on its yearly voyage through the scholastic year. Notwithstanding the fact that the Society has no permanent meeting place its members are assiduously working along those paths where real orators are made. The membership is at its highest, numbering something like forty-five on its roster. The latest ones to be admitted are Messrs. Duffill, Rianda, Joseph Sheehan, Brizzolara and William Lynch. This augurs well for the Juniorate branch of the Literary Congress.

For the unexampled prosperity of the body a vote of thanks is due, above all to Father Regan, our great-hearted, fair-minded and loyal moderator. His fairness to every member, his respect for every member, his untiring efforts with every member have won him universal esteem, and have won the J. D. S. an enviable place among all the institutions of Santa Clara. The effects of Father Regan's careful training are early discernible when our members are ever called upon in the class-room, in the dining-hall, or in the Student Body gatherings. Father Regan selects his debates with rare judgment; supplies debaters with matter from every source; is untiring in his efforts to force every one to make good. His motto is: "No Favorites," and hence the lasting good he has accomplished.

The Co-Op Through the keen business acumen of Father Sprague, our Student Body house of business has greatly picked up within the last few weeks. Indeed the good Father is on the job and looks after our interest with all the loyalty of our true friend that he is: Though greatly handicapped by outside places of business to which the students have access after breakfast and dinner, Father Sprague is working every spare moment of his time for the real interest of the Student Body. From him we shall be forced to draw to meet our current athletic expenses; on Father Sprague we depend for the wonderful season of athletics we have gone through and for the remaining part we have yet before us. His big

spirit does not confine itself to one or two; but to the entire Student Body and to every student in it.

Father Menager After several weeks of fruitless endeavor to secure passports for England, where he intended to complete his theological studies before ordination to the Holy Priesthood, Father Menager came by the sad news that it would require more time than he had anticipated. He sojourned amongst us for several days awaiting a place of definite assignment where he might continue his studies, pending the arrival of his passports. St. Louis University was the place chosen, where he is at present with Fathers McElmeel and Renshaw.

"Pep" The old pep is here. The old spirit has risen. The whole Student Body is agog with that certain Santa Clara something that makes us fight; that makes us contented. Pep filled the Auditorium on the eve of the Olympic game; pep called a couple of thousand ardent rooters from San Francisco and vicinity to the monstrous outdoor rally the night before the Stanford game; pep built the 75-foot bonfire; pep constructed that ring and filled it with so many scientific bouts; pep made us sing and pep made us yell; and it was pep that made the scribes of the dailies proclaim our rally "the finest ever and just like Santa Clara of old." Pep makes the real Santa Claran who never forgets and who is loyal to the end.

Fred J. Moran.
Louis F. Buty.

BY RESOLUTION OF THE FRESH-MAN CLASS.

WHEREAS, Almighty God in His Infinite Goodness and wisdom has seen fit to call to Himself the beloved father of our esteemed classmate and friend, Mr. John M. Jackson, and

WHEREAS, We, the members of the Freshman Class of the University of Santa Clara, desire to express our sincere sorrow and to extend our deepest sympathy to our bereaved fellow classman and his dear relatives in their sad affliction, be it

RESOLVED, That these resolutions of condolence be the instrument of our communication; that a copy of them be inscribed on the pages of our College Magazine, "The Redwood," and sent to the beloved relatives of the deceased; and be it finally

RESOLVED, That we have a number of Holy Masses said for the repose of his soul.

May he rest in peace!

Freshman Committee,
James Edward Neary,
Daniel Francis Donovan,
Robert Burns Guthrie.

RESOLUTIONS

WHEREAS, God in His infinite wisdom has seen fit to call to Himself the devoted mother of our dear friend and college fellow, Benjamin L. McCoy in a manner sudden, and humanly speaking, at a time when her goodness and charity would be most felt and appreciated by her loving son, and

WHEREAS, our duty towards the departed mother and our sincerest sympathies towards her sorrow-stricken son, our fellow student, demand that we be mindful of this, his great loss and sorrow;

BE IT RESOLVED, that a heartfelt expression of profoundest regret and deepest sorrow over the loss of the beloved mother of our esteemed fellow student, be conveyed to him and his sorrowing father;

BE IT FURTHER RESOLVED, that a copy of these resolutions be forwarded to our college fellow and that they be printed in the next issue of the official organ of the Student Body, "The Redwood".

(Signed)
Henry C. Veit, Pres.
Louis F. Buty, Sec.
Edmund Z. Coman, Treas.
Thomas E. Whelan, Sgt.-at-arms.
James B. O'Connor, Student Mgr.
Mr. J. O'Connell, S. J., Moderator.

This is the Football edition of the Redwood. But we must mention in it an important event which took place last month. It was the staging of Professor Sullivan's Smoker for the Engineers. Those who attended and enjoyed Professor Sullivan's hospitality, will remember the evening as part of many pleasant memories. The lawn in front of the home was illuminated by a spotlight on the roof, and served as a stage for the surprises which featured the occasion. First of all, the Freshman and Sophomores held a contest consisting of five events, namely: a boxing match, with the participants incased in sacks; a peanut race, won by the aid of a wad of gum; a paper fight, in which two worthy representatives of the classes demonstrated the brotherly love of the Freshie-Sophs; a fifty yard dash, in the winning of which much originality was displayed, and in which was proved the value of conscientious macaroni juggling; and finally, a rooster fight indicated clearly the worth of physical training and interpretative dancing. When the final count was compiled, the score read 71-45 in favor of the lowly Frosh. Though the Entertainment Committee was much in evidence, somehow or other it allowed as the next number on the program, an elaborate vaudeville act, which promptly was hit by the audience. Then the party crowded into the house to witness the Junior-Senior row. Here, amid the noise of the harmonious singers of the Engineering Society who attempted to accompany the willing accordion player, and while the spectators were being served with refreshments, the rival classmen plunged joyfully into a glorious game of cards. After the dreadful ordeal was finished, and the death toll had been taken, it was discovered that the Seniors and Juniors were equally clever with the popular deck. By this time the gaiety had calmed enough for a few speeches of thanks to be made; and finally, with a yell for Professor Sullivan, and the Engineers, the delightful evening was brought to a close.

And then too, at the Olympic Club-Santa Clara football game, the Engineers came within the range of public notice. With a touch of dramatic talent, they pulled off a stunt that held the interest of all present. In a dilapidated wagon, a remnant of the pioneer days, and hidden under oodles of "make-up", the Engineers conducted a fake survey that in the end resulted in the discovery of an ancient corpse, entombed in a petrified coffin. Under the deft fingers of the discoverers, the mummy was restored to life; and pranced off the field clad in the easily-recognized uniform of an American football player. The corpse was Mr. Di Fiori, and the other actors were Savage, Fowler, Heaney, Minahan, Ford and Flannery.

It would not do to omit mention of the building of this year's bonfire, for the Engineers were given charge of its design and erection. The pile was constructed in two days, and, owing to the lack of time and materials, which seriously affected the size of the structure, this must be considered noteworthy. At present, the entire attention of the Entertainment Committee is being given to the staging of a big picnic of the Engineering Society, and the results of this body are being awaited with expectant interest.

Alfred J. Abrahamson.

Once again the Alumni of Santa Clara have evinced their spirit of loyalty to Alma Mater. On the occasion of the opening of the New Stadium, on Sunday, October 12th, and on succeeding Sundays the "old boys" appeared in great numbers to watch the Varsity battle their opponents.

Among the most prominent of these was George Woolrich, Exchange Teller of the Wells Fargo Bank in the city. Good work, George, we hope to see you at all of the Varsity games.

'09 Another old boy who came came down to witness the Olympic Club game was Ray Kearney, now a prominent lawyer in San Francisco. He reports that he was only recently discharged from the army where he served as an officer in the Aviation Corps.

Ex '12 Another Alumnus to hear the wedding bells ring during the past month was Ben Fowler. His bride is Miss May Canelo, sister of Adolph, Clarence, and Harry, all former students of Santa Clara. The entire Student Body extends to Mr. and Mrs. Fowler their sincere wishes for a long and prosperous life.

'13 The month of October so it seems, is a popular one for weddings amongst our alumni as reports have reached us that several of them have deserted the fickle ranks of bachelorhood. Jack Bale of the Class of '13, has set the example to his younger brethren by recently announcing his marriage. We extend to the happy couple our congratulations and best wishes for a happy and prosperous married life.

Ervin Best paid us a long deferred but welcome visit during the month. Ervin was a clever athlete during his undergraduate days, being one of Santa Clara's mainstays in football and track. We hope he may find time again very soon to thus agreeably surprise us.

Ex '13 Harry Bennison was down to see the Varsity in action several weeks ago and after the game expressed himself as pleased at the progress the men are making in this their first year of American Football. Harry was a track man in his day starring particularly in the distance events. He also holds coast records in the sprints and has won numerous trophies at various meets.

Ex '14 Word comes from the South that Bernard Higgins, star forward on our old Rugby teams and brother of Coach Pat, has passed through a serious illness. While attending a ball game Bernie was suddenly stricken with a hemorrhage, but managed to survive the crisis. We are glad to hear that he is now on his way to recovery.

'15 Herbert McDowell, a collegiate of the Class of '15, was down with Best to help him look the old place over again and to renew acquaintances with the good Padres who guided his early footsteps along the lines of scholastic endeavor.

Michael Griffith has lately moved to Fresno to engage in the practice of law. Mike was always a loyal Alumnus who has constantly kept in touch with his Alma Mater. The Redwood takes this occasion to extend to him its best wishes for his success.

Word comes from Grass Valley that Louis T. Milburn has become the proud father of a bouncing young heir. Louie's record at college is still well remembered. Besides capably handling an outfield position on the baseball squad for several seasons. Louie was a star in our old gridiron struggles with Stanford. As proof of his literary ability we need only to consult the files of the Redwood; as Student Body President he met with great success. When Louie, Jr., registers at Santa Clara he will have to step lively to live up to the "old man's" reputation.

The local papers recently contained a full account of the wedding of Dominie Di Fiori and Miss Pennington of San Jose. The ceremony was performed in the Parish Church by the "marrying Padre", Father Boland, with Rudy Scholz acting as best man.

'16 Another young lawyer to appear on the campus during the past month was Miles Fitzgerald of San Luis Obispo. Miles was always a hard working student and a man "learned in the law" as his winning of the Cyc prize in his Senior year will attest.

'16 After seeing over nine months active service as an Ensign in the Navy, Eugene Trabueco returned home to San Rafael, where he recently entered into partnership in law with Lloyd L. Lennon. Gene is still remembered by many of the friends at college, who wish him all kinds of success in his chosen profession.

'17 Howard Kelley, the "Pearl of Antioch", dropped in very unexpectedly a few weeks ago. Howard is connected with the Pacific Gas and Electric Company and is at present engaged in the construction of a sub-station at Newark.

'18 Jerry Desmond, our former Cadet Major, recently tore himself away from his arduous duties in a Sacramento law office long enough to appear on the campus and shake hands with his former buck privates. It will be a long time before his ringing commands and clean-cut military appearance are forgotten here at Santa Clara. Besides winning many class distinctions, Jerry was a prize winner in the Ryland Debate, starred on the baseball squad and ably filled the position of Graduate Manager of Athletics in his Senior year. We look to Jerry to accomplish great things in the legal profession.

Frank O'Neill, more commonly remembered amongst us as "Nux", and Craig Howard, Ex. '19, were both down on Columbus Day to cheer the Varsity on to a hoped-for victory against the Olympic Club. Frank will be remembered as our capable Yell Leader during several of the Big Games with Stanford. He expressed himself as highly pleased with the showing made by the rooting section.

According to latest reports Dan Ryan is still stationed with the Army of Occupation in Germany. Dan won his bars at the Fourth Officers Training Camp at Camp Fremont and shortly afterwards was sent overseas. Soon after his arrival the armistice was signed so he did not participate in any battles, but his regiment was one of the first ordered over the Rhine. In all probability he will soon be on his way home, but knowing Dan as we do, we are willing to wager that he will leave many tender and sad hearts behind him.

'19 James E. Clarke, of the Electrical Engineering class of '19, has been transferred from the San Francisco office of the Sierra and San Francisco Power Company to their Stanislaus plant. Jimmie is a hard worker and will undoubtedly advance rapidly to the top in the ranks of the company.

Ex '19 Darrell Daly, formerly a steady contributor to the Redwood and a member of the Staff is now working for the Northwestern Pacific in San Francisco. He has not given up his legal ambitions however, but takes law at night at St. Ignatius College.

Ex' 20 A baby girl has arrived to brighten the home of Mr. and Mrs. Loufburrough. We extend to the happy couple our warmest felicitations and trust that Roy will prove a kind and indulgent father.

Hoit Vicini is at present connected with the Internal Revenue office at San Francisco. Before the war called him away, Hoit was a star center on the basketball squad. Very likely he will play this position the coming season on a team representing the Olympic Club.

Jiggs Donahue and John Briare, erstwhile members of Father Ward's famous "Bulldogs", were down to see the scrimmage between the Varsity and the U. S. S. Nebraska team. Jiggs and his jovial pranks are even yet frequently recounted among the fellows. As for John, his quiet, studious nature made him quite popular among his classmates. The latter is at present occupied with the study of law at the night school of St. Ignatius.

Frank Conneally, the Secretary-elect of the Student Body for the present year, sends word of a high old time he is having with brother Tom down in the City of the Angels. Frank was an elocutionist of no mean ability, winning the Owl prize last year. He established for himself an enviable record while at school here. "Connie" was always a good student and displayed such remarkable deliberative abilities that twice he was chosen for the Ryland Debate. At present he is employed in Oxnard with a sugar manufacturing concern and from the latest reports he is doing very well. Frank is specializing in Chemistry and he will no doubt derive very much practical experience in his new duties. University of Southern California is his goal where he intends to procure a certificate. Latest reports have it that he is headed northward to visit the old hallowed walls.

Ex '21 Raymond Momboise of Petaluma is reported to be studying Pharmacy at the Affiliated Colleges in San Francisco. Ray is the possessor of a fine voice which he keeps in tune by singing in the choir of St. Mary's Cathedral.

Ex '22 James P. Carr was on the campus recently with the blushing girl of his choice, Miss Maude Francis Roberts. Jimmie reported that the ceremony was performed in San Francisco in the early part of October. The happy groom is still well remembered about the campus and his old classmates extend to him their warmest congratulations.

Ex '23 The following is taken from the Marysville Appeal:

"De Witt Le Bourveau, well known and popular young man of this city, will be married in Oakland on October 15, to Miss Oviedo Forni, daughter of a wealthy stock man of

Placerville, El Dorado Co., Cal. The wedding will be a quiet affair. After a honeymoon in the bay cities they will return to Marysville to make their home. Le Bourveau is well known in baseball circles throughout the Sacramento valley, having formerly been a member of the Marysville Giants in the Trolley League. During the past summer he made a splendid record with the Philadelphia Nationals, with whom he expects to play next season. His bride-to-be is in charge of the accounting office at Mare Island and has the distinction of being the only woman employed in the Navy Yard. She is an attractive and accomplished young woman."

Martín M. Murphy.

The Exponent

The October number displays a rather persuasive notice on the Alumni Notes as a feature of this issue, and we declare that they are quite interesting and amusing. This is a department of a college magazine that is not to be neglected or underestimated, as it forms a link between the past and the present. Yes, indeed, Exponent, they are quite worthy of notice, even if we live out here in "the wild and wooly West".

The verses of this number are of a good quality, and we particularly appreciated "Love's Chain". "Helium and Aerial Navigation" and "Industrial Cooperation" are both good essays on interesting and up-to-date topics; and the length of the former or the brevity of the latter are not in the least derogatory of their merits. The two stories, accidentally or otherwise, have the same back-ground—the conventional American rural setting; however, aside from a detective shadowing a detective and a bank robbery dramatically foiled, there is nothing very startling about them. We cannot overlook the fine spirit expressed in the editorials; and the subjects, moreover, are quite apropos.

As a suggestion, we would like to see a slight change in the design as well as in the size of the magazine; the color on the front-piece is not very proper, we think, and a slightly larger book would undoubtedly add to its attraction.

The Villa Marian

College magazines are usually sample literary productions featuring the prose and poetic instincts of some talented students. But what must we say, if, besides evidencing a high standard of literary attainment, we are brought into intimate contact with the inter-mural events of some distant fane of learning? Such, indeed, is the case with this charming little magazine. We have come to know all about the happenings in those eventful days preceding graduation, and have learned something of the sad pleasure of parting. The "Valedictory" strikes a distinct chord that to us sounds very appropriate. "Class History" and other kindred documents afford us an interesting peep into the inner life of this happy group. Somewhere, however, we noticed this sentence, which to us seemed rather poorly constructed. "She made her way up what marble steps could be located, and wandered about the building on a search for her sleeping apartments, lost to the world." A little simplification would suffice. "When Ireland's dream comes true" is a calm and hopeful prayer for the rosy-fingered dawn when that noble race shall rise over the wreckage of its oppressors to her throne among the nations of the world. "Roses" is a beautiful thought, artistically well developed; and is more charming than its name indicates. The opening lines of the class poem express a striking simile, and we would fain copy them. But listen to "Mystery" which struck our fancy and we betray ourselves with these lines:

"Or some Angel dreaming of Mary
Pause in the midst of a prayer
To breathe on the virgin canvas
That his love might be pictured
there?"

This entertaining magazine immediately attracted us, and we must confess that we feel somewhat partial to it.

De Paul Minerval Stories, essays, verses, philosophical and educational disquisitions are embraced within the neat covers of the commencement number of our Chi-

cago friend; and the arrangement is indeed quite worthy of approval as the reader, mentally struggling through the heavy verbiage of critical discussions, emerges on the smooth surface of interesting stories, and even soars into the ambient air of enthusiastic verses. "P. D." is a typical war story. But even though this variety of story is a bit out of date at present, and is consequently not so relished, still one like this is always pleasing and entertaining. In "For the Honor of the Family Name" the judge is made to remark: "The proceeding may be irregular;" but we would add: In fact, too irregular to appear plausible or possible. But aside from the misdevelopment of the plot in this detail, the noble purpose of a hero being innocently condemned to save the honor of a name is praiseworthy.

At one extreme, breathing a fervent poetic instinct, is "Heart, Art Thou Alone?"—the embodiment of a beautiful thought; while at the other extreme, "Only You;" is a bit of sentimentalism which may be excused on the plea that probably it was due to the emotional ebullitions instigated by the balmy atmosphere of the Lake City. "Kinky-Headed Coon," however, we enjoyed, because, notwithstanding its uncommonness in college verse, it is still better than many other poetic efforts we have met. The author of "College Short Stories" gives a clear and accurate review of the prevailing types of stories, and pleads for a greater effort towards this form of college production. And the editorials: they are fine examples of a true virilent spirit that needs rather to be imitated than commended.

More power to you, Minerval; and may you continue to uphold the standard of true Americanism and Catholicism.

Friendship, like the winds
That move a watery caravan,
Shapes the course along
Our life, with its short span.

The Canisius Monthly This sprightly monthly reached us after a tedious trip across the continent, through the midst of strikes and other disorders, without a scratch. And its literary efforts are well worth reading.

A strong didactic verse with a practical lesson on the foibles of fawning humanity is "Popularity and Disgrace," and another charming bit of verse with an apt and patriotic thought is "Spring in Peace"; both of which are quite creditable. Of course, we read "Diamonds and Make-Believes," and immediately and intuitively our mind wandered back to our reading of De Maupassant's story. To us it appeared almost as bad or quite as good, if you like, as a translation.

"Socialism and Labor" is a clear and terse exposition of the leading tenets of an economic "patented medicine," with a logical summary of its impractical applications. In view of the prevailing circumstances, it is, indeed, timely and worth reading. Whether or not one will agree with the author of "Making Good" as to the typical American girl depends upon the point of view—and not a little upon personal experiences. We, however, think the title of Amazon best suited for this reckless bit of femininity. Certainly there is a lot of dash and splash in this story. But, for whatever purpose our remarks have been clothed to serve, we cannot but assent to the thought that has made "Success" possible. This is a story with a wealth of meaning, a lesson of unquenchable mother's love and an inspiring self-sacrifice that is almost too noble for words.

Excellent! Canisius; and may we see more of such literay genius in your bright little magazine.

Morning Star As a star that suddenly twinkles through a rift in the clouds attracts our attention, and then as the space slowly widens, other celestial sapphires swing into our view, so, the appearance of this magazine through the midst of our engrossing activities, disclosed not a few literary gems of real worth. The poetry of this number maintains its excellent standard with "The Good Shepherd," "Longing" and "Their Dying Will," all of which contain a beautiful thought clothed in tasteful verbal adornment.

"Farewell to Graduates" is the ap-

plication of a simile that is quite familiar and frequently used. However, we
were consoled with the thought that
there is nothing new under the sun. A
story with an appropriate atmosphere
and a noteworthy lesson for everyone
is "The Last First Friday". The plot
is well developed and its activities are
not overextended. "Only a Hair" is a
pleasing effort; and the same may be
said of others. But we found some
fault with "The Mystery of Clare-
more:" The plot, besides lacking its

proper development, is too embracing
for such a story, and its activities are
so varied and unexpected that we are
led to doubt their probability. The editorials, in their turn, manifest a
breadth of vision that indicates an interest in things other than mere domestic college affairs. And this is what
they should be, Star; and may you
continue to aid in molding the opinion
of the public with whom you come in
contact.

Peter F. Morettini.

ATHLETICS

With the passing of the month of October, American Football has found a home at Santa Clara. Our squad of past Rugby stars has Harmonized into an eleven well worthy to uphold the reputation of the Red and White. This has been accomplished only through the strenuous efforts of Coach Bob Harmon, and the willingness of some thirty aspirants to present themselves day after day for grilling practices, and to abide by the various training rules and diets set down by our coach.

Realizing that the Preps of today shall compose the Varsity of tomorrow, a coach has been selected, and to realize the wisdom of the choice one but needs to glance upon the Santa Clara Prep team in action. In the years from 1901 to 1904, a certain Mr. A. J. Roesch attended the Prep school of Lawrence University, but this failed to prevent him from holding down the position of right half back on the varsity of that institution during those years. In 1905 he enrolled as a Freshman at the Uni-

versity of Wisconsin, and found it no task to make a half-back position on the Frosh team. The year 1906 found him playing on the Denver University team, and allow us to reiterate that Bob Harmon was also a member of that eleven. The next year he entered the coaching life at the West Texas Military Academy of San Antonio. During 1911 he was the Public School Physical Director of San Bernardino, California. In 1917 and 1918 he coached the Mt. Tamalpais Military Academy eleven, and was the physical director of the San Rafael Public schools, as well as of the Citizens' training camp. Today we find him imparting football knowledge to the Preps of Santa Clara, and we doubt if there could be found a better man for the work than Coach A. J. Roesch.

The rooters section at any game is of great importance, and although many new faces are seen about the campus, all have learned the various songs and yells contained in the little blue book;

to whom credit is
nk . Chief Harter,
l Bill Desmond.
the highest degrees
, and the youth who
:ching the flickering
s gazing into the
"only dear one on
nould be urging his
is certain of a treat
sawdust. We state
isiness has been on
3 and S club.

Varsity 3

id of the "awful dé-
-e to receive at the
erienced winged O
; rumored that our
gby players, would
of their opponents,
the position of their
r 12, Columbus day,
he opening of Santa
ason, as well as of

igineers had baffled
with their haughty
llow advertisements.
;ame, and as soon as
ad eagerly witnessed
of the field by the
Student Body, a two
rie schooner rambled
Suddenly these wiz-
it located a cache in
eld. It proved to be
:e box.
presence of the curi-

ous spectators, a huge human form
clad in moleskins, leaped out. Old man
American Football was with us again.

From the moment of the kick-off until the last quarter had ended, the Varsity put up a game fight, their line
holding firmly the powerful drives of
the Olympic backs. Our visitors were
able to score only through the aerial
route, their passes being of the short
high variety, yet fate had it that a few
of them were successful. In the third
quarter Moose Korte made a beautiful
place kick from the thirty-five yard
line, thus netting our three points. Roy
Baker, the Tarzan from the South, has
a fancy for getting his man, and ofter
the spectators were thrilled by his low,
diving tackles. Mike Pecarovich, the
energetic lad from the Northwest,
played a fast game at center, and the
Olympic quarterback found it useless to
try plays through his position.

The following men lined up for the
kick-off:

Bannon	Left End
Manelli	Left Tackle
Ferrario (capt.)	Left Guard
Pecarovich	Center
Noll	Right Guard
Korte	Right Tackle
Whelan	Right End
Scholz	Quarterback
Baker	Left Half
Needles	Right Half
Cochran	Fullback

Referee, Braddock; Umpire, Huebel;
Head Linesman, Saxton.

Stanford Freshmen 13   Hooligans 0

On Saturday, Oct. 18, the Stanford Freshman Team lined up against the Santa Clara Hooligans. Now these Hooligans were the mystery boys of the campus, and the rumor ran wild that they were a pepless squad of grid warriors. The Stanford Frosh kicked off, and an ambitious Hooligan made a perfect catch. The observing spectators noticed that it required three of the Babes to stop him. On their first play they pulled an end run, and they ran such a perfect interference of the Sam Hill variety that it netted twenty-eight yards.

The Stanford Freshmen made wonderful gains in yardage through the fault of a Hooligan linesman being offside, and the first half ended with the score board reading Hooligans 0 and Stanford Frosh, 7. The second developed into a punting duel with one Ray Schall as a star. Once was Stanford successful in recovering a fumble near the Hooligans' goal, and putting the pigskin over, which added another six points.

Eddie Amaral and Nig Jackson in the positions of backs played a hard, driving game, while Beef Difiore, at center, displayed an unusual amount of football talent. The Hoolies' lineup:

Cronin	Left End
J. Muldoon	Left Tackle
Lewis	Left Guard
Difiore (capt.)	Center
Phelan	Right Guard
Heafey	Right Tackle
Kerckhoff	Right End
Neary	Quarter
Amaral	Left Half
Jackson	Right Half
Schall	Full Back

Varsity 60   U. S. S. Boston 0

To the gobs of the Batleship Boston much credit must be given. They have formed a team, and that team has been willing to battle any squad of warriors at any time or place. They have had the pleasure of crossing their opponents' goal line but once, yet their service upon the swelling blue has taught them to never say quit.

On Sunday, Oct. 19th, they lined up against the Varsity. It took the well oiled machine that represented the Red and White just six short minutes to place the pigskin over on straight line plays.

The Navy found a stiff defense in the Santa Clara line, and their attempts at end runs were sadly broken up by Hush Kerckhoff and Tom Bannon. Using the forward pass and off tackle plays frequently the Varsity found no difficulty in making their yardage. Rudy Scholz, at quarter, formed a habit of returning the Navy punts twenty and thirty yards, while Jim Needles often pierced their line for long gains. The end of the first half found the score, Varsity 40, Boston 0.

The Hooligans, their forms rather stiff from the previous day's game, were sprinkled into the line-up in the second half, in hopes that they would be taught football, through the only successful method, experience.

Although the pigskin seemed to have a fancy for slipping from their hands, nevertheless they added twenty points to the already swollen score. The following are the men who started in this game:

Bannon ....Left End
Manelli ....Left Tackle
Ferrario (capt.) ......Left Guard
Pecarovich ....Center
J. Muldoon ....Right Guard
Korte ....Right Tackle
Kerckhoff ....Right End
Scholz ....Quarter
Baker ....Left Half
Needles ....Right Half
Cochrane ....Full Back

Referee, Macomber; Umpire, Rosenthal.

Varsity 60   U. S. S. Nebraska 7

Sunday, Oct. 26, was scheduled as Color Day at Santa Clara. The eleven of the U. S. S. Nebraska was to furnish the opposition for the Varsity, while the Bears and Merchants, two loving baseball clubs of San Jose, were to do battle for supremacy of the diamond.

The Nebraska entered the gridiron with pep showing upon their faces, and throughout the game they never ceased to display it. After taking the ball fifty yards on line plunges, Manelli on a tackle around play, scored the first touchdown. The second score came soon after on the same play, while the third was made by Nig Jackson on a long end run. The Navy was forced to punt from behind their own goal line, but Bag Muldoon, played "Johnny on the spot" and blocked the kick. Not content with this honor he fell upon the ball, thus adding six more points to the score. A few minutes later Petri, playing right half for the sailors, intercepted a long forward pass and raced fifty yards down the side lines for the Navy's only tally.

In the second quarter the Varsity opened their style of play, but their forward passes often fell short or were fumbled.

Two injuries were received in this quarter which will undoubtedly cause a weakness in the Red and White line, Captain Fat Ferrario tearing the ligaments in his left leg, and Hol Lewis throwing his elbow out of joint. However, faith is placed in our two ambitious trainers, Doctors Argenti and Coman.

When the whistle had sounded for the end of the third quarter, the score stood sixty to seven. And as the sun was casting lengthy shadows, the game was called in order that the baseball nines would not be forced to play by starlight.

The following started against the sailors:

Whelan ....Left End
Manelli ....Left Tackle
Lewis ....Left Guard
Schall ....Center
Phelan ....Right Guard

Ferrario (capt.) ....Tackle
Kerckhoff ....Right End
Scholz ....Quarter
Jackson ....Left Half
Needles ....Right Half
Pecarovich ....Full Back

Referee, Cave; Umpire, Elliott; Head Linesman, Roesch.

Stanford 13   Varsity 0

Early on the afternoon of Saturday, November 8, found the students and the eleven of Santa Clara northward bound to do battle with their past Rugby rivals, Stanford. The day was ideal, for old Sol was as eager to witness the game as were the six thousand spectators.

Amid the roars of the rooting sections, the two Varsities jogged upon the turf at two-thirty. Some minutes later the shrill whistle of the referee pierced the snappy atmosphere, and from that time until the last moment of the game, here is what took place. Stanford kicks off. Cochrane advances the ball ten yards. Ferrario attempts a pass which fails. Manelli makes two yards on a tackle around play. Baker makes three through line. Korte punts to Templeton who returns the ball twenty yards. Stanford fumbles, but recovers. Wark loses two yards on end run. Tempelton punts to Scholz who returns four yards. Needles makes four off left tackle. Scholz makes two through center. Santa Clara makes their first down by Baker tearing off right tackle. Needles

makes one yard off tackle. Scholz makes two through center. Baker loses one yard on end run. Korte punts over goal. Stanford's ball on their twenty yard line. Templeton punts sixty yards with wind and Scholz fumbles, Stanford recovering the ball. Stanford offside, penalized five yards. They then made four yards around right end, but on repeating the same play failed to gain. Templeton, on a fake punt, makes fifteen around right end. Stanford makes five through line. Four off left tackle. Four off right tackle. Three off left tackle. Two through center but Needles recovers the ball from a fumble on Stanford's thirty yard line. Needles makes six through line. Scholz makes two through center. Needles makes one through line. Korte punts seventy yards to Templeton, who returns it thirty yards. Stanford gains two off right end. Seven off right end, and then one through line making their first down. On the next play they gain nothing through line. Six yards around right end. Four off left end. Holt makes seven through center. Holt makes four through center. Levy makes three, thus giving Stanford their yardage three times in succession. On the next play both teams were offside. Stanford gains four, two, and one yard, and then Templeton drop kicks from the thirty yard line, the ball going wide. Santa Clara has ball on the twenty yard line. Baker loses one yard. Needles gains five off left tackle. Needles gains two off left tackle, First quarter. Ball on Santa Clara thirty yard line. Score, 0-0.

Second quarter. Needles gains one yard through center. Scholz four through center. Needles three through center. Scholz gains two through center. First down for Santa Clara. Needles gains six on left end run. Baker four off right tackle. Again Santa Clara makes its yardage. Baker gains three off tackle. Signals miscarried. No gains. Baker runs thirty yards around right end. Needles four around left end. Needles three off left tackle. Scholz one through center. Baker makes one-half of a yard off left and the ball goes over to Stanford. Templeton fumbles on the punt and runs ten yards. Bannon relieves Whelan. Stanford penalized five yards for being offside. Santa Clara penalized five yards, offside. Templeton punts to thirty yard line and Scholz returns it twenty yards. Needles gains three yards. Baker does not gain. Manelli attempts pass, but it is incompleted. Korte punts to twent-five yard line, Templeton returning it eight yards. Levy one yard. Holt nothing. Stanford offside. Penalized five yards. Templeton punts to Scholz on twenty yard line, who returns it fifteen yards. Baker gains twenty yards around right end. Needles one yard through line. Forward pass intercepted by Pelouze on Stanford twenty-five yard line. Santa Clara penalized five yards for rushing Templeton while punting. Holt gains ten around right end. Levy seven around left end. Holt gains five through center. Stanford makes five yards off right tackle. Carroll replaces Levy. Carroll runs twenty-five yards around left end. Templeton makes two yards through center. Carroll nothing through center. Larson gains four yards around right end. Holt four through center. Holt makes two yards around right end. Holt then plunges through center of line but is stopped high, and a dispute follows, but Stanford is finally given the credit of a touchdown. Templeton fails to kick goal. Score, Stanford 6, Santa Clara 0. J. Muldoon replaces Ferrario. Stanford kicks off to Scholz on twenty yard line, who returns it twenty yards. Baker gains three. Scholz six around left end. Scholz loses three around left end. Korte punts to Stanford's twenty-five yard line. Templeton punts to Scholz on thirty yard line, who returns it to forty-five yard line. Forward pass by Santa Clara intercepted by Larson. First half ends with ball in possession of Stanford on their forty-five yard line. Score, Stanford 6, Santa Clara 0.

Second Half.

Third Quarter. Ferrario in J. Muldoon's position. Santa Clara pulls a trick kick off, and Ferrario recovers the ball on Stanford's thirty yard line. Baker makes fifteen through right tackle. Needles three. Baker two. Scholz three around right end. Baker one yard through line. Ball goes over to Stanford. Holt makes two off right end. Santa Clara penalized five yards for offside. Larson eight. Larson thirty around end. Phelan replaces Noll. Stanford penalized fifteen yards. Patrick gains two. Patrick punts to Scholz who returns the ball ten yards. Santa Clara penalized five yards for offside. Manelli loses five yards on a spread formation. Forward pass intercepted. Stanford makes three around right end. Holt gains nothing. Patrick gains nothing. Patrick punts outside. Manelli gains two around right end on spread formation. Scholz loses one yard around right end. Korte punts to Stanford's one yard line and the ball is returned by Patrick five yards. Patrick loses three yards. Stanford gains two through center. Patrick punts thirty yards, and Scholz returns five yards. Needles gains three yards. Forward pass, Manelli to Baker nets five yards. Forward pass incompleted. Scholz makes two through center, making the yardage. Korte gains one yard, Baker two, Manelli three. Korte punts fifty yards. Stanford has the ball on their three yard line. Patrick punts to their fifty yard line and Scholz receives it, but is tackled before he gains. Forward pass by Manelli incompleted. Again forward pass incompleted. Santa Clara penalized five yards. Korte punts to Patrick on twenty yard line. End of third quarter. Score, Stanford 6, Santa Clara 0.

Fourth Quarter. Santa Clara has ball. Baker gains three around right end. Scholz gains two through center. Amaral replaces Cochrane. Santa Clara penalized fifteen yards for holding. Korte punts forty-five yards, Patrick returning it ten yards. Holt nothing. Stanford ten through center. Patrick on a long end run gains fifty yards and places the ball on Santa Clara's two yard line. Kerckhoff replaces Baker. On the next play Caughy goes over for a touchdown. Patrick kicks goal. Score, Stanford 13, Santa Clara 0. Stanford kicks off, Pecarovich returning the ball fifteen yards. Pecarovich three yards. Manelli six, Pecarovich loses three on fumble. Korte attempts punt but it is blocked and Stanford recovers the ball on fifteen yard line. Patrick loses three on end run. Caughy gains two. Holt two around right end. Santa Clara recovers fumble and Korte punts out of danger. Patrick gains six around left end. W. Muldoon replaces Ferrario. Caughy gains three through center. Lilly replaces Caughy. Lilly gains three on right end run. Holt makes four around left end. Lilly gains three. The bleachers are roaring. Holt loses three yards and ball goes to Santa Clara. Bedolla replaces Kerckhoff. Forward pass by Santa Clara fails. Manelli loses four yards on a run from punt formation. Korte punts fifty yards, and Lilly returns the ball to his own fifteen yard line. Buty replaces Bedolla. Patrick gains ten yards. Stanford makes three off left tackle, two off left tackle, five off right tackle, and one through center. Daly replaces Buty, and Korte punts to fifty yard line and the ball is returned ten yards. Before the next play a shot rang out from the side lines, and the game was over.

The Red and White rooters gave their last yell with as much pep as their first, although they did feel an emptiness in their pockets, and the spectators drifted away satisfied that they had witnessed a fast football game.

Had the Varsity line held as it had been taught to hold, and had Baker and Ferrario been minus their injuries before the start of the game, then perhaps the score board would not have read as it did. A football team is composed of eleven men, and it is the aim of the Santa Clara Varsity to play those same men in a game as long as they are in the physical condition to move about the field.

The following composed the Varsity line-up:

Cochrane ....Left End
Manelli ....Left Tackle
Ferrario ....Left Guard
Schall ....Center
Noll ....Right Guard
Korte ....Right Tackle
Whelan ....Right End
Scholz ....Quarter
Baker ....Left Half
Needles ....Right Half
Pecarovich ....Fullback

Referee, Braddock; Umpire, Rosenthal; Head Linesman, Huebel; Field Judge, Macomber.

J. E. Neary.

THE PREPS.

Prep and pep are synonomous this year. Of all the Preps Santa Clara ever had, there was never a set more thought of, more honored, more deserving than our plucky bunch of this year. But four months ago, think of it! only four months ago, every one of them was a Rugby star. Two months of vacation over, they returned to the campus to find that the game of their infancy, the game they loved, the game that made them the envied of all the Preps of all California, was driven somewhere never-to-return and American Football, intricate, comprehensive and extensive American Football, rushed out to embrace our wondering Preps.

These peppery Preps leaped into their moleskins and after three weeks of grind were looking for fight. They journeyed to Palo Alto one fine day to try out their newly acquired knowledge with the Military Academy there. Well they won, 57-0.

Coach Roesch now took them in hand and the Preps never stopped learning. The game which they played against Centerville High and won by a 26-0 score made them look like a million dollars. Captain O'Brien was in the Infirmary and all the tears he shed to get out of the tender care of Bro. Anthony would have been enough to fill the water bucket. He pleaded, he furied, he argued, he did everything but threaten to get out and fight with his team. But the sage old Bro., though an ardent fan and an ardent lover of

American Football, loves his boys still better and would not yield to the peppy skipper of the Preps. Even this catastrophe did not discourage our team. Two hours before the fray little Joe Farrell, who never touched a football, was getting ready to play "Quarter" in place of Captain O'Brien. And say! That youth surely got away with a classy game. "Pat" Carey was a real star. Centerville's line bent and snapped in two when Pat hit it. He opened holes big enough for a taxi with both doors open to get through. And they got through for long gains every time.

Curley, Connell, the Geogheghan brothers, and Maggetti are positive gluttons for work and fight. They run low, hit hard, never fumble, and smile the whole time. Duff and Halloran and DeCazotte are likewise doing well:

The Preps of today are the Varsity of tomorrow. So there is every hope in the world for Santa Clara's future. Her fighting Preps are growing with her, and when they shall have reached their maturity in the very near future, Old Alma Mater need have no fear with Carey, O'Brien, Connell, Ryan, and the Geoghegans to defend her.

If you can't come over, then leave your Film at Madden's Pharmacy in your own school town.

Rex Theatre

SANTA CLARA, CAL.

. MORRIS   -   -   Owner and Manager

A Good Show Every Night

First Class Productions

First Class Plays

Courteous Treatment

If It's Made of Paper
We Have It !

The San Jose Paper Co.

hone San Jose 200
51-181 W. SANTA CLARA ST.

)UIS CHABRE & JEAN MILLET, Props.   Phone San Jose 4763

PARISIAN BAKERY
FRENCH AND AMERICAN BREAD
PIES AND CAKES

Pain de Luxe, French Rolls, Parisian, Richelieu, Rolls Fendu, Vienna Rolls, Etc.

utomobiles deliver to all parts of city   **251 W. San Fernando St., San Jose**

A. G. COL CO.
Wholesale Commission Merchants

Telephone San Jose 309

CONTENTS

Christmas

ONLY a babe on a truss of straw,
    Round whom the ice-winds play---
Yet prostrate at his tender feet,
    Faith learns the royal way.

Only a babe with arms outstretched
    To win a mother's kiss---
But hope adoring sees afar
    Our race redeemed to bliss.

Only a babe, but a babe divine
    Descending from above,
To give his all to us that we
    Might give our all in Love.

RUDY SCHOLZ.

The Redwood

Entered Dec. 18, 1902, at Santa Clara, Cal., as second-class matter, under Act of Congress of March 3, 1879

VOL. XIX.   SANTA CLARA, CAL., DECEMBER, 1919   NO. 3

The College Magazine

The Editor.

THIS is an age, apparently, in which nothing is stable except instability. We have ideas about everything, but of one thing only do we seem to be certain—that something else is lots better than the something we chance to possess. The result—Prohibitionists, Bolshevists, Socialists, those who have New Thought and those who have no thought; in short, a hundred and one self-constituted little deities who are perfectly sure that they could have made ever so much nicer a world than the one the Almighty created. Differ these radicals do, among themselves and in many things; still, upon their separate chariots of progress is emblazoned in characters so bold that he who runs may read, the slogan: Utopia or bust.

Were these "Ists" few in number or were their labors confined to matters of no interest to us, we would not

mind. But their spirit—the spirit of change—seems to be universal. Everyone is infected with it. Of course, the spirit of change is good in its way—in fact, progress without change is practically impossible. The trouble comes from the fact that change without progress is not impossible. Retrogression is, as often as not, the result of departure from means and methods which have been found for any length of time, successful. It is then rather important for anyone contemplating such departures to ponder long and carefully; otherwise his Utopian chariot is liable to turn off the highway of perfection and go careening down some unfrequented by-road whose terminus is in the quagmires.

Recently, a decided change has taken place in college journalism. The two, or four, or six-page weekly has appeared, and, judging by its steadily increasing popularity, it will soon steal the honors from the larger and more cultured monthly magazine. Now, it isn't our intention to hurl sticks and stones and nasty epithets at the little weekly newspaper. Far from it—there are too many points in its favor in which the monthly publication is undoubtedly not its equal. For instance, it is, or should be anyhow, newsy and full of the latest up-to-the-minute campus gossip. It is, or should be in intimate contact with college life in all its various manifestations. Published rather frequently, it has something of the power of the press, so far as its own little world is concerned. Thus, it is an admirable instrument for developing and fostering that something so important in American college life—"pep" or college spirit. Then again, financially speaking, the weekly is well-nigh independent. It is so small, usually, that printing expenses are comparatively insignificant. And to the college advertiser, the main source of revenue, it has inducements to offer which are capable of tempting forth his money. He realizes that here is an investment which is going to give him a substantial profit, and so he is a bit less chary of his aid.

But the monthly publication! Its advertising rates are necessarily much higher than are those of the weekly—higher in fact than its 'per capita' circulation would seem to warrant. And they must be, for the production cost is often quite considerable, whereas selling rates cannot be very great. The advertiser, considering as he does, only the return his money is going to bring, will naturally refuse to invest if he thinks that return will be negligible. Practically the only merchants over whom the monthly publication has any influence are those who carry on their business in the immediate neighborhood of the college and who have reason to fear a boycott on the part of the students. Such merchants are few though, and altogether insufficient to support a large magazine. Hence the necessity of falling back in such large measure on "courtesy" advertisements.

Moreover—for there's nothing like candor—the procuring of copy suitable for publication in a high-class monthly is becoming more and more a tantalizing question. There seems to be very little ambition these days among American youths to excel in literary endeavor unless they intend, as few do, to make literature their life-work. No wonder then that those charged with the duty of seeing that the magazine puts in a regular appearance are at their wits' ends around publishing time! The view-point of the youth is, of course, wrong, but who can blame him? He has only caught the utilitarian spirit of a very utilitarian age and is acting accordingly.

These obstacles and others are done away with in the weekly newspaper and we imagine that this very consideration has something to do with its present popularity. But, after all, is walking around a difficulty instead of meeting it squarely and surmounting it, the very best way to proceed? Or have we to confess that the struggle to interest the American youth in other and higher things than material prosperity is a hopeless one? If we're going to keep the literary monthly we assuredly have a task on our hands. There's no use denying that. But isn't it a task worth while? The monthly magazine gives something—a certain refinement and tone of dignity—to college activity which no newspaper, however "classy" can ever impart, and which is certainly worth preserving. As long as the monthly remains we have some kind of a remedy where that remedy is most needed, against the prevalent journalism craze which has so gotten hold of the nation. We have a means of counteracting the slovenly habit of intellect which is slowly, but very surely, rendering us a people incapable of appreciating true beauty in literature and in art. We're too much of a rag-time nation already without becoming more so, but what are you going to do if the only kind of English the college man is trained to enjoy is rag-time English—if the only intellectual nourishment he learns to care for is what may be found in the columns of a penny newspaper?

Twixt Dusk and Dawn

Henry C. Veit.

YEGG was the only name he had. At least it was the only name his pals had known him by. Surely it was not the name that his parents had given him when he was christened. Parents usually exercise a little discretion when time comes for the naming of the latest little swaddled arrival into this sordid world. However, regardless of what that choice might have been, Yegg was the peculiar title he had earned for himself during his long years in the underworld where he made a specialty of safes and strong boxes.

Like every other man claiming fellowship in the huge throng of crooks operating in and about that section of the country, Yegg was giving himself up entirely to a most careful and detailed study of the lay of his land. He thought it about time for another haul. The Strickler job brought him far less than he had expected. He admitted he was in need of a new wardrobe. One who claimed the distinction of being the best dressed individual in his profession must of necessity have a convenient fund to fall back upon in order to keep abreast of Dame Fashion. Yegg possessed a deal of pride in his distinction. Not even the disappointment in the Strickler outlay, which had caused his coffers an appreciable depletion, served to deter him from making at least two more hauls before he quit the little city of Du Bois.

Perhaps his love of the bizarre was the prompting agent in his desire to break into the Cathedral of St. Paul. When he would have succeeded in so doing, his list of jobs would have included every possible sort of place one might burglarize. At least it would tend to satisfy his taste for the unusual. Then there was the Norton home with its reputed content of precious gems and other valuables. If he could succeed in the last mentioned and with the former to grace his inner self as a personal achievement, he believed he would be satisfied with his spoils.

Thus he reasoned and in pondering, found himself eager to launch out upon both. Yegg was one to act quickly and he determined to attempt them before another day marked its passing.

It was growing dark and snowing. Yegg had no particular destination. He just walked briskly about the thoroughfares of Du Bois. He found the crisp air and the driving snow a stimulant for thought; he needed to think considerably, especially of the Norton job. It was all absorbing. There was the officer on the beat to cope with, then the demand upon his greatest skill to enter the home, capture his prize and make a successful get-a-way. These things filtered rapidly through his active brain. He was loathe to have failure epitomize what now appeared easy and a positive success. Much after the fashion of one so indulgent in every variety of theft, Yegg travelled over the course that was to witness his last job in Du Bois. He warily observed every vantage point and made a mental facsimile of the surroundings. Nothing escaped his sharp glances.

In the shadow of St. Paul's, a huge majestic pile of Gothic architecture, he drew his brisk walk to a saunter. Satisfied, he put his head to the gale and crunched on through the snow. Presently he confronted the Norton residence. Its apparent challenge in its seeming security from the possible housebreaker amused Yegg. To attempt the impossible is the acme of delight for any crook. Yegg was no exception. He lazily leaned against the lamp-post and imaginatively began an entrance, a good eight or nine hours in anticipation of his hoped for entry.

Yegg seemed to sense a pair of prying eyes in back of him. Turning he saw a boyish face beaming through the pane. The wreath of holly in the window should have told him of the Christmas season. He had almost forgotten it. Perhaps at another time when that face was not there he would have remembered the yuletide. As it was the reality did not possess him. There was a time, years back, when he had never failed to remember his little nephew at this time of the year. But his itinerary since then had carried him far into forgetfulness.

II

Jimmie Norton disliked the idea of being cooped up in his stuffy home on such a day. Though the gathering dusk should have told him he was better off as he was, he yearned to be out in the storm, romping about in the snow. For pastime he had viewed with curiosity the whole family album and proceeded to pester his mother with all sorts of questions as to the identity of every picture not already known to him. She condescendingly supplied the information, adding a bit of personal history to each one.

"That is Uncle Jim," she had told him in response to one of his queries.

Then, when the usual subsequent torrent of questions failed to come, she grew a little surprised. She turned from her sewing basket to find the youth intent upon something passing in the street. She was really glad. It might tend to distract him from a subject she did not care to discuss. Yet she disliked withholding the truth from him.

"Jimmy," she called.

"Yes, Mother."

"I want to tell you something about your uncle."

The youth eagerly sat himself at his

mother's feet. The bloom of boyhood was on his clean-cut features, and the upturned face suggested a few of the innumerable questions he was curious to have answered. In the past his mother had tactfully carried his mind away to other matters when he became unduly inquisitive. Now just the slightest incredulity seemed to possess him, yet he knew his fond parent to be sincere.

"Why doesn't Uncle Jim ever come to visit us, mother?" he asked.

"He'll come some day, Jimmie."

The youth's face was aglow. He recalled the stories his mother had told him of the days he could not remember, when his home had been in Chicago, and his uncle had been wont to come and fondle him and carry him about in his arms; then the array of presents given by him and which only in recent years Jimmie began to thoroughly appreciate. He remembered his regret at having to leave most of them behind after his father's death when they had moved to Du Bois so as to be near to the seat of the hugely lucrative enterprise his father had succeeded in building up shortly before he died. The prospect of a repetition of those days thrilled the youth.

"Do you think he'll come before Christmas?" Jimmie queried expectantly.

"I think not."

"Well, mother, when I go up to ring the little Angelus bells tonight, I'm go-ing to steal up to the altar and pray that he will."

Mrs. Norton beamed at this little display of great faith in her son. She recalled it was in matters of faith that her brother had been led astray. It pained her to think that it was his disbelief that caused him to set out upon a career of crime, the knowledge of which came to her only after his disappearance some dozen years ago. She linked together circumstances, recalled how she had pleaded, but in vain, for him to return to the creed of his fathers and how, when she had called into question his source of income, he had manifested a semblance of outward shame. Then, her subsequent learning that he was a crook caused her hurt. Little Jimmie's present manifestation of his faith, renewed that hurt, yet she found solace in the boy's sincerity.

She leaned over and kissed him.

"Yes do, Jimmie," she encouraged, "and pray that he'll come back to our faith."

The youth drew back non-plussed.

"Did he fall away?" he asked incredulously.

"Yes," she affirmed, "and because he lost his faith he became a thief."

The clock on the mantle shelf pointed to five minutes of the hour for the evening Angelus. He could just make it up to St. Paul's, four blocks away if he hurried. Bundling hastily into his wraps, and with the motherly admonition to take care against catching cold, he ran out into the driving snow and dashed up the street.

He could hear the clock in the town tower tolling the hour of six. Excited by the run he nervously closed the massive portals behind him and proceeded up the stairway to the belfry. The responding jangle of the bells to his pull brought with it the satisfaction that he had not fallen down upon his word to the good old sexton, who very graciously permitted the youth this nightly privilege.

The last reverberation was whisked away by the howling wind as he retraced his steps down to the vestibule. Reverently he pushed open the inner doors and advanced up the middle aisle. A holy quiet pervaded the interior. Up in the sanctuary glowed faintly the little lamp. Its soft crimson radiated a mysterious presence that enthralled the boy. Like an humble peasant in tattered rags, come into the luxurious court of a mighty potentate robed in the lavish purple of his office, Jimmie walked forward. He found a comfort in the hallowed stillness that was absorbing.

He thought the deep shadow on his left rather queer. Then he recalled the crib in process of building. Christmas was but two days distant. He could faintly discern beside the little manger the tiny new born Babe, the Mother; Joseph; and the meek shepherds. This too, served to put him at ease with the feeling that he was not alone in the stately edifice.

How long he had knelt there by the altar rail he was at no pains to determine. It was enough that he should be able to confide in and spiritually converse with the hidden King, laying bare his little troubles and requesting in earnest supplication, innumerable favors he had set his heart upon. He had not heeded the lapse of three full hours while so occupied. It seemed to matter little.

The realization of his waiting mother at home came to him. He could not recall a time when he had seemed so reluctant to depart from any one place. Perhaps it was the fact of his contentment that stayed him. Surely he was loathe to leave. Little did he realize what a hand Providence had taken in his earnestness. He was soon to learn.

Forgetful for the moment of all else save his predilection for prayer he permitted himself another few minutes at the altar rail. But the heavy hand of nature drew closed the lids of his eyes and he fell into a fast slumber, his head on his folded arms.

III

Yegg, in the attire of one about to enjoy the gaiety of a fancy ball room affair, stepped out of his rendezvous and hurried into the night. The illuminated clock in the tower told him the time was ripe for his job. He headed for St. Paul's. It loomed enticingly in the distance.

He had gained an entrance just as the hour of one pealed out across the snow-flaked night. The music sent a peculiar twinge through his system. He sensed a feeling of uneasiness. Perhaps it was merely the nervousness usually attendant upon first trials; nevertheless it galled him not a little. Yegg, who had launched innumerable and infinitely more difficult jobs successfully, with all their accompanying hazards, found himself lacking in his needed and customary confidence. He tried to shake loose the obsession from him, but it clung tenaciously. Angered by his timidity he felt for his "jimmy". It was the only tool he used. Outside of a varied assortment of skeleton keys he needed no other to aid him in his purpose. Deft fingers supplied the lack of the usual burglarizing instruments. Consoled and encouraged by its presence he advanced cautiously up the middle aisle.

Hardly had he reached the center of the edifice when a blinding white glare seemed to daze him. He turned his head for protection. Returning again to normality, he essayed a second look. Instinct rather than reason dictated to him to drop behind a pew for safety. Then the extreme brilliancy of the glare told him this was no natural light. Curiously, yet cautiously he peered over the top of the bench. He saw a transparent something come forth from the sacristy attired in the vestment of a Celebrant of the Mass. It was hoary and tottering, as if the weight of years had long overpowered its decrepit body.

Laboriously it reached the foot of the altar. Ascent was impossible. Apparently shackles deterred its willingness and effort to gain the top. Then forlornly it turned and re-entered the sacristy. As suddenly as it had appeared the blinding glare dissolved into the absorbing blackness around.

Yegg felt beads of perspiration surmount his clammy brow. He raised his quivering body to its full height and proceeded to convince himself he had not been dreaming. After a moment's deliberation, he revived his courage and proceeded on. Again the egress of the aged Celebrant from the sacristy and once more failure met his aim. Yegg for the second time saw blackness envelop what had before been light of incomputable candle power.

He set to reasoning. He recalled principles learned in many years gone by which rationally led him to the belief in the existence of a Personal God, a hereafter, one true church and many other fundamentals in the tenets he espoused when the wonderful gift of faith had been his. He had long since cast them overboard as useless, good only in an educational way but possessed of no objective truth. He had wanted to be free, to ply his profession without any subsequent qualms of conscience to nightmare him back to the old beliefs. He had thought himself successful. Now this appearance of a supernatural force seemed to upset his former convictions. He had been wrong. He must return to the dictates of right.

Yegg ended abruptly his train of thought.

"It's foolishness," he said to himself.

Annoyed by this dilatoriness he decided to quickly complete his job.

Again he advanced with renewed determination and again the revisitation of the supernatural. Like a mustang with its spirit broken, Yegg bowed to the powerful influence. He found the old faith revivifying his being once more, surcharging his whole soul with the ardor of his former staunch belief.

"There is a God after all," he said, "Lord I believe once more. Forgive me my transgressions. I repent." And he knelt in prayer.

He observed the Celebrant had gained the first step, beyond that no further. For the first time he noticed little Jimmie Norton still asleep at the altar rail.

The youth moved, straightened and awoke to the confronting apparition. The glare bewildered him. Frightened, he gazed about. Emptiness was everywhere. He too became aware of the unnaturalness of the light and the more did he become interested. His first thought was that the early Mass had begun; then what was mother doing over his absence; then he wondered if his prayer for the return of Uncle Jim would be heard.

A touch on the shoulder arrested his mental processes. He turned to see at his side one apparently just returned from a fancy dress affair. Jimmie grew curious. The possibility that his prayer in part had been answered caused him to whisper:

"Are you my Uncle Jim? God! You answer prayers quickly!"

Yegg looked at the youngster puzzled. He recognized the face he had seen in the window of the Norton home late in the afternoon.

"The old priest wants an acolyte," he said, "will you help me serve?"

Yegg brought to play his remarkable memory and allowed himself a few brief moments of brushing up in the duties of an acolyte. He had served upon the altar for years. Now he found he had forgotten little if anything.

The venerable Celebrant smiled wanly as he turned and saw the two by his side.

Yegg's metamorphosis had been complete. In spirit he followed the sacrifice being offered before him; the condemnation; the pain-exacting way to the heights of Calvary; the ignominious death on the Cross; the glorious resurrection. All this confronted him with startling reality. It caused his heart to well over in true sorrow as he reviewed his past life. He could recall no former occasion, in the years before his erring footsteps carried him far afield in crime, when he had so thoroughly appreciated the Holy Sacrifice.

Before he was fully aware of the fact the Celebrant had done and was following him into the sacristy. He had observed long before the reality of the old man's transparency. There, before his very eyes he saw the venerable priest slowly fade away into nothingness. The two prior visits of the apparition had convinced him that its disappearance was to be expected. He would have been surprised had it not taken place. Nothing but a faint glow remained and then settled once more the majestic silence pervading the cathedral.

A moment the two hesitated, awed by what had just transpired; then a voice was heard to say:

" 'Tis a holy and a wholesome thought to pray for the dead.' A soul is loosed from purgatory this instant by your assistance. I promised to say a Mass for a departed parishioner which I had forgotten to do. Full many a night have I come in this manner, always to fail because no one was here to assist me. I'll remember you both when I get to Heaven."

IV

That morning Jimmie Norton was giving a detailed account of his night's experience to his worried mother. She in turn was relating how she had enlisted the whole police force to scour the country in search of her missing boy.

"I'm so glad it all happened, mother," he was saying, "and—and my prayer was answered! Oh! I'm so excited I can't tell you."

The next moment he was rushing to the outer door.

"Come on mother, and see Uncle Jim. He has come to spend Christmas with us."

Grey Sails

LOVE! I watched thy silent ship go down
    The West, and with each golden ripple creep
Away from me; and thy dark misty sails
    Droop in the trackless fathoms of the Deep.

Ah Love! long, long I waited through the night
    For thy return; and then through weary days
Of throbbing fear---though well I knew thy sails
    Would never light the shadow of my ways.

But Love! 'tis only while the stream of years
    Runs swiftly on that we must parted be;
Not many tides may flow before---as thine---
    Grey Sails of mine will fade away at sea.

A. J. STEISS, JR.

Dicta on Feminology

Peter F. Morettini.

"What a piece of work is a woman!
How noble in sentiment, how infinite
in cunningness!
In action how like a butterfly!
In apprehension how like an oracle!
The beauty of the boudoir, the paral-
lax of men!"

THESE words, in gracious apology to the bard of Stratford-on-Avon, were but the philosophical ebullitions of another youth, who had rashly attempted to solve the mystery of a modern Medusa, and was ruthlessly cast aside. Woman, after all, is but true to her nature: for does not the word itself convey an ominous meaning to anyone who possesses masculine self-respect and hauteur? Syllabify the word, and we have "woeman". Coincidently, it was at this stage of his mental argumentation that the erstwhile hero paused and ruefully ruminated :

"Yea, woe to man, when a woman comes bearing gifts."

Even to us, in our youthful simplicity and inexperience, woman has appeared not exactly a mystery, but rather a problem—a miscellaneous construction of analytics, calculus, mechanics, and algebra, with a good coating of lacquer, cream, and powder. Now, with such a combination, can any mathematician, with the assistance of Solomon and Nat Goodwin, really give us an intelligible solution? But referring to facial ornamentation, the modern female has mastered all the technique of the art which flourished in the days of the Babylonians, Assyrians and Greeks; in fact, has far surpassed them all, and today the fabled "fountain of youth" would be as useless as the German Navy or the League of Nations.

Personally we dislike any female who seeks to disfigure her countenance with any of the amorphous or gelatinous preparations which the ingenuity of the drug store has concocted; and we prefer them innocent, natural, and unaffected as they came from the hand of God. Our view in this matter is not at all singular and exceptional, since we can boast of as great an authority on this

118

question as Horace. "Vultus teretisque integer laudo" is his poetical conclusion. And now what modern Adonis dare dispute it? Of course, we have said nothing of powder, as great minds differ on its merits as well as to its effect; but the greater weight of authority, supported by a long line of decorous decisions, hold that a little powder is altogether good for feminine attractiveness. Moreover, in company with a gentleman friend, it has a highly stimulating effect; provided, however, the scent is at least within the range of her partner's nasal activities. More than that, it has the charitable virtue of overcoming ill temper and self-imposed taciturnity, if the pair should be so unlucky as to have pledged themselves to a domestic career.

In logical sequence we should next mention her capillary attraction, and its intrinsic worth. But we balk at so expressing ourselves, except to say that we do not appreciate bobbed hair in any way, or on any occasion. This is a period of Americanization, and nothing that is in the least suggestive of a parlor bolshevist can call for our sympathies, much less our few stray pennies.

Again, at the force of logical sequence, we are led to inquire of the phrenological cavern, sometimes completely camouflaged by a hat as to its extent, and by lachrymose eyes and quivering lips, as to its nature and disposition. 'Tis true that our schools are crowded and our offices filled with this branch of the human race, but still we frequently hear the remark that women are senseless and the girls are so silly. Possibly though, our feminine population has subconsciously become so remarkably intelligent and artful that to the hoi polloi they pass as mere ignorant and worthless creatures. We hasten to add that this observation is true on principle from our own experience. By analogy, how often has it been that we have launched forth in an attempt to explain to the inner circle of the family, or to some less educated acquaintance, or even to the benignly docile, but insidiously treacherous, members of the faculty at the orals, the difference between truth and beauty, the nature of evil, or the hypothesis of innate ideas? And were we not pitied when our explanations failed to convince and our arguments vanished like bubbles in thin air? Then, perhaps, we can understand the nature of a woman's whimsical vacillations: for, indeed, they may really be on a higher intellectual plain than we collegiate products.

An example may probably make our reasoning clearer. We have been apprised of the fact that a certain female student at one of the nearby educational institutions boasts of a record of seven years of Latin, and six years of Greek. Talk about educated! She has enough classical training to pass for high priestess of the vestal virgins, if they existed today, or of the rhythmic dancers, should they provide an equally lucrative position. In fact, almost any girl can tell you the kind of cold cream

Mary Pickford uses, or how frequently Norma Talmadge pencils her eyebrows —but, what fair damsel, whose shapely fingers and velvet hands have done no harder work than brushing her teeth, can tell the simple ingredients of a comely biscuit or cake, and can really master the intricacies of cooking an honest and digestible meal without maternal assistance?

"O judgment! thou art fled to another planet,

And girls have lost their common sense!"

Still, many persist in tempting the troubled sea of matrimony without the compass of a cook book or the chart of domestic responsibility.

And does anyone blame the dubious young bachelor for balking at such a bolshevistic future? Rather he is to be praised than blamed. Yet they say that love is blind: probably that is why young people are always bumping into each other. If the young man could only see with the calm eye of reason, unbiased by any affection, he would undoubtedly avoid any such responsibility as frequently terminates in the court room. But, speaking for ourselves, if we should ever arrive at that stage in life where "two heads are better than one", and should awaken to find ourselves balancing a knife and fork across the table from a charming young wife, our fondest hope is that we may be able to conduct our own household without the aid or interference of a flock of domestic servants and parasitical relatives. This is strictly confidential, and under the table cloth. If this were not the case, then it would cost as much to manipulate a family as to launch a presidential campaign. And under the present conditions very few are financially equipped to cope with such a disheartening situation. Our ambition is to engage profitably in the legal profession, from the income of which to construct a home on the sunny slopes of the Western Coast line, "far from the madding crowd's ignoble strife"; and "along the cool sequestered vale of life" we hope to spend our days as peaceful Acadians. But all such ambitionings are worse than useless if the female commodity maintains its present high cost of living, and manifest its foolish cravings for unsubstantial knowledge.

Still, "Hope springs eternal in the human breast": and we vow not to desist in the pursuit of our heart's desire until the silver locks gather around us and the palpitations of life's throbbing hour slowly ebb away. In our sober moments we unconsciously recall the reflections of Edmund Burke with the words—

"But the age of chivalry is gone . . . never, never more, shall we behold that generous loyalty to rank and sex, that proud submission, that dignified obedience, that subordination of the heart, which kept alive, even in servitude itself, the spirit of an exalted freedom.''

Recovering from such profound depths of melancholy asseverations, we cast about us an optimistic glance, weighing in the scale of accusation and reproach our own shortcomings and idiosyncrasies, with the happy faults of the weaker sex, and then, from the hesitating beam, we recall to mind the proverbial lines—

''There is so much good in the worst
   of us,
And so much bad in the best of us,
That it behooves none of us
To be too hard on the rest of us.''

Snow-Flakes

T IS day---and like a million tiny clouds
In pity sifted by some angel hand,
Slowly the snow-flakes fall and softly rest
A virgin raiment o'er the war scarred lar

Night---and the pale moon's limpid, shimmerin
In glist'ning radiance mingle with the snow---
A path of silv'ry glory from His throne
For peace to come to aching hearts below.

And Lo! from out the stillness of yon plain,
Ranging in solemn order, row on row,
The crosses of dead heroes rise to tell
Not of death, but of the joy they know.

A. J. S., Jr.

The Manikin

Lloyd Nolan.

IT is peculiar—the fascination which the weird or ghostly seems to exercise over the mind of a man. Here I am now, old—so they say—but hale and hearty and, so far as I know, without a reason in the world why I should incline to the morbid and gloomy rather than to the pleasant and cheerful things of days that are past. Yet, whenever my mental gaze wanders along the perspective of memory it invariably fixes upon one image, particularly uncanny; an image which embodies recollections of the saddest and most repulsive event of my whole life—the image of Dr. Philip Evernon. Poor old Phil! We had been boys and playmates together, then classmates and finally fellow-graduates. As a lad he had always been a considerate and accommodating companion. Good-natured, on the whole, and affable, yet, when occasion arose, as full of the devil as a nest of angry hornets, there was never a bit of mischief or a prank afoot but that he was in it. There was only one big fault in Phil—he was a mighty poor loser. That I discovered the day we made the raid on Lartner's apple orchard and Lartner caught us—almost. Everyone managed to get over the fence in time except Phil, and he got the neatest horse-whipping of his young career right then. It was a painful and humiliating thing, no doubt, but, whereas most boys would have forgotten their resentment when the smart of the lash had ceased, with Phil it was different. I knew then—something told me—that Lartner had made an enemy who would hate him bitterly till the end of his days. The sequel proved me right.

It was after an absence, if I remember correctly, of some twelve years, that I returned to my native village where earlier I had left Phil—then the "village doctor"—in possession of quite a comfortable practice. My first thoughts, of course, when I had come back, were of him, and without stopping to enquire of anyone as to what changes might have taken place, I made my way to his office. Opening the door without knocking, as in past times I had been accustomed to do, I beheld him, his back toward me, sitting in a chair, his hair dishevelled by fingers that twitched ceaselessly. The neatness and tidiness which before had been the characteristic of the place had quite disappeared. Books were lying around in careless confusion; papers littered the floor; rugs were ruffled and out of place—even the back of my old friend sensed of untidiness.

"Phil!" I said.

With a cry of alarm he sprang from his chair and faced me, but with an expression of countenance so different from that of the man whom I had known in past years that I was thoroughly startled.

"You, George? God, how you frightened me!" He sank back with a sigh of relief and rested his head on his hand. I stood for a moment, too surprised to speak, and then, thinking that, perhaps, my presence might not be acceptable just then, I turned to go. He held up his hand:

"Don't go, George. Don't go. Pardon me for neglecting a word of welcome after all these years. You see I— I haven't been any too well of late and —that is—subject you see to nervous attacks and all that sort of thing. Come in! Come in!"

Encouraged, I advanced into the room and shaking hands, sat down in the hope of starting some kind of a conversation on old times. There was something besides nervous disorder troubling my friend—that was evident. I believed that by adroit manipulation of the talk I might be able to find out what it was. As we conversed, he struggled to regain his composure and once in a while he essayed a smile. It was a pitiful attempt, resulting in a kind of ghastly grin that sent cold little shivers running up and down my spine. Dark lines furrowing his unshaven face told but too plainly the story of sleepless nights and troubled

days. His words came from his lips in false jerky tones. There had been a time when I had numbered among all my acquaintances no better or more pleasing conversationalist than Phil Evernon. But the change! His former smooth command of language, his gift of giving interesting utterance to entertaining thought had vanished. Now his sentences were disconnected; often, indeed, a mere jumble of words without apparent meaning.

It was not until he reached into an inner pocket for a cigarette that I noticed the floor beneath his desk covered with stubs and ashes.

"Just a newly acquired habit, George," he said, following my glance. "My nerves need something to soothe them now and then."

"Phil," I answered, shaking my head. "There's something very much the matter with you. You're a doctor and certainly know better than to treat yourself so carelessly."

Again that uncanny grin passed over his face, but he said nothing. I arose and walked about the room, commenting on the changes that had been made since my last visit. Once I turned to question him about a book and caught him sitting bolt upright in his chair, watching my every movement narrowly. His countenance was a picture of suspicion and mistrust. I set the book down then and directed my attention to another addition to his queer collection. It was a large wax model of a man, such as you often see in scientific exhibits, standing inside a glass case. Upon the surface were sketched roughly the principal blood-veins of the human system. Evidently it was the work of a novice, being too grotesque, too untrue in proportions to rank as skilled modeling. As I surveyed it, Phil watched me intently and, I thought, a little fearfully.

"Nice work, eh George?" he rasped.

"Not a bit of it, to my mind," I answered.

He shifted uneasily at this and I imagined I saw a menacing expression creep into his eyes. It began to grow plain to me that he did not take kindly to my examination of his curios, so I went over to the table, and, in lieu of any better way to bridge over a rather embarrassing moment, began to read aloud various little articles of news from the morning paper.

"Why, Phil!" I exclaimed suddenly, "what's this? 'Mr. Daniel Lartner, well-known citizen of this town is still missing. All clues as to his whereabouts have proved misleading. It is stated by his friends that previous to his disappearance he had been somewhat ill and was contemplating an operation.' Do you remember him, Phil? The old crank that gave you the beating the day we raided his orchard?"

Phil's only answer was an incoherent mutter and I read on:

"Everything possible is being done in the matter. Two of Pinkerton's best men have arrived and are now at work. As yet, however, nothing of importance has been discovered. Some advance the theory of murder. If such be the case we have no doubt as to the final victory of the law. 'Murder will out,' and so—"

A shriek rang out that chilled me to the marrow. I glanced at Phil. God! May I never have to look at a face like that again! The man was a raving lunatic. His eyes gleamed with insane hatred. Foam trickled from the corners of his mouth. Staggering across the room, he stumbled against the table and paused, laughing drunkenly. Laughing? No, the sound was more like the cry of some wild, terror-stricken animal. It would rise, then die down, then rise again in crazy cadences. Suddenly he began to speak.

"George! George! listen to me! What was that they said? Murder will out? Is that it? Ha! ha! Murder will out! But I say it won't—do you hear me? I say it won't. It won't, it won't. They lie. I know a murder that will not out. It's in. It'll stay in. They're fools—fools. I'm too smart for them."

He tittered childishly, hysterically.

"You asked me, George, if I remembered Dan Lartner. Remember that hound? There wasn't a day of my life that I didn't. There wasn't a day that I didn't swear, over and over again that I'd get even on him for that beating. And I did. O! I did. And they'll never find him, George, they'll never find him. I'm too smart for them. Too smart! He's hidden where no eye can see. Where he'll never raise his hand again to hurt a child. Listen to me, I'll tell you."

He had grown somewhat quiet by this time and his talk was a bit more coherent.

"He came in here a fortnight ago to tell me—me of his troubles. Oh, George! I was wily. I told him that such an operation could be performed without risk by a doctor of my experience—that I could do it then in my room. The fool believed me. He consented. He allowed me to strap him to the operating table. Only then did he ask about a nurse. 'Dan Lartner,' said I, 'no helping hand is needed for that which I am about to do.'

"Then only did he suspect the truth. He looked into my face and was frightened. Ah, George! It was sweet to see the fear in his features as he glanced at the bonds that held him. It was music to my ears when he whimpered that perhaps an operation was not needed after all. He requested—then commanded—then beseeched me to release him. I never answered for there was no need. I stood above him, knife in hand, and gloated in the terror that possessed him. He thought I would butcher him alive. But I didn't. I'm too smart, George. I would spill no blood. I took my ether mask and held it over his mouth. Then I removed it. Then I held it there again—O! but it was joyful to have him there. I held the ether over him till he slumbered. I held it till he slept—the sleep of death."

He ceased talking and was gazing past me into the window. A terrible look was on his face. Suddenly he began to tremble and as sure as I am writing these lines I saw the hair stand upright on his head.

"George!" he hissed, "George!"

"Be calm, Phil," I commanded, though I myself was sick with fear. "What is it you see?"

"I see him," he whispered in a voice scarcely audible. "Look, there he comes."

Whatever object his delirious eyes beheld seemed to be approaching closer to him and he shrank back like a threatened cur. Then in a fit of insane rage, he cried aloud, and seizing a vase hurled it at the apparition. Books, chairs, whatever he could find, followed the vase. The apparition seemed to disappear, for he suddenly stopped. Then his unearthly eyes caught sight of the wax figure.

"Gad! Gad! Get away! For God's sake, stop! There, go!"

With the last words—his last, indeed upon earth—he seized a heavy volume and hurled it with all his remaining strength at the figure and then fell to the floor, dead.

The book crashed through the glass and hit the model with such force that it toppled and fell, smashing into a thousand bits. And there before my eyes, wrapped in yard after yard of linen, lay the body of the missing citizen —Daniel Lartner.

Nocte Silente

A. J. Steiss, Jr.

LOWLY young Carlos ascended the rugged path as it wound upward among the meadows. His destination, the ancient castle of Don Pedro, stood above him, shrined in the climbing vines of five hundred years. Below him, nestling in the fertile plain of old Castile, lay his home, the village of Santander.

As he came closer to the object of his journey, he passed a vineyard, from which the fragrant odor of ripening grapes arose. The breeze which generally fanned the heights of smiling La Grande, had died away, and, as Don Carlos paused on the hillsides, the solemn stillness of nature pervaded the fields. The view from the lofty station was sublime, encompassing all the land from the purple Pyrenees to the north, where stately mountains raised their snow-white caps, to the verdant plains below them, dotted with tiny hamlets, barely discernible in the creeping evening mists.

Of a sudden, a wild, melodious song awoke the vines; and the notes rose in pleasing contrast to the gloomy stillness of the pile wherein they echoed. The young man's steps involuntarily turned in the direction whence they came, but he stopped sadly.

At that instant the singer emerged from the tangle of rows, and came into the view of Carlos. The vision, lithe and small and slender, was clad in a soft white mantle, which reached her feet, and obscured the rest of her raiment. The features of her face were small and dark, while her jet-black hair was well offset by a brilliant scarlet rose.

Her gaze rested on the youthful Spaniard for a moment; then, in a blush of confusion, she darted back quickly into the garden,—but her song had ceased.

And, like the lilting melody of the maiden, any song that might have lingered on the thin, red lips of Carlos had also ceased, and he said slowly, and in a barely audible voice:

"To think, that perhaps she might be my own, if we had not quarreled! But it was cruel that anything should have come between us when we were so happy. And it was all about guardian angels. Certainly no guardian angel led me when I made light upon that subject before her beautiful face!"

He hung his head and turned about, and the tears were glistening in his deep, brown eyes.

In a moment, however, he was on his way again, and just as the sun was setting into the valley, he entered the precincts of the castle beneath a turbulent arbor of wild "Granadilla."

But in the vineyard there knelt a Senorita, weeping as if her throbbing heart would break. Just as Don Carlos entered the massive castle, she saw him again, and wondered what took him there. Soon she arose, and slowly wended her way to the cottage, in thoughtful, melancholy silence.

As evening progressed, and the maiden sat lonely in the garden, she brooded more and more on the subject of Carlos' purpose in visiting the castle. No explanation occurred to her, but, as the soft, warm tears of love stole down her cheek, and the Spaniard still remained the leading object of her thought, she asked herself if perhaps she yet did love him.

Then, in that easily aroused anxiety of love, she wondered over and over, if the safety of her lover, who had so lately entered the ruin, was assured; and, as the question repeated itself more forcefully in her feverish mind, she grew more and more apprehensive that such might not be the case. Alarmed by this startling conjecture, she rose to her feet, trembling with fear and nervousness. At last, she recited a fervent prayer to the Virgin, and proceeded slowly to her room.

In the castle, Don Carlos had finally made his way to a tiny chamber, high in the grey stone tower. The retreat was dark, and dusty, and had an atmosphere of damp decay about it, which,

in no way improved the humor of the Spaniard. The place was devoid of furniture, save for a rotten bench in a corner, and with a snort young Carlos turned to the window. Below him stretched the garden—wild and overgrown through many years,—and sunset colors only added to the riotous hues of the flowers. Farther down the hillside lay the vineyard, and Carlos gazed at this a longer time.

"Well, I was a fool, indeed," he said, turning again, "to wager on the election of Alcalde for the city, since now I must spend the night in this clammy ruin, and may catch my death of cold."

He threw himself down on the bench and soon sank into a deep and heavy slumber.

The singer of the vineyard, Dona Margarita, had slept in peaceful oblivion for some few hours, when she awoke with a start. Something, someone, told her of immediate danger to her lover, and she quickly arose and dressed. Softly she slipped from the house, and swiftly glided through row upon row of vines.

When Carlos awoke, the moon was shining brightly, and the chiming of the bells in the cathedral of Santander, told him that it was twelve o'clock. At first, on recalling his position, he was too greatly frightened to arise, but attracted by the charm which the moon imparted to the landscape, he crossed to the window, and stood, admiring the singular beauties of the garden.

Clambering vines that grew on walls

and tree-trunks, glistened like winding cords of silver thread, while turbulent Granadilla passion flowers had shimmering golden petals. Even the stern, drab walls of the castle were softened by the mellow flood of light.

He had remained in this position for a time, when he became conscious of voices somewhere, far, far below him in the castle. His first wild impulse was one of flight, but a stronger feeling of curiosity prompted him to remain.

Slowly and with as little noise as possible, he pushed ajar the door to the apartment where he had lain. Darkness, fearful and palpable, yawned at him through the aperture, but he resolutely pushed forward into the enveloping gloom. His wanderings brought him to the staircase by which he had gained the castle tower the previous evening, and feeling his way along the walls, he blindly descended; down, down, down.

Far down a gloomy passage-way, he noticed a single gleam of light, and he made haste to follow in its pursuit. But in his eagerness, he slipped, and came to the floor with a crash that was intensified by the silence that had preceded. Instantly there was a commotion; someone cursed, a chair was overturned, and before Carlos could possibly have escaped, two huge, old Spaniards in the care-free garb of banditti, emerged and captured the thoroughly terrified Senor.

Forthwith, he was dragged to the chamber in which the band sat assembled, and he then fearfully comprehended the fact that he was in the hands of outlaws.

On a table, which stood in the center of the room, various articles of plunder were scattered, gleaming in the light of a single candle. The robbers were seated about the collection on chairs and boxes, and as the captive was produced, they all rose to their feet.

"Miguel, what shall we do with this spy?" asked a swarthy fellow. "We cannot let him go for he knows our hiding place."

"That is true, Pedro, but neither can we take him with us now, since we shall be very busy before the night is over. Here, bind the prisoner, and we shall return for him ere daybreak. Make haste, for 'tis after twelve!"

Without a word they tied his hands and feet, and the men trooped noisily away. But Carlos breathed a thankful prayer as their footsteps died in the distance, that the candle still flickered on a chair.

How long he remained on the floor of the room, in the position in which he had been left, he could not have told. But suddenly, far down the passage-way, and coming ever nearer and nearer to his prison, he heard a faint, quick, rustling sound. Soon the light of the burning candle shone on the figure of a Senorita, in the doorway, and Carlos cried joyfully, "Margarita!"

"Hush," warned the apparition, "for it was only through the help of my guardian angel, and your light, which

guided me here, that I have been enabled to save you. But now we must
hurry and depart from the ruin, before
your captors return.''

Young Carlos was too much astounded to utter a word, but he followed the
Señorita in dumb obedience. Quickly
she led him forth into the open air, and
under the light of the stars and the
great full moon they made their way to
the vineyard.

Here they parted, and the exhausted
Castilian again gave way to his drowsi-
ness, and in a short time was dead to the
world.

He awoke in the morning, with sweet
odors round about him, and the warmth
of a summer sky beaming upon the
earth. Not a great distance off stood
the castle, gleaming in sunny brightness—but Carlos knew its mystery—
and to him it did not look bright.

*   *   *   *   *

Later a pensive Spaniard was seen,
knocking at the vineyard gate. When
it was opened, the slender form of a
Senorita appeared, and slowly the gate
swung shut behind the two. Here our
little story closes upon the lovers, but
we are assured that in the subsequent
conversation they spoke at length of
love, and castles—and Guardian Angels
that watchfully care for man.

The Redwood

PUBLISHED BY THE STUDENTS OF THE UNIVERSITY OF SANTA CLARA

The object of The Redwood is to gather together what is best in the literary work of the students, to record University doings and to knit closely the hearts of the boys of the present and the past

EDITORIAL STAFF

EDITOR-IN-CHIEF	HENRY C. VEIT
BUSINESS MANAGER	TULLIO A. ARGENTI
ASSISTANT BUSINESS MANAGER	JACOB E. HEINTZ
CIRCULATION MANAGER	EDMUND. Z. COMAN

ASSOCIATE EDITORS

EXCHANGES	P . F. MORETTINI
ALUMNI	MARTIN M. MURPHY
UNIVERSITY NOTES	LOUIS F. BUTY FRED J. MORAN
ATHLETICS	JAMES E. NEARY

EXECUTIVE BOARD

EDITOR   BUSINESS MANAGER   EDITOR OF REVIEWS

Address all communications to THE REDWOOD, University of Santa Clara, Santa Clara, California.
Terms of subscription, $1.50 a year; single copies 25 cents

EDITORIAL

Yuletide

"Glory to God in the Highest and on Earth, Peace to Men of Good Will." It was sung sweetly by myriad angel voices two thousand years ago in homage to the New Born King of Bethlehem. The year of our present writing finds its music once more reverberating in our midst bringing peace to men of good will. It savors of a wealth of good cheer and present-giving. Not only has the Christmas spirit pervaded the atmosphere, but it has found scope for ample expression in the field of journalism as well. Pens are being assiduously applied, forming trite ideas into novel shapes about the snow, the Babe in the Manger, the Three Wise Men and kindred Yuletide subjects.

The REDWOOD has absorbed this

131

contagion. However we succumb gladly. It means so much to the most of us,
especially the members of the staff.
Aside from that "big dinner" and the
presents and all that, it makes for us
satellites of the journalistic profession
a period of rest and willing abandon
from all that smacks of literary work.
So in passing, let us take this opportunity of wishing all our friends, old
Santa Clara men here or still abroad
and Alma Mater, through the pages of
our publication, a very Merry Christmas and a Happy, Prosperous, Christian New Year.

Resume   Half the battle is over,
but as the wise man
once so aptly put it, the
worst is yet to come. What we have
to do now is to make the coming semester a critic of the last. Many of us
rolled up our sleeves last August with
the determination to get in and do some
real honest-to-goodness study and

work. Some of us even ventured so
far as to promise a poem or a story or
an essay to be printed in the RED-
WOOD. About the latter we can only
say they were all most conspicuous by
their absence. However as far as you
were concerned, that was only of minor
importance, although we will admit
when you failed us it assumed gigantic
importance when we were brought into
direct concern thereby. It is rather the
other that must give us all pause.

In the quiet precincts of home, when
nothing weighty arises to annoy or dis-
turb, you can take inventory of the past
six months work. Find out where you
have to increase your speed, where the
shadows must be deepened, the ill ways
corrected, the acquisition of virtue ac-
celerated. Be frank and honest with
yourself and then when that is done be
prepared to return and begin the New
Year properly. Get off to a good start
and remember the good New Year resolutions you have made and follow them
out. Then you are bound to win.
ADIOS.

University Notes

3rd High vs. 4th High

On November 16th those members of the student body, and they were many, who gathered in the gymnasium to witness the widely advertised basketball game between the Third and Fourth High teams were treated to ar evening of real sport.

As preliminary to the main event, a program of boxing bouts was arranged by Father O'Connell and Jack Hartford, who guides the destinies of the manly art. It may be remarked that greater interest is being manifested in this popular sport day by day. More over,.it is rumored, that the roped arena is fast becoming a field of combat; where injured honor may seek redress.

Somewhat of an innovation for such occasions was introduced by having the Jazz Orchestra—"Turk" Bedolla, "Zeek" Coman, and Bill Desmond— render some of the latest in their line between the bouts. Perhaps the spirit displayed by the contestants could to no small degree be traced to.the effort: of the jazz dispensers.

The program was opened with a bout between Larry McDevitt and "Army" Irving, both boxers being blindfolded

and having bells tied to their feet. The boys displayed admirable footwork— that is to say, they stepped to a merry tune. The bout proved interesting, and it is hoped that these two warriors may meet in the future without the handicaps.

One of the feature bouts of the evening was the fast engagement between Johnny Barrett and Walter De Martini, paperweights. This bout was judged one of the best exhibitions on the program, and resulted in a well-decided draw.

Another pair of faithfuls to don the mitts were Karl Koch and Ethelbert Giambastiani. These lads were exponents of the more scientific style of boxing, and very little damage was occasioned by their stay in the ring.

Kid Alfredo, bedecked in a pair of sky blue tights with embroidered chyrsanthemums, and a discolored optic met and defeated "Red" Cotter in four rounds. Inasmuch as the optical adornment of the Chihuahua Kid found its cause in the "Red" one's trusty right, some days previous, the fruits of Alfredo's victory were doubly sweet.

"Battling" Rose, the pride of Irvington, and "Kid" Lambrosa, of New York, engaged in four rounds of fistic bombardment, which earned their bout the distinction of being the best on the program. In fact, their efforts were so strenuous as to lead one to believe that another case of injured honor was being settled.

Then came the basketball game. For weeks previous, when Third High threw out their challenge and Fourth High duly accepted, a high state of excitement existed between the two classes. Yell leaders were appointed in each class, and daily practices were held, with the result that both teams received the benefit and support of organized rooting throughout the game. For Third High Nolan and Florimont lead the yells, while Rianda and Smith were in charge of the Fourth High rooting section. The teams were evenly matched and the game was fast and interesting. At the end of the first half, the score stood 11 to 10, with Third High leading. This narrow lead was maintained throughout the second half, the final score being 17 to 16 with Third High on the long end.

THIRD HIGH		FOURTH HIGH
Regan (Capt.)	F	Shelloe, E.
Corbett	F	O'Brien
Burns	C	O'Sullivan
		(Capt.)
Hamilton	G	Shelloe, R.
O'Neil, J.	G	Toner
Carney	Sub	Brunetti
Referee: Coach Harmon.		

Thanksgiving Vacation

Through the good-will of Father Murphy, the usual Thanksgiving vacation was lengthened this year, from four to six days, thus enabling many, who otherwise would have been prevented, to enjoy their Thanksgiving repast at home. Needless to say, this decision of Father President coincided with our feelings in the matter, and very few voices of dissension were noticeable among the student body.

For those whose homes were situated too far distant to enable them to travel conveniently for the holidays, a sumptuous turkey dinner with all the trimmings was served in the refectory.

Basketball

With the passing of football, basketball has come to the front in the line of college athletic activities. While the 'Varsity squad will acquire the better material, students in the collegiate department will be encouraged to participate in this sport by the formation of a league, somewhat resembling the "Mountain League" of baseball. The plan of such a league is to bring out the smoldering rivalry and pep existing between the various classes, and rival organizations about the campus. The idea has been given quite an impetus, and already several teams have been entered.

For instance, the "Iodine Apartments" have already submitted a list of their representative quintet. Such men as Bull Montana Moroney, Don Burke, Zeek Coman, Mike Pecarovich, and Skeet Whelan will form the nucleus of the representatives of Bro. Anthony's rendezvous. Poverty Row will most likely put out a strong quintet, with such men as Flynn, Cronin, "Pop" Jackson, "Joe" Kerckhoff, Baker, Schall and Bill Muldoon to draw from

Senior Hall will undoubtedly put two teams in the running, while the Good Ship has a wealth of likely material, and should be able to give a good account of itself.

With four or five such teams entered a successful season is anticipated.

Olympic Club

As a fitting close of the season, twenty-two members of the Varsity football squad and the Olympic Club team were the guests of the Olympic Club at a Thanksgiving dinner, immediately following the game at Ewing Field. The shackles of training rules were thrown aside with a vicious assault upon the national November objective, turkey. After the final entrenching processes had been completed, speeches were heard from Mr. Jack Spaulding, Football Commissioner of the Olympic Club, Coach Lieut. Rosenthal of the Olympic Club, Coach Harmon, and Captain Ferrario.

The fine spirit displayed by both teams on the field and hopes of continuing the same pleasant relations in the future were expressed by all. Coach Harmon tendered the Olympic Club, through Mr. Spaulding, the thanks of the squad for the excellent treatment which they had received, and for the assistance and co-operation displayed throughout the season.

At the conclusion of the dinner, the nineteen-nineteen football squad disbanded for the year.

Fr. Mark McNeil

Fr. Mark McNeil, S. J., of the New York-Maryland Province, lectured to the Student Body on the Japanese and Japan. For the last five years Fr. McNeil has been engaged in the missionary work in that country, and has been selected by the Imperial Government as Professor of English in the Imperial University. His brief talk treating some of the many customs of the Japanese was both educational and interesting.

Requiem Mass

Tuesday, December 2nd, the entire Student Body assembled in the Chapel to assist at the Solemn Requiem High Mass for the departed members of the Student Body and Faculty of the University. Fr. Boland was the celebrant, with Fr. Brainard and Fr. Sprague, deacon and sub-deacon respectively. A deeper significance clothed this year's Mass, mindful as we were of the names added to the list and the cause for which they gave their last. There is not one among us who, having been touched by the martial spirit, is not proud of the fact that he attended the same University where these heroes of "Over There" were once taught. Noble, indeed, was their example, and may we, through God's Providence, equally deserve the prayers of our Alma Mater. Requiescant in Pace.

Notre Dame Benefit   In order to defray their debt of taxes and to pay the cost of actual necessities which exceed the meagre tuition they receive from pupils, a benefit in the form of an entertainment was given by the Alumnae of the Convent of Notre Dame, for the Sisters of that school. Ever mindful of the kindness these good Sisters have shown them, the young women graduates of the Convent exert every effort to make a success of the annual affair. This year's program was, in all probability, the best of those thus far rendered, the spacious University Auditorium being crowded to the doors on the evening of the performance. Among the excellent numbers of the show were dainty Miss Gallagher, the youngest soprano to grace the footlights; little Miss Cavanaugh, the elf-like pianist of wide renown; and not least in the realm of theatricals were the dramatists from our own midst, Mike Pecarovich, Bill Desmond, and "Pop" Rethers, who thrilled the audience with the one-act play, "Murder Will Out".

ENGINEERING NOTES

The coming of Christmas has halted the march of accomplishments of the Engineers' and delayed until next semester the fulfillment of further ideas. Last week the Society held its last regular meeting of 1919. During the session, a new batch of pep was displayed, which promises to reach a climax in the hidden "doings" of next year.

To summarize the activities of this semester would be hard. In fact, no one desires to listen continually to a catalogue of deeds which may, or may not, be just cause for pride and boast. Suffice it to say, that the Engineers intend not to boast of what they have done, but resolve to be proud of what they are going to do. The members certainly are not "a bunch of deadheads". And so the officers, realizing that the Engineers of Santa Clara have need for diversion as well as education, have mingled a fair sprinkling of social and athletic functions in the literary and scientific program. The field of athletics offers a special challenge in basketball, baseball, track, and perhaps swimming. Prudence cautions us to forget boxing. The social experiments begin with the big picnic, for which all preparations have been made; and end with the banquet, that will even better last year's well remembered one.

The work of the officers, and that of the various committees, could not have been accomplished without the support of the members who sacrificed individual opinion and desire for the good of the whole Society. This long-sought spirit of co-operation is due to the democratic ruling of the Society, and is the power that will compel success to crown the events of the future.

Alfred J. Abrahamsen.

137

'86 Once again we are indebted to that loyal old friend of Santa Clara, Mr. George Woolrich. His generosity this time was in the form of a gift of an elegant, hand-worked linen cloth for the Boy's Chapel. Mr. Woolrich has ever had the interest of Santa Clara at heart and for this his latest remembrance, we are deeply grateful.

'03 It is pleasing to note that many of our old boys, if they are unable to visit the school in person, at least keep in touch with us by dropping an occasional line. Bill Regan has shown a good example in this regard, which his fellow alumni might well profit by.

We were indeed pleased when we heard of the appointment of Archer Bowden to the office of City Attorney of San Jose. Mr. Bowden has succeeded in building up quite a practice in the neighboring city and this latest achievement is but a recognition of his uncommon ability. Congratulations, Mr. Bowden, Santa Clara is proud of you.

'06 After eighteen months of duty abroad as a welfare worker of the Knights of Columbus, Martin Merle returned home in time for Thanksgiving dinner. It was he who conceived the novel idea of furnishing the doughboys with cigarettes by dropping them from the air. In regard to this feat, Merle is quoted as saying: "At first the Doughboys thought the Spad machines were manned by the Huns, and were a bit bashful about picking up the hundreds of small packages which came fluttering down. But when they spotted the "Casey" mark they lost all fear. Thereafter the idea became a general one and was tried in the Argonne when the Lost Battalion failed to make a liaison with the right and left flank."

Mr. Merle is well remembered as the author of "The Mission Play of Santa Clara", a production which brought a great deal of credit to the young play-

138

wright and his Alma Mater. Since his college days Mr. Merle has written many successful plays and scenarios. The war of course interfered with his vocation, but now that he is on the job once more undoubtedly we will soon hear from him.

'07 August Aguirre and family paid us a visit during the Thanksgiving Holidays. "Augie" was one of the cleverest fun makers that ever attended Santa Clara and together with his team mate Harry McKenzie afforded amusement for dozens of audiences in the old Auditorium. For his recent bereavement, the loss of a dear father, we extend to him our sympathy and condolences.

An old classmate of Aguirre's, Walter (Steamboat) Schmitz, followed his good example and motored down from Madera where he is managing his mother's ranch. "Steamboat" acquired his picturesque cognomen in his old gridiron days by the manner in which he waded through his opponents. He expressed himself as being pleased at the supplanting of rugby by the old brand of football 'in which he starred in his Varsity days.

'08 The local papers recently contained an account of the wedding of Joe Martin and Miss Lucille Carnes. The young couple intend to make their home in San Jose, where the groom is employed in a remunerative position. We extend our heartiest congratulations to the happy couple.

'15 The following, taken from the San Jose Mercury Herald, speaks for itself: "An interesting wedding took place in the historic St. Claire's Church in Santa Clara, on Thursday morning last, when Miss Gladys Kartschoke became the bride of Carl F. DiFiori of Berryessa. The ceremony was performed at eleven o'clock by the Rev. William Boland and was very quiet and simple in its appointments. Mr. Leopold DiFiori acted as his brother's attendant.

"Immediately following the ceremony the young couple departed on a motor trip throughout the state and upon their return they will make their home in a cozy apartment at the Don Felipe. Mrs. DiFiori is the daughter of Mr. and Mrs. Kartschoke of this city and is a graduate of the Washington school with the class of 1918. Mr. DiFiori is the son of Mr. Frank DiFiori of Berryessa. He graduated in Civil Engineering from the University of Santa Clara with the class of 1915 and later attended the University of California and is at present associated in business with his father."

Shortly after his arrival home from service in France and Germany with the Army of Occupation, Percy O'Connor was appointed Assistant Deputy

District Attorney of San Jose. We sincerely hope that his old friends at Santa Clara may shortly have an opportunity to congratulate him in person, both on his safe arrival home and on his success in securing this important appointment.

Ex '18 James Lyons, S. J., is at present studying philosophy at St. Michaels, Hillyard, Washington. We anticipate that he will soon be in our midst again, this time to guide the more youthful of his Alma Mater's sons along the proper lines of scholas tic endeavor.

'20 Armand Robidoux, S. J., is in the last year of his junior ate at the Sacred Heart Novitiate, Los Gatos. Armand, during his undergraduate days, had a habit of copping eight or nine first honors and several prizes each year; one of these latter being the Day Scholars medal awarded to the student deemed first in morals and conduct.

Ex '22 After enduring the rigors of a Siberian winter and passing through many weird and dangerous experiences, B. Lettunich recently surprised his many friends at college by appearing on the campus, after an absence of several years. "Letty" has many interesting reminiscences of his army life, but was well pleased to don the old "civies" once again.

Paul O'Neil, Ex. '22, was another welcome visitor. "Slim" is at present attending the University of California, where he is showing a lot of form on the Freshman basketball squad. Paul was one of our mainstays on last year's baseball team.

IN MEMORIAM.

Once again it becomes our painful duty to record the passing of several whom God, in His Infinite wisdom, has seen fit to call to Himself.

On the seventeenth of November, Father Neri, after an extended illness of several weeks duration, quietly passed away. It is needless to attempt here a description of Father Neri's unquestioned piety or of his wonderful achievements in the world of science for such knowledge is already common information.

Suffice it to say that he was one of California's greatest pioneers of learning. His inventions along scientific lines were such as to astonish the scholars of the early days and to bring everlasting glory to the Order he represented. Although stricken with blindness about ten years ago, this wonderful man memorized the Mass and continued to perform this Sacred Office until a short time before his death. In his passing Santa Clara has sustained a great loss.

The sad news has reached us of the

death of Father Gregory Leggio, S. J., in Vancouver, Wash. Father Leggio is known to many of the older boys here at Santa Clara where he taught for several years. As Father Neri was noted for his scientific knowledge, so was Father Leggio known for his ability along literary lines.

It was with the sincerest regret that we heard of the passing of Mr. Nicholson, the grandfather of George and Ed Nicholson, both prominent members of the Alumni Association. Mr. Nicholson was among the first settlers of Santa Clara Valley.

We have lately been called on to mourn the departure of the mother of Richard O'Connor, a member of the Class of '22. To Dick and to all of the afflicted relatives and friends of the departed here mentioned, the Redwood takes this occasion to extend its most heartfelt condolences.

Requiescant in Pace!

Martin M. Murphy.

The Fordham Monthly

Although the peace treaty has not been ratified, and as a consequence, we are told, a state of war still exists between this country and Germany, nevertheless the fact remains that our streets resound no more to the martial tread, and, among other things, war stories have failed to satisfy us any longer. So it was with slight misgiving that we read "Where Shadows Fall", and this was deepened into uncertain appreciation when the plot unfolded itself as a queer and weird war drama, in which we were left in doubt as to who was the real hero. But the portrayal of the various emotions, and the description of the scenes were uncommonly good, and above the ordinary in present day college literature. As a pleasing bit of reading which does not require any great amount of mental effort, we would recommend "A Trial of Fragmentary Thoughts"; while for one's more sober moments, when the mind craves something profound and instructive we suggest "Rene Descartes". We found mental satisfaction and a confirmation of our views in reading "Apologia pro Classicis", with its quotation in original Greek, for whose translation we had recourse to the dictionary. To think that our knowledge of Greek, which once had been so assiduously acquired, seems at last to be slowly and unconsciously ebbing away! That reminds us that the B. C. Stylus also treats of the same subject in its October number. Too much, however, cannot be said in favor of the Classics. The verses of this number do not display the same imaginative representation and fervid expression as the verses in the Holy Cross Purple. To tell the truth, Fordham, we think that they are slightly below the standard of last year. Still, it is not too late to make up the deficiency, as the season is yet young. "Away to the West" is noted for its peculiar rhyme and verse construction, and "God's Seance" contains a poignant argument that is well presented.

The Boston Stylus

With the same good measure o literary quality and with the same sense of lettered refinement, The

Stylus makes its initial appearance of the season from the "Athens of America".

And, indeed, we can do no more than quote the words of the editor, that every "poem, essay, or story . . . . . is the result of diligent care and arduous labor." The result, therefore, attained by this magazine is not at all surprising. A thoughtful insight into and pleasant reminiscence of the indomitable spirit of a people struggling, at last with some glimmerings of success, towards the dawn of liberty after seven centuries of oppression, is "The Singer". Quite a queer title! The well-written essay on "The Value of Classics" is a clear and logical exposition of the advantages—mental, material and spiritual—of the study of the ancient languages. Needless to say, we concur in and ratify the author's stand without amendments or reservations. The stories, however, are not of the same high order. "Better Than Gold" has an uplifting plot with a good moral, although the incidents are somewhat obscured. On the other hand, "A Man for a' That" may properly not be called a story, but rather an incident; still it uncovers quite an appealing side of life. The best verse of the issue is "My Garden of Dreams" with its dream-argosies wafted before Fancy's eye. "Absolution" portrays a beautiful thought with the aid of an accurate and powerful simile, while "Vignettes"—well, it set us thinking.

For quite a while we have been thinking of something, but have always hesitated, fearing, perhaps, to offend the cultured sensibilities of our Eastern friends, until finally, steeled with the "native hue of resolution" we politely inquire: Should not The Stylus also boast of an Exchange department? Perhaps it is a personal interest that prompts us to speak, you may say, but we have not entirely forgotten what the staff of The Purple complimentarily ejaculated about the literary messenger from Chestnut Hill: "The one of the two or three most literary magazines in the country," Again we recall from our philosophical perigrinations that goodness is diffusive of itself; and, doubtless, this also applies to the B. C. monthly. Then, how could The Stylus better bestow some of the radiance of its literary form upon less gifted creatures than through an Exchange column?

Georgetown Journal

In these days of marked centralization tendencies on the part of the government, and, as a consequence, of a continual efflux of reading matter from our Palatine on the Potomac, it is indeed exceptional, but none the less pleasant, to have something of literary worth make its appearance with all the senatorial eclat that surrounds a great name. Accordingly, the outside guard did not require the usual pass word, as the blue and gray cover of the Journal was sufficient evidence of its quality to be allowed to pass unmolested into our inner sanctuary.

The first number contains a pleasing array of verses in company with a good essay and article; but,—well, probably it is too much to expect a short story in the first issue of the year. "The Gloaming" is well expressed in appropriate imagery; although there appears to be a somewhat halting tendency in the lines. "A Smile" also is quite approvable. "The Road to Stars" is a verse of whose exact meaning we are rather uncertain. Is it the money-madness of the present generation, or an appeal for renaissance of that pure and indomitable American spirit? The author of "Kosciuszko" has again given a clear and concise portrayal of another great historical character. His open and unaffected style is appreciated in this essay no less than in his similar effort of last year, "Beaumarchais". As a contribution against the prevailing spirit of the times, it is no mean aid in reestablishing that spirit of unselfish nationalism that today seems to be derided and all but neglected in the pursuit of the luring mirage of internationalism.

"An Impression of Cardinal Mercier" is a personal reflection on the character of this world figure. It contains very little, however, that is not already known to the world; still, subjective impressions are always novel and interesting.

Holy Cross Purple

Once more The Purple enlivens the atmosphere with its presence, bringing in its train stories and verses in measure overflowing, that unfold an added interest in that commonwealth to us inhabitants of the sun-set shores of the Pacific. The first number of this season contains a wealth of verse that certainly augurs well for the future; and all of it, moreover, is of a high standard of excellence.

"Eddystone", besides expressing a rather uncommon thought, gives to the reader, in its peculiar strain, an idea of the ship cleaving the foam-crusted waves, with the lines—

"Bowling along on the crests of the seas,
Then sweeping down in the trough,
Scoffing the sea salt, snapping the breeze,
She races along to the north."

"Song of the Scouts" also expresses an excellent thought; the imagery, especially, is quite notable. Coming to another excellent bit of verse, "Petals of Memory", we must confess that we are rather partial to it, by the apparently simple thought adorned in such an appealing mode of expression. In "Dies Dolorosi" the title is somewhat misleading, but in reading it one is well repaid for the effort. The short lines with their peculiar rhyme certainly add to its attractiveness. In our rather partial and immature judgment we selected "To an old Coin" as the best piece of verse in this issue, for its thought, imagery and rhythm. The bold expressive imagery may be particularly remarked in the lines—

"Then I had looked on many a golden town
Walled by the endless pasturage of stars,
And over all the pale moon looking down
Out of her gold-flaked, visionary bars."

The other verses, also, are not far behind in charm of expression. Turning to the stories, we find that they are of a superior quality. "Kaiser, The Demon", loses nothing by being a war story, and the incident, skillfully portrayed, commends itself to us. "The Chance" is a record in modern salesmanship methods, and also quite interesting. A noteworthy feature of this issue is "Baccalaureate" that makes profitable and instructive reading.

But, among all the genius and talent displayed in such lavish profusion in the organ of this Hellenic center of American College life there is not to be found an Exchange Column from which other less favored mortals may imbibe the nectar of literary grace and excellence!

There is a certain room located just off the training quarters, that is packed high with battered head-gears, torn socks, and mud-stained football pants, for Santa Clara's entrance into the American game is now history. To train a Rugby star to the American game and make him a success at it in one season is far beyond the powers of any coach, but in a short period of practice that we have had, and the small schedule of games we must give the highest praise to the work and results of Coach Harmon.

The football that has been taught by our coach will now have a few short months to rest in the uppermost portions of our team members' bodies, and when Captain-elect Manelli leads his eleven upon the gridiron for the opening game of next season, well, watch Santa Clara.

Nevada 41   **Varsity 7**

On Thursday evening, November 20, the team, accompanied by Coach Harmon, Manager O'Connor, Moderator Fr. O'Connell, Trainers Drs. Argenti and Coman, and Representative Camarillo, pulled out for the city of untied knots. After being forced to arise at the chilly hour of seven to partake of the usual mush, coffee and two "softs", in the Capitol City, we returned to our private Pullman hoping against hope that the engineer would demonstrate a little speed. The climb over Sam Hill was a nagging one. And for lunch we were placed upon a diet of baked beans and coffee, for the head of this restaurant politely informed us that that was all she had. The high altitude had its telling effect upon our appetites and during the remaining part of the ride through the chain of snow-

146

sheds our finger-nails suffered considerably.

The citizens of Reno turned out in their furs to witness the game, and we must admit that they are one and all for their school. At 2:15 P. M. Santa Clara kicked off, and the Nevada eleven advanced the ball down the field on line-bucks mingled with long end runs and after five minutes of play put the ball over.

The altitude was having its effect upon our Varsity, but we hoped to overcome this before the half had ended. After this touchdown Santa Clara received the kick off, but failed to make yardage and Korte was forced to punt. It was at this period of the game that Mike Pecarovitch injured his shoulder, and Tom Bannon received a broken nose, but nevertheless they continued their playing. On the next play the Nevadans fumbled and Santa Clara recovered. We then made our yardage twice, but when within a few yards of the goal a place kick was attempted on the fourth down which missed by inches. Nevada again fumbled and Santa Clara recovered. Line bucks and end runs proved unsuccessful in making yardage. Nevada returned the ball to their twenty-five yard line and there the quarter ended.

In the second period the Varsity weakened although they displayed all the fight that could be asked of them. They tackled harder than in previous games, but failed to hold their man. It was in this quarter that Bradshaw, the speedy quarterback of the Nevada team, started his long end runs, and when the whistle had sounded for the end of the first half the score stood: Nevada 14, Santa Clara 0.

A few moments after the start of the third period silence came upon the spectators, for it seemed as if the Varsity had at last found themselves. After making their downs on a shift play, Roy Baker plunged over the line, and Moose Korte converted. They found Mother Nature difficult to defeat however, and the high altitude was playing its game. Throwing a long forward pass which was caught over their goal line, or should we say end zone, the Nevadans made the count 21, and in the last period Bradshaw ran thirty yards after receiving a pass, but not content with this honor he tore off two end runs of 50 and 40 yards, which caused the score board to read Nevada 41, Santa Clara 7.

The lineup:

Cochran ....Left End
Manelli ....Left Tackle
Noll ....Left Guard
Schall ....Center
Ferrario ....Right Guard
Korte ....Right Tackle
Bannon ....Right End
Scholz ....Quarter
Baker ....Left Half
Needles ....Right Half
Pecarovich ....Fullback

Substitutions: Whelan for Bannon; Amaral for Whelan; Neary for Amaral; J. Muldoon for Ferrario; W. Muldoon for Noll; Jackson for Cochran.

Referee, Cave; Umpire, Norris; Head Linesman, Hassmen.

Olympic Club 6   Varsity 0

With a high wind blowing, and the spectators shivering in the cold, this Thanksgiving day game at Ewing field was the last appearance of the Varsity for the season. The first half was scoreless although both goal lines were in danger several times. The Olympics found no difficulty in making their yardage when in the center of the field, but time and again they were held for downs when within a few yards of a touchdown. The winged O eleven hammered the Varsity line through guard and off tackle, and it was the secondary defense that stopped them. Throughout the game they failed to gain through center, for Beef De Fiori, who rose from the ranks of the famous Hooligans, was playing his best game of the season, and often he dropped an Olympic back as he started on an end run.

It was in the third period that the Olympics scored their lone tally. Santa Clara kicked off, and after pounding the line for yardage, Morrison made fifteen yards around right end, while Clark repeated the act around left. This brought them within a few yards of the Santa Clara goal line and on their fourth down, Morrison plunged through tackle for a goal. During the remainder of the game both teams op-

ened their style of play, and in the last few moments of the battle Cochran threw a perfect pass to Needles, who had a clear field and but ten yards to go. A Varsity end was off side, however, and the play netted nothing.

Although Captain Ferrario and Mike Pecarovich were on the injured list, the Varsity showed a vast improvement over their first game of the season, and we have good reason to believe that the winged O eleven will find themselves on the short end of next year's score. To them we extend our hearty thanks for the Thanksgiving dinner that they served to the Varsity squad at their club after the game.

The line-up:

Whelan ....Left End
Manelli ....Left Tackle
J. Muldoon.....Left Guard
De Fiori ....Center
W. Muldoon..Right Guard
Korte ....Right Tackle
Scholz ....Right End
Neary ....Quarter
Baker ....Left Half
Needles ....Right Half
Cochran ....Fullback

Substitutions: Jackson for Whelan; Lewis for J. Muldoon; Daly for Jackson; Bannon for Daly.

Referee, Huber; Umpire, Elliot.

BOXING.

Santa Clara has always had the pleasure of turning out clever mitt artists, and if present indications speak for the future the list shall be greatly increased. Chief Jack Hartford is by no means a new man at this game.

During a career as an instructor in the army he met some of the best men that the Northwest had to offer, and perhaps his hardest match was a four-round bout with Jack Abel at Camp Lewis, which resulted in a draw. Allow us to remind you that Abel was the champion of the A. E. F. forces.

For the obvious reason that he was in the service, Hartford met men of both amateur and professional standing, but as the contests were always for the benefit of his fellows in khaki he received no financial recompense and therefore retains his amateur standing.

Every afternoon a class of one hundred turns out in the gym. The rudiments of the game have been taught, and the boxers are now in training, as matches are in order at every turnout. Among the men who have donned the gloves are several football players, Roy Baker, Mike Pecarovich, Harold Cochran, Ray Schall and John Lewis. Copeland, Fiorino, Duff and Rianda are also promising in this sport. In the near future contests are expected with California and Stanford, or with any other school that takes up amateur boxing.

SWIMMING.

This popular sport is again coming into our midst through the efforts of Dick Julian. Dick has no small reputation as a swimmer, and when the va-

rions dark horses of the present class are composed into a team, we can expect surprising results. On every Wednesday afternoon, the class, which contains seventy members, holds its workouts and those who are displaying an unusual amount of talent in this pastime are: Bob Gardner, who competes in the dashes; Tub Nolan, who attempts nothing less than a mile, the fancy high divers, Harris, Reddy and Harney, who have made the Kingfisher jealous; the natural-born swimmer, Hip Hanaberg, who spends his summers in the foaming waves that break upon the Hawaiian shores; and last, but always first, Hol Lewis, the graceful cup-winner in the dashes. In due time, the team which is to be selected, shall, we hope, have the pleasure of competing with the various clubs and schools of the state.

J. E. Neary.

PREP NOTES.

S. C. Preps 12   Mt. Tamalpais M. A. 6

Is an Irishman ever licked? Boy, page Mt. Tamalpais Military Academy. On November 16 the fighting Preps journeyed across the bay to San Rafael the better to instruct the denizens of said institution in that matter. Undoubtedly the instruction came somewhat as a surprise to the M. T. M. A. lads, for, but a few weeks previously they had invaded our sacred precincts and ground down the Preps to a 54 to 0 defeat. Then to Santa Clara came canny Coach Roesch and ere long he had whipped the Preps into an eleven easily the match of any high school team in the state. The boys, under his tutelage, began to find themselves and to thirst for revenge against the team that had so humiliated them. They got it, and it was sweet.

The most notable feature of that second Tamalpais game was the vicious fighting spirit that the Preps displayed. They started the game with eleven men and finished it with the same eleven— not a substitute being called upon during the entire play. Ryan and Connell, the Prep tackles, were particular stars. Their brilliant work it was, aided by the rest of the line, that enabled the back-field men to crash through Tamalpais for gains of from ten to fifteen yards at a plunge. Three different men were used by Tamalpais in an effort to stop that "little black-haired guy"— Connell. But he simply was not to be stopped. In the back-field Halloran's long end runs featured the Prep play. Time and again he was away with the pigskin for thirty and forty yard

gains, and it was only Muth, the fearless safety of the Tamalpais team, that prevented him from as often crossing the counting line. Pat Carey was as usual a mountain in the Prep defense. Malley as an end has the ear-marks of a real player and unless we mistake very much will be varsity material in a couple of years. But the Geoghegans, Louie and George. Watch them, that's all we say.

PYGMIES.

They say a real football player must begin early to acquire the instinct. If so, Santa Clara should have no fear for the future, for the pygmies under the leadership of Captain Jimmie Daly are certainly learning the game. True, they only played two games during the season. But the first was a victory and the second, against the far heavier second team of Santa Clara Hi was a tie. They're scrappers those pygmies and a scrapper is always a good footballer.

Frank Maloney.

WEBB'S PHOTO SUPPLY STORE   94 S. FIRST ST., SAN JOSE

CONTENTS

TO HIS GRACE,

Most Reverend Edward J. Hanna, D. D.

Archbishop of San Francisco,

This Old Missions edition of "The Redwood" is
affectionately and gratefully dedicated

The Redwood

Entered Dec. 18, 1902, at Santa Clara, Cal., as second-class matter, under Act of Congress of March 3, 1879

VOL. XIX	SANTA CLARA, CAL., FEBRUARY. 1920	NO. 4

FOREWORD

Daniel P. Meagher, S. J.

THE natural tendency of the human mind upon observing some strange phenomenon, is to ask: Why? Such, we presume, will also be the attitude of those interested in the "Redwood", in its prosperity or adversity, upon the appearance of this, the "Mission" number. Those resident in California are in all probability quite able to answer the question for themselves. For the benefit of others, we may state that after a period of what seemed inexcusable indifference, the sons of America's land of loveliness have at last awakened to the realization that by far the greater and the sublimer portion of the beauty, poetry and romance of which they are so justly proud, breathes and has its being in and about our mission ruins. Accordingly, a movement to shield these sacred shrines from the destroying hand of time has been inaugurated, and, thanks to the patronage of His Grace, the Most Reverend Edward J. Hanna, D. D.; Archbishop of San Francisco, is now well on its way toward a successful termination. In the spirit of this movement and from a desire to co-operate in some small way in so holy a venture the "Mission Redwood" has been prepared. That it is but a feeble attempt, imperfect in many details, we realize, but we have done our best. We can but hope that it may attain in however small a measure, the purpose toward which any efforts expended upon it have been finally directed; that it may commemorate, and in commemorating do honor to those heroic men, the Padres. of whose lives and labors and sacrifices the missions should be preserved as lasting monuments. They were altruists,

those men, but altruists of the most Divine type, who learned their altruism at the Cross of Christ. They shed undying lustre of glory upon California. To them we owe much of what to-day we have and are. May we
never forget them.

**Acknowledg-
ments**
It is but fitting that the staff of the "Redwood" here express its gratitude to those whose generosity has made this
number possible. They are: Capt. Peter B. Kyne, in whose
liberality, certainly, there has been no trace of self; Frances Rand Smith,
whose zeal and disinterestedness have aided so materially the researches
of the California State Historical Survey Commission; Dr. Owen C. Coy,
Director and Archivist of the Historical Survey Commission; Judge John
F. Davis, to whom we are indebted for the true facts of that sweetest of
romances, the story of Concepcion de Arguello; Charles B. Turrill, well-
known historian and collector of relics of the ancient days of California;
Mr. H. C. Peterson, President of the Palo Alto Historical Society; Frs.
Englehardt and Steck, O. F. M.; Fr. Z. J. Maher, S. J.; Mr. Charles D.
South, A. M.; and Mr. Martin V. Merle, A. M., author of the Mission Play
of Santa Clara. To each of them we extend our sincerest and our most
heartfelt thanks with the assurance that their thoroughly unselfish kindness is not likely soon to be forgotten.

A Tribute
To the Rt. Rev. Monsignor, Joseph A. Gleason, of Palo
Alto, we feel that special gratitude is due. His has been
the wisdom, his the interest, that has guided us throughout. By kind counsel, ready suggestion and best of all, by unfailing encouragement, he has ever shown himself a true and invaluable friend.
So much so, indeed, that without him, we fear our task would have been
too great for our inexperienced hands. His goodness has been unfailing—
our appreciation, we hope, will prove the same.

Due to an oversight unnoticed until all the pictures had been printed,
the caption on the photograph of Msgr. Gleason has been made to read
"Very Reverend", instead of "Rt. Reverend" as should have been the
case. As any reprinting of the pictures would have involved quite an
expense, it has been decided to allow the caption to stand as it is, with
this explanation.

VERY REV. MONSIGNOR JOSEPH M. GLÉASON

The Historical Survey of the California Missions

Owen C, Coy, Ph.D.,

Director and Archivist of California Historical Survey Commission.

THE old Franciscan missions even as they stand, are probably the most valuable legacy now left to us from the earlier generations of Spanish padres and conquisidores. Much that made up the life of this religious and romantic people has passed away, or been submerged under the later flood of Anglo-American immigration. The greed of the officials of the Mexican regime took the missions from the watchful care of the padres, and the vandalistic hand of the settler and the unrestrained destructive forces of nature soon reduced the greater part of them to a state of ruin.

Even in their ruined condition they have ever attracted the admiration of all who have an appreciation of the work of past generations. The artist never tires of the missions as subjects worthy of his brush; the writer finds delight in describing the beauty of the ruined walls and in weaving romantic tales about the mission as a center; architects have come to appreciate the beauty of the arcade and tiled roof until the mission style of architecture is recognized by all; while the tourists in ever increasing numbers visit these old monasteries to pay their respect to the mechanical skill and religious zeal of the Spanish padres. Is it not strange that the people of this great state have not long ago been aroused to the importance of caring for these historic treasures?

That these old edifices of adobe and stone should be preserved from complete destruction has to some extent long been recognized by many for religious, historical or artistic reasons. In some cases the missions have been preserved very much as they were under the Franciscan fathers, in other instances efforts at repair have rendered the buildings suitable for religious use, but the utilitarian motive sacrificed both historic and artistic ideals in an attempt to make the buildings habitable. Indeed, the lack of careful historical evidence, combined with an insufficiency of funds, made proper restoration seemingly impossible. Cases where recent repairs have robbed the missions of their original form and beauty are too numerous to require specific mention. On the other hand there is another small class of persons of extremely aesthetic temperament who consider it an artistic sacrilige to attempt even to stay the destroying hand of nature. They believe that the glory of the missions can better be displayed in their ruined walls than by the "desecrating" hand of the restorer, no matter how skilled he may be. Unfortunately, the outcome of the latter policy would inevitably result in the complete disappearance of all the missions at no far distant date. It seems logical then that some kind of restoration is both desirable and necessary, and that if it is to be accomplished properly it must be done along lines prepared as the result of careful study, both of the history of the mission buildings and of the extant remains.

In keeping with this latter view the legislature in 1917 declared it to be the duty of the historical commission of the state to make a study of the physical history of the Franciscan missions, and to prepare ground plans, sketches and models. Before the report upon any mission is complete the commission is required to hold a public hearing at which any interested person is permitted to state his views and present his evidence, if it in any way makes addition to or conflicts with the work already done. After this hearing the law provides that the commission may declare the plans and models thus drawn up to be the official California model. By action of the church authorities all work of restoration is required to be done in accordance with these official reports.

This commission has now on file in its office reports on San Carlos (Carmel), Santa Cruz, San Diego and San Antonio missions. These reports are the work of Frances Rand Smith of Palo Alto, who has for a number of years had a keen interest in studying the architecture of the California missions. One of these reports, that relating to the San Carlos mission, has been submitted to the public at a hearing held at Carmel, October 31, 1919. As soon as the reports upon the other missions have been carefully checked other public hearings will be held.

It is the aim of the Historical Survey Commission to make its work both historically and scientifically accurate. This requires a discriminating study, not only of all written historical documents relating to the mission in question, whether in the form of official reports or descriptions of travellers, but also a study of all early sketches and drawings, photographs and surveys. To this must be added a careful examination of the buildings or ruins now extant.

For historical information Mrs. Smith and the commission have drawn heavily upon the manuscript documents in the Bancroft Library which contains transcripts, not only from the church archives but from the Spanish and Mexican archives, of which many of the originals were destroyed in the United States Surveyor-General's office during the fire of 1906. That office now has the survey plats and field notes made in the fifties and sixties when the mission property was patented to the church by the United States Government. The narratives of La Perouse, Vancouver, Mofras, Duhaut-Cilly and others who visited the California coast during the eighteenth and early nineteenth centuries abound in descriptions of the various missions and many of them contain sketches and ground plans which are very helpful. For example, the earliest picture of the San Carlos (Carmel) mission is that accompanying the description of Vancouver's visit in 1793. These sketches, while full of helpful suggestions, are not fully reliable because of the inaccuracy or imagination of the artist. Photographs eliminate this factor and furnish some of the most essential evidence, the earlier ones being exceedingly valuable in preserving the record of walls and buildings now no longer to be found. The opinions of old time residents is also of importance in determining many things which cannot be otherwise established, but human memory at best is treacherous and all evidence of this character must be weighed with great care.

One of the unique features in reference to the mission buildings is the fact that they seem in many cases to have been built as opportunity offered without a definite plan and careful measurements. This is especially so of the smaller structures surrounding the mission court and its buildings. Close observations and careful measurements are therefore necessary in order to prevent errors in reconstructing ground plans and elevations. This may be illustrated from the San Carlos mission where the writer has recently been engaged in making surveys. Notwithstanding the fact that the court gives the general appearance of being a parallelogram, accurate measurements show the opposite sides of the court to be 350 and 362, 258 and 293 feet respectively. The position of the stone church, the most important edifice at the mission, is found to be at an oblique angle to all other buildings. Furthermore, the width of these buildings, although appearing to be uniform, has been found to vary considerably. All of this gives mute but reliable testimony to the handicaps under which the Franciscan fathers labored—without adequate instruments or tools and aided by the unskilled hands of the natives.

On account of the many lapses in the historical evidence available it frequently becomes necessary for any one endeavoring to reconstruct these ruined edifices to draw upon his imagination. Unless it is carefully guarded by all available facts these deductions may lead to serious errors. This has been the crime of many of the so-called restorations which have been drawn up by artists and others who had but slight opportunity to obtain the facts. On the other hand, if properly and cautiously done many structures long since completely or partly gone can be reconstructed along lines closely approximating the original buildings. In order, therefore, that the plans and models may be complete it is the policy of the Historical Survey Commission to supplement those parts which are based upon irrefutable historical evidence by using other data, which, according to all applied tests, agrees with known conditions, even though it may itself be unsupported directly.

It may be of interest to the readers of this article to know that the recent study of the ruins at Carmel indicates to the writer certain features, which, although at present not fully supported, are nevertheless worthy of consideration since, if confirmed, they would aid greatly in locating some of the places closely connected with the intimate life of Father Junipero Serra. It is his belief, based upon fairly strong evidence, that the original quadrangle of the mission was located in the space now surrounded upon three sides by adobe ruins. This is only about half the area of the larger court, but corresponds closely in size to the court described by Father Serra in his report of 1773. This court doubtless served as the center of mission life and was the only court from 1771 until enlarged when the stone church was completed in 1797. The original buildings were of wood with which the coast at that point abounds, while the present remains are of adobe, but it is probable these may have been constructed during the years before the erection of the church. A sketch of the mission made in 1793 locates with a fair degree of exactness the church built by Father Serra. A study of the ruins shows foundation stones corresponding closely to the building shown in the sketch, at one end of which are large stones which may well be the foundation stones for the original altar near which the body of Father Serra was buried. It is probable that subsurface excavations will help to refute or verify these suggestions; until that time it is of interest to speculate upon the possibilities of future investigations which must be made before the work can be considered complete.

The Historical Survey Commission is not engaged in the actual work of mission restoration, as that is entirely in the hands of others. It is, however, concerned in the matter of acquiring definite information relative to the history of these missions and their method of construction. In this work it has secured the hearty cooperation of the church authorities who have made available to it many much needed records and other information. On the other hand its observations are at all times available for the use of those authorized by the church to undertake the work of reconstruction. By means of this full cooperation it is earnestly hoped that the work of restoration be done in a manner worthy of its importance and that once again the people of California may be able to look upon the old missions as they were in the time of the Franciscan fathers.

San Francisco and the Redwood

Francis Borgia Steck, O. F. M.,
Santa Barbara, Calif.

S AN FRANCISCO and the Redwood — a strange combination of names, indeed! San Francisco, surely, the metropolis of California; and the Redwood, well, the Golden State's far-famed tree. But, what in the world has the metropolis to do with the tree? If San Francisco should stand for the glorious Saint of Assisi, the lover of nature's beauties, then I could establish some connection between his name and the Redwood, one of nature's most striking beauties. But I must go on; perhaps, by San Francisco the city is meant after all.

Those who have read and studied the early history of California will remember that in December, 1602, Sebastian Viscáino, while sailing along the coast of that State, came to a fine port which, in honor of the ninth viceroy of Mexico, he named Monterey. Standing on the high land elevation that formed its southeastern border and viewing the undulating plains that stretched far to the north and east, he remarked that here would be an ideal site for a mission. Accordingly, that subsequent explorers might not pass it by unno-ticed, he described it very minutely, closing his account by observing that from the elevation where he was standing the bay resembled a large O.

But more than a century and a half elapsed before an exploring party set out to profit by Viscáino's discovery. It may be of interest to know who took part in this expedition. The military officers were Governor Gaspár de Portolá, Captain Fernando de Rivera y Moncada, Lieutenant Pedro Fages, Engineer Miguel Constansó, and Sergeant José Francisco de Ortega. Under their command were twenty-seven leather-jacket soldiers and seven Catalonian volunteers. Besides these, there were four Indian servants and seven mule-teers, while fifteen convert Indians from Lower California had charge of the supply trains. Two Franciscan priests, FF. Juan Crespi and Francisco Gómez, accompanied this memorable expedition. Portolá had orders to travel by land along the seacoast until they reached Monterey Bay as pointed out in Cabréra Bueno's Navegacion, a copy of which they had with them.

It was late in the spring of 1768, about a year before Portolá set out on his exploring tour. The Franciscans

under the leadership of Fr. Junipero
Serra had just been appointed to take
over the proposed missions of Upper
California. To make the necessary preparations for their departure, Don José
de Gálvez summoned Fr. Serra to La
Paz.. When they had determined how
the six Fathers destined for this new
field of labor were to travel, Gálvez advised the Fr. Presidente as to the sites
and names he had been instructed by
the viceroy to assign for the missions.

"The first," he said, "is to be erected in the Port of San Diego and dedicated to the Saint of that name. The
second shall be established at the Bay
of Monterey and named San Carlos; of
course, the bay has first to be found,
but I am sure Portolá will succeed in
doing this with the minute description
he has of the bay. For the third mission
a suitable site should be selected somewhere between San Diego and San Carlos and its name is to be San Buena-
ventura."

Fr. Junípero looked troubled.

"Sir," he faltered, "is there to be no
mission for our Father St. Francis?"

"If St. Francis wants a mission,"
the Inspector-General returned playful-
ly, "let him cause his port* to be discovered and a mission for him shall be
placed there."

(*) For the benefit of the reader it must
be stated here that what is now called
Drake's Bay was visited by Sebastian Rodri-
guez Cermenon in 1595, seven years before
the discovery of Monterey Bay, and was
named by him in honor of St. Francis.
Bueno's Navegacion contained a minute description of it.

On Friday, July 14, 1769, at four
o'clock in the afternoon, Portolá with
his men and the two Franciscans set out
to find the harbor of Monterey. For
twelve long weeks the hardy band pursued their northward course along the
coast, trudging over hills and prairies,
and picking their way through forests,
marshes, and arroyos. Finally, on October 1, after marching four days down
the Salinas River, they pitched camp
near what is now Morocojo, a little railroad station north of Castroville. It
was Sunday, a day on which the two
Fathers generally said Holy Mass.
Wishing to explore the beach, which
was only some four miles off, Portolá
accompanied by Fr. Crespi, Miguel Cos-
tansó and five soldiers sallied forth,
following the river's course. Coming
to an elevation about eighty feet high,
now known as Mulligan's Hill, they
scrambled up its sandy slope. How
great was their surprise when on reaching the summit they beheld a grand en-
señada or open bay, its silvery surface
extending far to the north and south.
Full of expectation, they took out their
surveying instruments and consulted
Bueno's description.

"See those two points yonder?" said
the commander; "the one to the left is
covered with pines. That must be Bueno's Punta de Pinos. And over there
to the right is Punta del Año Nuevo.
Then the Bay of Monterey must be near
by."

"Perhaps right here at our feet,"
suggested Fr. Crespi.

"Hardly," Portolá replied, "for where is the large O which Viscáino says the bay resembles? No, not here, but somewhere near by must be the bay."

"Well," Fr. Gómez ventured, "it's a long time since Viscáino was here; the topography may have undergone a great change. Who knows," he continued, "perhaps, in the course of those 167 years, so much sand filled in the bay that today it is no longer such as Viscáino saw and described it."

"Why, General," broke in the engineer who had meanwhile adjusted the surveying instruments, "we aren't in the latitude at all designated by Bueno; we must go farther north."

Puzzled and disappointed the party returned to the camp. Rivera with eight men was next sent out. Twice he passed along the entire southern coast of the bay; but in vain did he look for a port resembling a large O.

The following day was the feast of St. Francis. In honor of their Seraphic Father, the two Franciscans celebrated Holy Mass. All attended, imploring the Saint to intercede for them that they might find the much-desired harbor. That same morning, Portolá convened a council. The officers and the two Fathers were asked to state freely whether in their opinion the expedition should proceed or turn back. All voted for breaking up camp and continuing the march northward; St. Francis would hear their prayers and lead them to the port where the packetboat with

men and provisions would be waiting for them.

Portolá, however, decided to make one more attempt. He ordered Ortega with his men to explore the northern coast of the bay. But when these returned two days later and declared that no harbor such as Viscáino described had been seen, he lost hope and commanded that on the morrow the march should be resumed.

Accordingly, on October 7, they decamped and proceeded in a northerly direction. The country they entered now was exceptionally beautiful. Like the Poverello of Assisi, Fr. Crespi had an eye and a heart for the charms of nature. The flowers on the prairie, the herbs and shrubs along the bank of the river, the trees of the forest, the birds starting up at his approach—he knew them all by name and understood the language they spoke. Enthusiasm is contagious and Fr. Gómez was not proof against it. He, too, was filled with admiration, especially when they came to the El Rio de Pájaro that courses tranquilly through a fertile valley girt on either side with a luxuriant growth of trees and underbrush.

Portolá and his company forded this river and were now traveling in a westerly direction. They had already passed out of a timber, when a charming spectacle met the gaze of the two friars who were bringing up the rear. To their left some two hundred yards away stood a grove of trees more handsome than any they had so far seen.

"Aren't those magnificent trees?" remarked Fr. Gómez.

"Indeed," repled Fr. Crespi; "I, too, was admiring them. How tall and stately they are—especially that one over there at the edge of the grove; sure, it must measure some two hundred pa$_l$m$_{os}$ in height."

"At least," his confrére corrected.

"And their dense foliage, what a vigorous green. How massive those reddish trunks are, tapering upward so gracefully. And high over all, how beautiful those pyramids of leaves pointing heavenward to their Creator."

"Do you know the name of this tree?" Fr. Gómez asked when they had reached the grove.

Fr. Crespi picked up a handful of cones that lay on the ground and examined them closely. Then he looked up at the branches inserted with slender acute leaves and terminating in a red-brown cone.

"No; it is entirely new to me," at length the friar replied; "at college, as far as I remember, neither our professor nor our text-book ever made mention of a tree of this kind. How strangely beautiful! See, the bark is red," he added, pulling off a piece that was loose.

"Why, it seems the entire trunk is red," Fr. Gómez put in, pointing to where his companion had removed the bark. "And it isn't a cedar either," he continued, "for it hasn't the odor of a cedar. I just wonder what name botanists have given this tree."

"Very likely it is indigenous to these regions," Fr. Crespi explained, "and consequently it has till now not been named and classified."

"Well, it is up to you then to give it a name," the other returned good-naturedly.

"And a name it shall have; we'll call it **Palo Colorado**."

"Fine!" applauded Fr. Gómez. "**Palo Colorado—Redwood,** a name as beautiful as the tree that shall henceforth bear it."

Meanwhile, Portolá and his officers were pushing on. They were bent more on finding the Bay of Monterey than on discovering and naming unknown trees.

"We must find that bay," he said to Fr. Crespi, when the latter had caught up with him; "we must find it, no matter what it costs."

"And we shall," the friar replied cheerfully; "St. Francis is guiding us."

Onward then the company marched —three more weeks of suffering and privation. Luckily, the condition of the sick men was improving, insomuch that toward the end of the month they were able to leave their litters which had been strapped to the backs of the mules.

It was on October 31 that the party arrived at the foot of a hill. Not suspecting what was in store for them, they wearily scaled its rugged side. But what was their joy and confusion when the officers and the Fathers reached the top of the hill and beheld a grand roadstead before them.

"What have we here?" exclaimed Fr. Crespi.

"The charts!" demanded Portolá.

"Is it possible?" the general mused, after briefly comparing the scene before him with Bueno's account. "Exactly! There, almost due north, the point of land; yonder, farther west, to the left, the farallones; and to the northeast, the estuary. Is this—"

"Yes, General, the Bay of San Francisco," Fr. Crespi continued.

"Then we have left the one of Monterey behind us?"

"Everything points that way."

"But we must make sure of this," insisted Portolá, much perplexed.

Next day was the feast of All Saints. When the two Fathers had finished saying Holy Mass, Portolá ordered Ortega with a squad of soldiers to explore the entire coast and to report in three days. They set out immediately. By the time they returned, however, conjecture had grown into certainty. A party of soldiers, having left camp on All Souls Day to hunt deer, returned that same evening with the glad tidings that to the northeast a mighty arm of the sea extended into the land—the magnificent San Francisco Bay.

"General," said Fr. Crespi, "St. Francis is a trusty guide; we didn't pray in vain to him on his feast day."

"Well," came the glad reply, "our expedition was not in vain, after all. We missed the Bay of Monterey, but found the one of St. Francis."

"Where, I trust, he will soon have his mission," good Fr. Crespi concluded.

San Francisco and the Redwood—the fortunate discovery of the one and the beautiful name of the other, the result of an error hard to account for. Did St. Francis petition God to shut the eyes of Portolá and his men and to direct them to his bay in order to secure his mission? Further, did the sainted lover of nature want one of his sons to give California's most beautiful tree its name? But, no matter; only for the explorers' failure to recognize the Bay of Monterey this story would not have been so strangely entitled SAN FRANCISCO AND THE REDWOOD.

Black Robes and Brown in California

Z. J. Maher, S. J.

Courtesy of the "Catholic World".

HEN the old Spanish caravels stood out for new seas and new shores and prows which till now had headed North and South in quest of discovery and adventure were dipped in Western waters fabled to lap the base of golden cliffs, side by side with the daring mariner sailed the no less daring friar. One ran up the royal ensign, the other held up the standard of the cross; one sought new lands for the crown, the other new souls for Christ, and from out the first small boat that grounded on a new-found shore there leaped the cavalier and there stepped the friar. The flag was unfurled, the cross was raised and there on the beach to the boom of cannon and the roar of the sea Mass was said and God was asked to bless the land and all that were to dwell therein.

Be it said to the glory of Spain that she ever sought to christianize her discoveries, or rather she sought to discover that she might christianize.

It was therefore but in accord with the usual procedure that friars were found in Cortez' party when he landed on the coast of Lower California in 1535. The Spaniards scurried after gold, the friars mingled with the natives, and tried to tell them of Heaven and the things of the soul. Difficulties were overwhelmingly great and after a year of fruitless effort the friars were compelled to give up in sorrow.

Sixty years later a second attempt was made, determined and persevering, but it too ended in failure.

The Brown Robe had come and suffered and labored and gone.

Meanwhile Ignatius of Loyola had founded the Society of Jesus and filled it with a world-for-Christ conquering spirit. Its movements were swift and sure. Ignatius planned, Xaviers executed. In ten years it had spread over Europe; in thirty it had entered Mexico, opened colleges, founded missions and soon counted 120,000 converts. All this was on the mainland; across the gulf, on the peninsula, nothing was done until the arrival of Frs. Salvatierra and Kino, S. J., about 1680.

Unfamiliar names these, yet the names of the men who thought out and set in motion that vast mission system which for 150 years was to creep steadily Northward from Lower California up past San Francisco to Solano, reaching out and gathering in souls for Christ till it was crushed by a counter

164

COURTESY THE MONITOR, SAN FRANCISCO

movement which in its last analysis was planned and set in motion by the supreme hater of all that is holy and divine.

Kino was a German Tyrolese whose real name was Kuehn, mellowed by the soft-tongued Spaniards into Kino. A splendid mathematician, he gave up his chair in the University of Inglostadt for the missions. His first taste of California was had while acting as royal surveyor to a company sent out to map the gulf coast. Deeply struck by the misery of the natives he sought permission to labor among them but was refused.

Salvatierra was a Milanese and like Kino a University man, but now fired with zeal for the conversion of the Californians. Kindred spirits these, but civil and religious superiors alike opposed their plan; the country was a useless desert, the missions could never support themselves and the government would not lend them aid. Salvatierra met this difficulty with the determination to have the missions endowed. He would beg. He would gather funds on the interest of which the missions could be maintained. In six months generous Spaniards in Mexico had contributed $45,000. Salvatierra invested the money in certain holdings in Mexico City; these were to belong to the missions, to be devoted exclusively to their support, to be administered by the procurators of the Jesuit college. Thus was begun the famous pious fund, destined to play so important a part in the foundation and upkeep of every mission in Upper and Lower California.

Permission was finally obtained to begin the work. Salvatierra and Kino threw themselves into it with the pent up fervor of ten prayerful years, and on October 19, 1697, founded the first of the California missions.

Fifty thousand creatures, one is loath to call them men, then existed on the peninsula. Whence they came they neither knew nor cared; some said from a bird, others from a stone or worse. Tall and robust, dark, with heavy features and low forehead, they much resembled the Digger Indians of Upper California or the Yumas of Colorado. They built no wigwams, but lived in the open, under a bush or behind a heap of stones. They cultivated absolutely nothing; day after day they searched for food, talked, slept and rose to search for food again. They were near brutes, eating anything and everything— roots, seeds, flesh of all kinds, cats, rats, owls, bats, snakes, worms, caterpillars. "Nothing" one of the missionaries notes, "was thrown to the European pigs which the California Indian would not gladly have eaten." Twenty-four pounds of meat in twenty-four hours was not too much for them; sixty such gormandisers once consumed three steers in a night.

It will startle our Commissions on Hygiene to learn that neither gout, apoplexy, chills, fever, smallpox nor venereal diseases were known among these creatures before the white man came to live among them. A California Indian never grew sick. He just died.

We have lifted a corner of the veil that hides their physical degradation; we dare not do as much and show their moral wretchedness. There was no law nor order among them. To quote our outspoken missioner:—"In government they resemble nothing less than a herd of swine which runs about grunting, to go here today, scattered tomorrow. They live as if they were freethinkers and, salve venia, materialists."

Family there was none. When the young Californian had been taught to catch mice and kill snakes his education was complete; it mattered little to him whether he had parents or not. He could count to three or at most to six, though some say twenty, surely not beyond, for fingers and toes then failed. Why count at all? Whether they had five fingers or fifty mattered not, the succession of days mattered less. Every day was eating time, idling time; every night was sleeping time, dancing time. They had no concept of a Supreme Being, no idols, no temples, no suspicion of the immortality of the soul. Some writers tell of a belief among them, strangely resembling the Incarnation, of a Creator of land and sea one of whose three sons had lived on earth and had been killed by the Indians. So write Venegas and Clavigero who never saw California, while Fr. Baegert, a missioner of seventeen years residence, states that he could find no notion of a Supreme Being among them.

Such were the creatures whom the Black Robes undertook to Christianize in 1697. He won his way to their hearts by soothing their stomachs. Any of them would listen to an instruction for the sake of a meal, ready cooked and savory, but none of them was willing to work for it.

In sheer playfulness they would mimic the missioner as he fetched stones, mixed clay, felled timber, cleared the ground, dug, plowed, herded cattle. All day long, day in and day out, these priests, men of culture and refinement, toiled like slaves, offering their labor as a prayer that God might give the Indians grace to see the truth and strength to follow it. Wearied by a day of toil, they would gather the Indians at eventide to instruct them and once more satisfy their craving for food. It was discouraging work. The Indians were slow to understand, the Fathers slow to baptize. Some they did baptize, but even these could not keep continually at the mission. Lack of water and arable land precluded the establishment of pueblos or towns; there could not be that constant dwelling of neophytes round the church, so necessary for successful mission work, which we see in the reductions of Paraguay and in the missions of Upper California. Some few however they managed to keep near them for weeks at a time. These they would assemble in the church for morning prayers, Mass and instruction. Breakfast followed, after which the Indian went to mimic the patient missionary at work. A long rest was enjoyed at noon; in the evening all assembled in the church again to recite the rosary and evening prayers.

With difficulty could the natives be induced to live in rude huts, with greater difficulty could they be persuaded to clothe themselves. Then of a sudden they would off to the mountains when the cactus fruit was ripe, but what could the missioner do but forget and forgive when the fruit was gone and the memory of the mission meals brought the wanderers back?

Though revolting to every finer sense, work among the Indians ever attracted fresh recruits who pushed Northward into the country, founding new missions as they advanced. The martyrdom of two of their number inspired the others with a greater love for a work that might end in blood. We cannot give the results of their labors in figures. Records are wanting. This we know:—the Jesuits in Lower California explored the whole peninsula, Kino alone doing 20,000 miles, rediscovered the Colorado's mouth, constructed a wondrous system of aqueducts, raised cattle and crops while all the wise heads of Mexico said they must fail. Best of all, they founded eighteen missions and saved hundreds of souls. For six decades of years had fifty-six sons of Loyola labored, forgotten and ignored, till of a sudden, Don Gaspar de Portola arrived with peremptory orders to ship every one of them back to Spain. It had been discovered in the highest court of a Catholic country that men who had forsaken all to labor and sweat as farmers, menials and cattle-men, who had submitted to insults the vilest and had breathed in an atmosphere of physical and moral filth that they might raise a tribe of Indians a few degrees above the level of the brute and thus effect that the blood of Jesus Christ might reach and ransom a few more souls, were a danger to a king who hardly knew of their existence and a menace to a nation that had yet to learn who they were and what they were doing.

They were soldier-priests, these sons of Loyola, and their pass-word was 'Obey'. The clothes on their backs, three books in their hands, no more they took away with them when they boarded their prison ship amid the tears of their neophytes who now had learned to love them.

The Black Robe had come and labored. He was led away, prisoner of the crown.

There was one consoling thought in all these trials—the ship that carried them away would return bringing Franciscans to take up the sadly interrupted work. The Brown Robe was returning to his own, led by that sweetest of western missionaries, that self-forgetful, winning Francis of the West, Fra Junipero Serra. Spain claims his birthplace in Majorca, but California claims his resting-place in the lovely Carmel valley within sight and sound of the sea, under the clear blue sky, down by the river side in the meadow-land at the foot of the purple hills of Monterey, where the cypress and the pine stand eternal watchers at his tomb.

Difficult indeed was the task the Franciscans undertook; the natives eyed them with suspicion, judged them supplanters of the Black Robe and friends of the civilians who had hastened to rob the mission stores, but the sweet spirit of their founder was with them to win the confidence and love of the natives. In three years they baptized nearly 1731 neophytes, blessed 787 marriages, buried 2165 dead. Surely in the economy of grace the sufferings of the Jesuits, who during these same years were being shipped over the seas like cattle and flung into prison holes like felons went up a mighty prayer to God, winning for the Indians grace to see the truth and to welcome it.

It needed but a glimpse of Upper California to convince Junipero Serra that the energy he and his friars were spending on the peninsula would produce far greater fruit there. Eager to begin, but loath to abandon the work he had but lately undertaken, Serra welcomed the Dominicans who offered to take charge of all the missions, five years after the Jesuits had been driven away.

Faithfully the Dominicans labored on till 1840; constant friction with an irreligious government wore down the mission chain and one day it snapped asunder. Mexico then, as Mexico now, was no lover of the church and was restless till the work of the Jesuits, Franciscans and Dominicans in Lower California lay a dismal ruin.

We turn in sorrow from the scene to view the marvels Serra wrought in Upper California.

Cabrillo and Viscaino had long ago sailed up the coast and claimed the land for Spain. Russian boats came sailing down the Pacific seeking sealing grounds and harbors. It was high time for Spain to assert and maintain her claim. The country must be settled, the natives subdued. Instead of soldiers, friars were requisitioned, for flags the cross, for forts a church, for the play of artillery song and psalmody, for the death-like grip of war the loving kiss of Christian peace. The army that conquered California for Spain numbered fifteen friars, led by Junipero Serra who came up overland and on July 16th, 1769, founded the first of that long chain of missions whose crumbling ruins today tell of the enterprise and the devotion of the friars of half a century ago.

They found themselves in a wondrously lovely land. "Many flowers and beautiful," writes Serra, "and today I have seen the queen of them all, the Rose of Castile."

This fair land was fair in all that lived in it but man. There was no one tribe, no great nation as Iroquois or Mohawk, but a multitude of smaller tribes, differing in language, customs and manners. Twin brothers of the Lower California Indian, they were

slow, sluggish, immoral, inexpressibly filthy. "In not one of the missions," Padre Palou has left in writing, "was there found any idolatry, but only a negative infidelity." Father Englehardt, who is taken to be the greatest living authority on the California missions, writes:—"The California savage had no religion whatever. Of the pure and reasonable worship of the Creator he had no conception. As he, brutelike, aimed only at filling himself and gratifying his animal instincts, the subject did not interest him."

But the missionaries saw in these poor creatures nought but a soul to be saved, a heart to be won and a body to be trained to labor. The tendency today is to call the friars humanizers, working for the uplift of the race, and to honor them as such; they were all this and more, for they had the secret of all uplift—the Cross—which itself was lifted up with its precious burden and must be lifted up and set in the hearts of men before the race of red or of white men can be led out of the darkness of a paganism, refined or barbarous, into the light of a nobler Christian manhood.

A study of the methods pursued by the missionaries must be of interest, for the results obtained were marvellous.

The site of a future mission was not chosen at random; arable land was sought for, abundance of water and good pasture. Each mission at its foundation received $1,000 from the pious fund, each friar an annual stipend of $400 and to members of the Society of Jesus it is pleasant to think that not a mission was founded in either California which was not due in this little measure to the early efforts of the zealous Fr. Salvatierra. Yet the money never reached the friars as money; every last peso went to purchase church goods, farming implements, iron ware and supplies. The balance went to pay the freight, for the ships would carry nothing gratis either for the friars or for God.

All the buildings were erected on a similar plan; a square was laid off, the church erected on one corner, next to it the friars' residence, into which women and girls were never admitted, then the dwelling for Indian boys who acted as domestics, then shops, granaries and stables forming the sides of the square. In the rear was the "monjero", the so-called nunnery for girls under twelve who were whole orphans, for unmarried girls over twelve, and for wives whose husbands were away. The intensely carnal passions of the Indians made these precautions necessary. Here the "monjas" were locked in at night by a trusty matron; during the day they could go about, visiting relatives or friends or could, if they wished, stay near the mission learning the tasks of Martha.

The kindness of the patient friars could not fail to quiet the fears of the Indians. They came seeking for good. Why should they wander searching for rats and roots when they could get better and a plenty if they sat down and heard a man talk for an hour? So they gathered round the friar who told them the story of creation and redemption. Once baptized, the Indian was scarcely ever allowed to leave the mission. This had to be. If left to himself the Indian would revert to his former habits; the little learned would be quickly forgotten were he allowed to wander at will over hill and dale. To save his soul he had to be kept near the mission, to keep him near the mission he had to be fed; to feed him and teach him to care for himself in a manner differing from that of the brute, this was the task to which the Franciscans next addressed themselves.

The neophytes were largely employed in agriculture, but besides they were taught cattle raising, the care of sheep and various trades, carpentry, blacksmithing, the making of bricks, tiles, saddles, candles, soap, etc. In every task the versatile friar was the master; there he stood in his coarse brown robe, guiding the plow, forging, building, planting, herding—made all things to all men that he might gain them all to Christ.

His bodily needs thus cared for, the Indian was content to dwell at the mission. To reach his dull mind and to impress upon it the chief truths of Religion the Padres made free use of paintings, pictures and processions. The beautiful liturgy of the Church was carried out in all its grandeur. Visitors to the mission today are struck with the richness and completeness of the liturgical equipment, while the paintings on the walls and ceilings tell them, as they told the neophytes, albeit crudely and in vivid color, of death, hell, purgatory and the mysteries of religion. In spite of all this instruction not many could grasp the meaning of the Blessed Sacrament, the great central point of all Catholic liturgy; hence, but few were allowed to receive Holy Communion. As time went on, the children, always objects of the missionaries' special care, sang at Mass, at Vespers and at Benediction. Sweet indeed and peaceful were the Sundays at the mission with Morning Prayer and Mass, Rosary and Litany, all in sweet succession. God was blessing the missions, and the friars felt that their labors had not been in vain.

Yet withal, excesses were to be expected, the more so as the white man mingled with the red. For various faults gentle reprehension was at first used, then persuasion. To lock an Indian up was useless; nothing pleased him better for it freed him from work. Hence fasts were imposed, hard labor and for grosser carnal crimes the lash, but never with the cruelty which the bigots assert. The number of strokes was fixed by law at twenty-five, nor were they ever administered by the friar himself, nor more than once a day and never more than once for the same offence. This punishment was first introduced by the Jesuits in Lower California who found it the only way to make the natives feel that to do certain things was very wrong indeed.

Such was the life, such the system adopted at each of the twenty-one missions founded in quick succession during fifty-four years. God blessed the friars and their work. In the height of their prosperity. they harbored and clothed and fed thirty thousand neophytes at one time, while the combined missions owned 268,000 head of sheep, 232,000 head of cattle, 34,000 horses, 8,300 goats, 3,500 mules, 3,400 swine.

These figures are all the more striking when we reflect that there had been no livestock of any kind in California before Junipero Serra drove a small herd up from Lower California. when he had come to found the missions just fifty years before this time.

The friars however were never left in peace. Greedy officials hungered for the mission goods and snapped at the Padres who kept them at bay. For this they called them misers, self-seekers, greedy for gold—them the barefoot sons of poor St. Francis who had sworn a solemn oath never to possess a peso. They meekly bore the slander and the lie, but when inroads were made on the mission goods then they showed their mettle. Mission goods were Indian goods, to touch them was to wrong the Indian and as long as the Franciscans had a pen to write and a tongue to speak they protested against the injustice done their neophytes without fear of the consequences to self.

Yet there was a subtler opposition behind it all. To see its cause—for its effects were all too pitiful—one must go back to the libraries of France where Voltaire and the Encyclopedists thought out a false philosophy of life, of the equality of man, of liberty, fraternity and the rest. Their ideas were caught up in France and carried over to Spain whence they spread even to Mexico, influencing the political situation there as elsewhere. Secularization of the missions was the form it took in Mexico. Secularization was said to be the emancipation of the Indian. Till now he was on a lower social scale—but he was equal to the white and therefore he must live as the white; his liberty was hampered by the friars, he must be given freedom for all men are born free. the friars must give way to the secular clergy; community life at the mission must stop; pueblos or towns must be built, and the Indians elect their own officials and govern themselves. The lands and goods were divided among the Indians in a way that left them about twenty thousand acres, leaving over a million acres of land and a like disproportion of livestock at the hands of the government. This was called secularization; a shorter name and a truer would have been—theft.

The friars protested vigorously, but to no avail. Mexico had declared itself independent of Spain in 1821 and California accepted the new order of things. The grand old flag of Spain was lowered at Monterey fifty-three years after it had been raised by Portola. It fell as it had risen, bloodlessly. The political history of California under the Mexican rule would be ludicrous were it not lawless; new governors were set up and deposed after revolutions in which never a gun was fired nor a man injured. Street brawls and petty jealousies installed new governors. What cared the Spanish Californian, who ruled the land? As long as luscious grapes blushed purple in a setting silver green, as long as his fields went rippling away in golden laughter up to the mountain side where his sleek cattle grazed, what cared he who issued manifestos at Monterey? He would swear by any governor, any constitution. And so he kept on swearing. And when Commodore Jones, U. S. N., sailed into Monterey and raised the Stars and Stripes, he would have sworn by Jones had not Jones concluded he had made a big mistake and sailed away before the gay Hidalgo had had a chance to swear.

What could the friars do amid these incessant changes They feared for their missions and prayed for their neophytes, for evil days were come upon them. Each new governor agreed with his predecessor only in meddling with the missions and pushing secularization ahead till even the California Indian, who was no warrior and was much too lazy to be angry, rose in rebellion. Then the friar stood for authority and taught the Indians to obey while once more he showed the governor the injustice of his policy. It was useless. They tampered with the missions till 1845

when Pio Pico stole and sold the missions as never pirate stole at sea. Mission La Purissima, worth $67,000 ten years before, went to John Temple for $1,100. Capistrano, which but thirteen years before owned 11,000 head of cattle, 5,000 sheep and 450 horses, went for $700 to Messrs. McKinley and Wilson. Soledad, with 10,000 sheep, and 7,000 head of cattle thirteen years before, went for $800—and so on through the sad litany of the missions. Interference had depreciated them, these "sales" ruined them. Appraised at $2,000,000 twelve years before this time, they were estimated at $150,000 in 1845.

The ruin of the mission system was complete. For 76 years 146 noble sons of St. Francis had labored, two had died as martyrs—and now their work was all undone. Under their care and guidance the Indians had harvested 2,200,000 bushels of wheat, 600,000 bushels of barley, 100,000 bushels of lentils, 850,000 bushels of corn, 160,000 bushels of beans.

Had the friars done naught but this they would deserve full meed of praise. But they did more. They baptized 90,-000 Indians, blessed 27,000 marriages and buried 70,000 dead.

All honor to the Brown Robe! He taught the Indian to serve his God and his king, he taught him to respect himself, he taught him trades and agriculture, he explored and mapped the state, built roads and aqueducts, brought in live-stock, fruits and grapes, wheat and corn—and for this his missions are ruined, his lands are plundered, his neophytes disbanded. And what had he to say? Only this: "You ask me who caused the ruin of the missions? As one who saw and suffered I can only try to close my eyes that they may not see the evil done and my ears that they may not hear the endless wrongs endured." Sweet spirit of St. Francis, living, forgiving in your sons as in yourself!

Here we must weave in the story of the pious fund. We noted its beginning by Salvatierra in 1697. It totaled some $400,000 in 1784, while in 1842 it was valued at one and one-half million dollars. On the suppression of the Society of Jesus, the King of Spain acted as its trustee to be succeeded by the Mexican government in 1821. Too sweet a morsel to be placed where it might not be nibbled at at will, Santa Anna declared the property formerly incorporated into the national treasury and ordered the sale of the real estate, acknowledging an indebtedness of 6% on the total proceeds of the sale. Thus matters stood when Commodore Sloat, U. S. N., sailed into Monterey bay and hoisted the Stars and Stripes, though war had not been declared with Mexico. War did come and California was ceded by Mexico on July 4th, 1848. With California thus lost to her, Mexico ceased paying any share of the proceeds of the fund to the missions of Upper California. The California bishops protested before the American and Mexican Mixed Claims Commission in 1869.

Sir Edward Thornton, the umpire, decided for the bishops in 1875, awarding them $904,700 in Mexican gold, this being the accumulated interest from the year 1848 to the year 1869. Mexico paid the award, stating at the same time that she considered the claim settled 'in toto' and made a last payment in this sense in 1890. Naturally the Bishops demurred and claimed payment of interest due since 1869. The cause was finally settled at The Hague in 1892, being the first international claim there arbitrated. Mexico was thereby compelled to pay the United States $1,420,682.27 Mexican, this being the annuity of $43.050.99 due from '69 to '02. She must moreover annually and perpetually pay the United States on the 2nd of February, $43,050.99 in money having currency in Mexico, this being, in round numbers, $22,000 American. This sum is divided between the three Bishops of California.

The U. S. Commission on Indian Affairs tells our mission story in four words: "Conversion, civilization, neglect, outrage. The conversion and civilization were the work of the mission Fathers, the outrage and neglect mainly our own."

The beginnings of this outrage and neglect hastened the death of the first Bishop of California, Diego y Moreno. Padre Gonzales, a Franciscan, was appointed administrator. The mad rush for gold was now on; that frenzied struggle with man and beast and sand and snow and mountain and plain, that furious scramble up the Rockies and down the Sierras; that wild race to pan the gold that had glistened for ages in the California river beds.

There were but eight priests in the whole state. Help must be had and in God's providence it was to come from that same Blackrobe who had laid the first beginnings of the mission system which now lay in ruins all along the gulf and up the coast. He came down from the North from among the Couer d' Alenes and the Flatheads, the Spokanes and the Gros Ventres where the great De Smet had founded the Oregon missions.

Frs. Nobili and Accolti set sail for California on St. Xavier's day and passed through the Golden Gate on the night of the feast of the Immaculate Conception in 1849, so that, writes Fr. Accolti, ''the next day we were able to set foot on the longed-for shores of what goes under the name of San Francisco, but which, whether it should be called madhouse or Babylon, I am at a loss to determine, so great is the disorder, the brawling, the open immorality, the reign of crime which, brazenfaced, triumphs on a soil not yet brought under the sway of human laws.''

Meanwhile a new Bishop had been consecrated for California. A Dominican, Joseph Sadoc Alemany. On the 19th of March, 1851, he placed Fr. No-

bili in charge of the abandoned mission of Santa Clara. Eighteen years earlier it had counted 1,125 neophytes in its mission family; on the eve of that St. Joseph's day ''the church and ornaments were sadly out of repair,'' notes Fr. Nobili. ''The few buildings attached that were not either sold, bestowed or filched away were in a condition of dismal nakedness and ruin. The gardens, vineyards and orchards were in the hands of swindlers and squatters.'' The 10,000 cattle, 10,000 sheep and 1,000 horses were grazing on other pastures.

Here then, on the ground prepared by Franciscans, at the behest of a Dominican Bishop, did the Jesuit Fr. Nobili, with $150 in his pocket and unbounded trust in Providence, lay the first beginnings of SANTA CLARA COLLEGE.

The Turin Province of the Society of Jesus took over the rising mission and sent as helpers exiled subjects who were working in the East; Fr. Maraschi, professor of Philosophy at Loyola, Baltimore; Fr. Masnata, professor of Rhetoric at Frederick; Fr. Messea, professor of Chemistry at St. Louis. The two latter went to Santa Clara. Fr. Maraschi remained in San Francisco seeking a site for a church and college. ''Build it over there,'' said His Grace, with a sweeping gesture. 'Over there' were rolling sand dunes, shifting sands that sank into the sea. Fr. Maraschi built it 'over there' in the hollow of the hills. Ninety days later a college was opened, a college with classics, science and philosophy, in the rollicking, happy-go-lucky, devil-may-care city of San Francisco in the days of '55· Nobili at Santa Clara, Maraschi at San Francisco, and the Blackrobe had come back to California.

The Brownrobe never left the state; praying at Santa Barbara mission, he awaited happier times. Today he is working up and down the coast, yet he holds but two of his twenty-one missions.

His modest figure is loved by all in California. We treasure every mission ruin as a shrine for pilgrimage; we are retracing the old mission road, El Camino Real, and in lieu of mile posts we hang up mission bells—out in the valley, up in the mountain, marking mile by mile the road that Serra trod from San Diego up to San Francisco. Even in the heart of the city where the rush for gold is as mad as it was in '49 all stop and pause a moment, for the mission bell is being hung; it marks a mile on the road to Mission San Rafael. There he stands above the crowd, brown robed son of St. Francis, symbol of all that is deepest in faith, purest in love, noblest in self-sacrifice. He blesses the bell and bids it swing out and tell the passer-by that in the long ago his bare-foot brothers gave up home and self and all they loved to care for the body and save the soul of the California Indian.

Theirs was the highest altruism, for they are the noblest of our race, truest friends of their fellow man, greatest benefactors of society who shape their lives in imitation of the gentle Son of God who cured all ills of body and then laid down His life to save the soul.

Fulfillment

ACROSS the epochs stretching in your train,
The spirits of your holy founders glide;
Reaching at last your portals, now in chain,
Eager to swing them far apart and wide,
Longing to lift you from the ages' dust,
Where crumbling in your ruin you have lain
Seeking fulfillment of a sacred trust;
The glory of your past to rear again.

Proud temple wrecks, still regal in your fall,
Rise up as when you were but pioneers;
For your appealing cries have torn the caul
That overspread the span of slack'ning years.
Know that at last new life your age surrounds,
For God, by man will bind your bleeding wound

MARTIN V. ME

176

Remarks on Art

Peter B. Kyne.

JUBAL and Tubal-cain, according to Chapter 4 of the Book of Genesis, were the great - great - great-great grandsons of Adam and Eve. We have the same authority for the information that Jubal was the father of all such as handle the harp and the organ, while Tubal-cain was an instructor of every artificer in brass and iron. I take it, therefore, that these two were the first creative geniuses, and they were true geniuses, too, for God made them such at birth. I have been unable to find any record of the person who wrote the first poem, short story or serial novel; it is probable that David with his Psalms and Solomon with his Proverbs are the first authentic authors we know of. For my part, however, I refuse to believe that at a period in the history of mankind when longevity was the rule rather than the exception, mere boys of from a hundred and fifty to seven hundred years of age loafed around Tubal-cain's blacksmith shop all that time without some long-haired lad among them helping himself to one of Tubal-cain's cold chisels and a hammer in order to write a picture story in the lime-stone cliff hard by. I'm a trifle hazy on ancient history, but I seem to remember that the Egyptians did more or less stone writing thousands of years before Christ and the thought occurs to me: Where did the Egyptians get the idea? Well, if human nature was fundamentally the same then as it is now I can well imagine one of Adam's Hebrew descendants declaring to an unsympathetic world that the Egyptians had stolen his stuff.

What interests me chiefly, however, is not the identity of the first creative geniuses in music, sculpture, painting and literature. What I'd give a ripe peach to know is the name of the fellow who, when Jubal appeared in concert for the first time with his home-made organ, seized his nose 'twixt thumb and forefinger and cried in agonized tones: "Rotten!" That's the information I'm after. Who was the first Knocker? Nobody will ever know, I fear. However, nobody who ever saw a pteradactyl also photographed the creature and wrote a monograph on pteradactyls, based on first-hand information and study of a live specimen, but for all that scientists have reconstructed not only the pteradactyl but other prehistoric monsters, and in such a clever manner that even the very stupid among us can gain a very fair idea of what these creatures looked like. Inasmuch as I have had more or less experience with Critics of Art and Knockers of Honest Artistic Effort, covering a period of more than ten years writing fiction for national (and latterly) international consumption, I am going to venture to reconstruct The First Critic and present him to you as I am confident he actually was back in Jubal's day. In order to identify him I shall christen him Fooey.

Fooey wasn't a bad sort of chap to begin with. He possessed an alert intelligence and tremendous ambition to be famous. The weak spot in his nature was his vanity. He desired the applause of the multitude; failing to win that he still desired their notice. He wanted to be talked about and in a pinch it is probable that he would have accepted notoriety as eagerly as he would have accepted fame. Fooey could take a kick in the face and take it smilingly, but to be overlooked, neglected or forgotten, hurt him cruelly.

Now, Fooey was reasonably fond of music and the first time he heard Jubal practicing My Figleaf Babe out back of the barn he was fired with ambition to go and do likewise. So he contracted with Jubal to make him an organ and as soon as Jubal delivered it Fooey hied him away to a quiet spot and started one-finger exercises. At the end of a month he concluded he was just about as good as it was possible to be, so he called around to astound Jubal with a demonstration of his Art. Imagine his horror when he discovered Jubal playing the organ with both hands and his eyes shut!

Hurrying back home Fooey started to work with his left hand. At the end of a year he was doing very well for an amateur, so again he called on Jubal—and lo, Jubal was tickling the ivories with his bare toes and playing an accompaniment with his hands on his latest invention, the harp; alternately he sang or whistled and banged a bass drum with his right elbow. His oldest boy was pumping the organ. Quite a number of friends and neighbors were standing around, cheering for Jubal, and among them Fooey noticed the charming daughters of Irad, one or both of whom he planned to marry, an extra wife or two not being considered an encumbrance in those days.

In a fit of jealousy Fooey fled the gay and festive scene. His feelings were lacerated: Nobody had ever applauded his efforts—that is, nobody for whose opinions he cared three whoops in a hollow—and applause and fame were what he desired. It was a matter of indifference to him whether or not he could play the organ as Jubal played it, provided he could, in our modern phraseology, "get by". He was much concerned with what the Irad girls thought about his Art, but not with what HE thought about it. In fact, he didn't think about it at all. He thought about himself. He said: "I'm all right, but why this Jubal bird can perform so wonderfully and seemingly without effort, and in such a manner that those two Irad girls simply cannot make their feet behave, is a mystery to me.''

After much brooding Fooey concluded he had found a clue to the mystery. The Irad girls were more or less bovine; they didn't appreciate good music when they heard it—that is, when they heard it played by a Genius, for by now our hero regarded himself as such, since the wish is ever father to the thought. We all know that to strive to appeal to such natures as the Irad girls possessed (according to Fooey) is as hopeless a task as attempting to popularize the Gregorian chant in a modern cabaret. No, these light and frivolous creatures whose approval he secretly coveted, did not appreciate him; they could not understand his Art, and a profound wonder stole over him that anybody could cheer for the careless, sloppy art of that fellow Jubal!

Fooey continued to brood. Eventually it dawned upon him that he could not hope to excel Jubal as a musician, but nevertheless he evolved a plan to keep the spotlight on himself and belittle Jubal. He resolved to become a Critic! He affected a solemn and melancholy cast of countenance, dressed differently from other men and lavished great praise upon Jubal's students, no matter how awful they were. Jubal he ignored, unless some enthusiastic admirer of Jubal eagerly demanded his opinion of Jubal's art, when Fooey would say: ''Jubal's playing is pleasing at times; in fact he does rather well with those minor, simpler melodies, which serve to screen his appalling lack of technique. However, since the ballad is the commonest and simplest form of music, originating as it does among the ignorant and illiterate of all nations, it is not surprising that as a troubadour of the proletariat Jubal is immensely popular. It is to be regretted that a man of his undoubted native talent should sacrifice his future by practicing the catch-penny tricks of the professional entertainer. Posterity will have none of him.''

Hearing Fooey speak thusly certain persons, who then, as now, have no individuality and prefer to have their thoughts manufactured for them, and being quite impressed by Fooey's judicial pronouncements and artistic poses, credited Fooey with being a great Artist and a Learned Man—one whom it would be well to imitate. Gradually it became the fashion in certain circles to criticize adversely and cruelly not only Jubal's art but Jubal himself. Persons who desired to know Jubal but whom Jubal could not afford to know because they wasted his time calling upon him when he had need of practicing, resented his aloofness and ascribed it to hauteur and the swelled-head. So they spread little scandals about him; gradually it became known that Jubal had stolen another man's idea when he invented the organ and had taken advantage of the extreme poverty of the real inventor of the harp to purchase the manufacturing rights at a starvation figure. Later it was reported on good authority that he owed everything he had to his wife, who was his inspiration and had taught him how to play. He was reported to booze considerably in the privacy of his home and to be the possessor of a dreadful temper. It was stated that he never paid a bill he could possibly evade paying and that he was grossly "commercial". Fooey once stated in public that the clink of silver had drowned the voice of Jubal's art; with sorrow he was forced to state this accusation. No, Jubal knew nothing about Art.

Nevertheless, Jubal continued to prosper in worldly good and gear and his popularity increased by leaps and bounds. He was what we term now-a-days "a riot". He brought such joy to his neighbors that they would give him almost anything they possessed and which they didn't particularly need at the moment, provided he would play for them. Also, Jubal derived quite a thrill out of the knowledge that he had successfully produced an organ and a harp; he was tremendously happy because he could play and his own music never failed to thrill him. Of course he took the silver folks threw at him because Lamech, his father, was a poor man and needed the money, but the fact of the matter was that Jubal would have played just as long and just as well for nothing. He had music in his soul and it had to come out; also he was thrifty by nature and hated to see a good thing wasted. Likewise he was unselfish and loved to share a good thing with his neighbors, and if people listened to his music, that appealed to his thrifty, unselfish soul. It is natural for man to enjoy that which appeals to his nature, and when we enjoy a thing we are happy and desire more enjoyment. Jubal was that way. He desired more happiness and the only way he could get it was by perfecting better and sweeter organs and harps and learning to play newer and sweeter melodies upon them. After a while people who had been wont to sit around nodding solemn approval, commenced to applaud a little. Soon they discovered that this method of expressing their approval was insufficient, so they stamped a little and the young men whistled shrilly between their teeth, while dignified old gentlemen cried "Bravo, Jubal! Bravo!" Finally Jubal became so good his audience just naturally threw back its respective heads and howled! Jubal only quit through sheer exhaustion and wanted to hug everybody who appreciated him. He was so happy that when Lamech, his father, who had always regarded his son as a peculiarly, worthless, wool-gathering and impractical fellow who would come to a bad end, booted Jubal for neglecting to feed the goats and milk the camels, Jubal didn't mind it a bit.

For Jubal was an artist. He didn't know anything about art and he didn't have to. God Almighty had attended to that. I suppose Jubal frequently wondered how he happened to be so different from other men, and why, from the practical business of providing food for his belly and clothes for his back in his old age, his mind had wandered to organs and harps. It used to cause him vague uneasiness when Fooey passed him by with a cold sneer; Jubal always wished devoutedly that he would eventually develop into such a marvelous player that his art would bring a soft and luminous light into the cold green eye of the Critic. He yearned to hear Fooey cry "Bravo, Jubal, bravo! Good work, old scout. I knew you'd get there in time." But, alas! Jubal never succeeded in eliciting from The Critic anything more tangible than a sneer or a cool, patronizing smile. And it broke Jubal's soft heart. He did his best to be artistic, but somehow he couldn't improve his playing. He wondered what this mysterious thing Art was, that Fooey and the other brethren of the Intelligencia talked so much about; there were times when he considered himself exceedingly stupid because he couldn't understand this prate and agree with it. Fooey and his friends had evolved a glib patter to describe the efforts of others to bring joy to mankind, and after they had gotten through talking poor Jubal used to take his corrugated brow in his hands and try to puzzle out what it was all about. He wondered what technique could possibly be; he marveled much that he should have so many enemies, and marveling always, eventually he

died and his spirit took wing and appeared before the bar of Heaven.

St. Peter* looked up from his interminable bookkeeping as Jubal presented himself for admittance. And the old saint smiled. "Welcome, Jubal," he cried kindly. "Now, at last, we shall have a Master to lead the Angelic Harpists."

"Ah," wailed poor Jubal, "do not jest with me. I am commercial.. I know naught of Art. Unlike Fooey I could never learn."

St. Peter smiled. "My son," he replied, "art is a gift from God and those upon whom the gift is conferred are never aware of it because they have always had it in a greater or less degree. Art is something that happens. Money cannot affect it, for money is but a sign of appreciation. Jubal, you have made a great many people happy, have you not?"

"It has seemed to me that all but a few persons have enjoyed my music," Jubal admitted.

"You have changed sobs to laughs; you have wiped away tears and the discord in human souls has melted before your melody. Your music was but one of the infinite expressions of beauty and beauty makes the majority of people happy; ugliness appeals to none. Jubal, you have drawn great contentment from the knowledge that, regard-

---

*Note—Since writing the above, I have ascertained that Jubal preceded St. Peter to Heaven by some years.

less of the faint praise of Fooey and his ilk, you have made countless persons happy. That is Art. Making people happy is the sole excuse for an artist's existence."

"But—but—" sputtered Jubal.

"But me, no buts," the good saint protested. "First door to your right, Jubal. They'll measure you there for your crown and issue you a harp that's a harp! Bless my soul! If he hasn't fainted!"

Methods of Study for the California Missions

Frances Rand Smith.

THE present movement to restore the architecture of Spain as it was when introduced in California, demands the exclusion of any pretense or apology for inconsistent modifications. To follow this trail of research it is essential that the topic should become a thoroughly familiar one, for the reconstruction should be based upon a technical study of the problems presented and a thorough knowledge of the history of the mission. In the compilation of valuable historical material and the comparison of the data, there should be an elimination of all errors as far as possible. As it has been requested that I should sketch somewhat in detail the course I have followed in the twenty years I have studied the missions, I will touch upon a few of the many important incidents which served to bring me more closely in touch with the romance of California and the importance of its early history.

In the summer of 1906, I stood before the altar of San Juan Capistrano, the most imposing to be found in all the missions, and realized that the time alloted to my visit was too brief to allow me to comprehend in some small measure the magnificence of the structure or to record the significance of its details. I fell feverishly to work and came away with one detail in color which I can proudly claim as the first copy of mural decoration produced at San Juan Capistrano. I made my way to San Luis Rey eager for further knowledge. There we were held under the spell of the very friars of the Franciscan order who were performing the tasks at the mission in an altogether somber manner. As though by way of contrast, Father O'Keefe in his genial and kindly way asked if we cared to see the mission under his guidance. From the moment he turned the key in the great doorway of the church, we followed, losing not a word, for we were listening to one of the best known of the scholars in history, from the Franciscan Order of Santa Barbara. The variations of form and color were emphasized by Father O'Keefe and I was better able to appreciate the charm in Harmer's reproduction of the altar of San Luis Rey.

Another journey to the southward brought me in touch with the remarkable mission of San Fernando. It was an exceedingly warm Sunday morning when our little party stepped into the cooler air of the long corridor of the mission tavern. Aroused by the approach of strangers, a laborer arose and with the courteous manner of a native of Louisiana asked if he might explain the attractions of the mission. We passed through the various rooms consisting of the quarters of the priest, the original chapel, the wine cellar, the kitchen blackened in the early days with the use of charcoal. Finally we were led into the great dining-room and seated at the plain wooden table, where we were served royally and in masterful fashion, for we were told the trip would not be quite complete unless we partook of the old-time mission hospitality. Before we bade adieu to our guide, he expressed his longing to know something of the history of the mission, the reason for its existence and the life of those who had lived there. His was a thought that was in my mind also and I wondered if I might accomplish something in gathering data which would bear upon the old mission. As a result I arose many a day in Los Angeles at half past four, that I might catch the first train for San Fernando. I gave little heed to the heat of those long summer days or the number of hours in which I felt it was a great privilege to work. I was in an unrecorded field, the wealth of material was mine and into my note book I put the many interesting stories I gathered pertaining to the mission. Susceptible as I was to the charm of the surroundings, I might easily have imagined that I was there to greet Helen Hunt Jackson as she rode up before the main entrance, in the wonderful stage coach of early days. Later as I passed through the village of Fernando I heard the call of "Ramona" go out to a little brown-eyed maiden. She was the granddaughter of Mrs. Lopez to whom I became indebted for an explanation of the courts and buildings, as fourteen of her girlhood years were spent at the mission. In this manner I made my beginning of an accumulation of material not only for San Fernando but the other missions as well.

I found that California contained within its length and breadth much material of value and not infrequently the southern part of the state held in its collections what was most needed for San Antonio de Padua, or the required data for San Diego had long been treasured in the archives of the north. Gradually I became acquainted with many of the old residents, and during interviews collected pictures, drawings, maps and books. Through library investigation an important field was entered, which many of the older publications have hardly been touched upon. A continuation of these pilgrimages through twenty years, and a comparative study of all this available material and the checking up of sources of information resulted in reducing to maps and architectural drawings a considerable number of missions of California.

The field is a broad one and the opportunities for investigation will be open for many years to come. No better introduction to Spanish architecture in California could be had than what is to be seen now and will be produced through the restoration of the Carmel mission. The methods employed were much the same as in other missions, the elaboration of details varying in each group of buildings. Broad expanses were built upon because, in general, ground levels were necessary and were available. Extensive walls built of blocks of sandstone or adobe bricks moulded from the adaptable soil are the dominant features of the work of the Spaniard. Their purpose was to build consistently, to adopt methods which conformed to the necessities of the particular site chosen for their location and by a duplication of the simplest proportions they built their missions, constructed towers for their chimes, gave strength in great buttresses and added an indefinable beauty in the arches of their corridors.

The period of prosperity for the California missions was exceedingly brief. Among the descriptions written in those early and unfamiliar days are those by the sea-captains whose ships bore the flags of different nations. The Frenchman Laplacé saw the Santa Cruz mission when its tower was the principal attraction but when Farnham from an Atlantic port sailed into the harbor, the tower which had been seen above the treetops was gone. An earthquake, always a fearful menace, had despoiled the mission of its most pleasing feature. There were those who wrote of storms and high water and all too soon the stories came of devastation among the various communities. Thus have the people of this state become accustomed to the mission in its form of ruin. So, long ago was the mission of San Diego in its state of perfection that its full beauty has never been known to our generation; and the early environments of Carmel hardly can be pictured today.

A period came when partial restoration placed several of the missions out of the list of actual ruin and these are the sites of greatest historical interest today. The numerous missions still to be cared for offer opportunity for restoration of the same character and arrangement as they had originally. The old outlines followed will produce a unity and beauty and final development of Spanish architecture deviating little from the original design which embodied simplicity and distinction.

History

THOU art too fond of idol-worshiping,---
    Clay idols, armor-clad and helmed and plumed,
Gold-spurred, brass-gauntleted, steel-brandishing,---
Thou unctuous eulogist of despot king
    Or world-enslaver whom thy scribes have groomed
    To noble semblance. Nor oblivion-doomed
Are sceptred bawd and pander. Why wilt bring
Archaic fetishes on classic scrolls
    And leave us all too meagerly illumed
    With the unselfish great, the broadly wise,
Who teach mankind to strive for higher goals,
    Who strip from crime its cloaking glory-guise,
    Who seek by love to end old Hatred's tolls,
    By truth to purge thee of thy royal lies!

                     CHAS. D. SOUTH.

186

COURTESY ARCHITECT AND ENGINEER, SAN FRANCISCO

Early Photographers of the Missions

Charles Beebe Turrill.

HE present Statewide interest in the restoration and preservation of California's old Missions creates a desire to know something of those who have left us pictorial representations of these interesting Landmarks.

We old Californians have been too slothful in preservation and backward in appreciation of the wonderful architectural heritage the good Franciscan Fathers left us. We have been too prone to regard them as only mud walls erected by strangers whose every desire and ambition were alien to our own. Not until stranger tourists swarmed across our borders did we wake to interest in our Missions. Prior to that period the old buildings were either ignored, or, if handily located, were used as cow-sheds by a generation of farmers who gave but casual inspection as their plow-shares turned to the light of a modern day some crude agricultural instrument with which, in the forgotten past, an Indian neophyte had broken virgin soil to plant the strange seeds of grains and trees from those strange lands whence came the good Padres who taught of stranger and better lands beyond.

Fortunately, however, there were a few exceptions among our people who were not unmindful of the architectural harmony, structural symmetry and historic interest of the Missions. A few beheld and comprehended. These have left to us most important and priceless pictures of the by-gone time.

Our search of pictorial material carries us back to a period when drawing and sketching were considered integral parts of a fair education. Many of the most important illustrations of California scenes and incidents are preserved to us only through the painstaking sketches of early travelers or pioneer residents. Of the latter was Edward Vischer who left much most valuable, and in some sections the only, contemporaneous illustrative treasures. He, more than any other, loved the Old Missions, the work of a generation anterior to his, for themselves and for what they represented.

A few artists accompanied early exploration expeditions and have embellished the volumes of travel with occasional Mission sketches. These were simply searching for illustrative material and carelessly portrayed a few of the leading architectural features of a strange and distant region. Perhaps the most ridiculous of such sketches is that of Mission San Luis Rey in the atlas of DeMofra's Voyage, where the French artist has depicted a beautiful building on the apex of which flies a French flag over a Spanish Mission located in Mexican territory. Were the flag the only discordant feature we might excuse the patriotism of the Frenchman, but so many liberties have been taken in embellishing a beautiful structure that critical forebearance ceases to be a virtue. The artists who illustrated Vancouver's Voyage and Forbes' "California", have been more true to nature. When those accompanying the U. S. Government survey for a Pacific railroad entered the pictorial lists we received a picture of Mission San Diego. In that work the new and unusual received illustrative notice and the Missions had to compete with plants, fossils, reptiles, etc., in the proportion of one Mission to about a dozen rattlesnakes.

But it was different with Edward Vischer. While he has left important sketches of California life and scenery these, in his mind were of little worth in comparison with his Mission sketches. His works, done mostly during the '60s and drawn with photographic detail, are our only source of pictorial data of the condition of the Mission establishments before the hand of neglect had crushed their roofs and left their walls to the mercy of winter rains.

In the early '50s the Daguerreotype was popular. Daguerrean Galleries were common in all the larger settlements and in most mining camps. The chief work undertaken was portraiture but a few hardy artists essayed views. Thus we have had Daguerreotypes of the Missions of San Diego, San José and Santa Clara. These were made by J. M. Ford, who also had galleries in San Francisco and San Jose. Probably owing to this fact two different daguerreotypes were made of Santa Clara. One of these seems to have disappeared, but had been copied by Watkins. The other and earlier is at the University of Santa Clara.

Hamilton and Company were early San Francisco photographers. There is no evidence that they made more than one photograph showing a Mission. In a wood-cut inscribed "From a photograph by Hamilton & Co.", we get a distant view of Mission Dolores.

Undoubtedly the first to photograph the Missions in any thorough manner was Carlton E. Watkins, the best view photographer California has seen, whose superb work did more to make known our State's superior scenic attractions than all the other photographers combined. Mr. Watkins was not only a most accomplished and painstaking artist, but he was possessed in a superior degree with the perception not only of the artistic but also of the historic importance of old landmarks. About 1876 Watkins visited Southern California traveling with his covered wagon in which he not only transported his photographic equipment, but also developed his wet plates. On that trip he photographed the Missions of San Diego, San Luis Rey, San Juan Capistrano, San Gabriel, San Fernando, Santa Barbara, San Luis Obispo, Santa Inez, La Purissima, San Miguel, Soledad, San Antonio and San Juan Bautista. Later, when the Del Monte Hotel was completed, he visited the Monterey region and made several photographs of San Carlos. The earliest of his Mission Dolores pictures was a copy of a photograph made by an English tourist who stopped in San Francisco during his return trip from the Orient. The Watkins photograph of Mission San Jose was his copy of the Ford Daguerreotype. In his later years Mr. Watkins assembled and copied pictures of the Missions he had not personally photographed and planned an album of views of the Franciscan Missions which got no further than being copyrighted. He also made a superb collection of 16"x20" transparencies of the Missions which was destroyed with his possessions in the great San Francisco fire of 1906.

During the '60s and '70s the demand for views of cities called into being the View Photographers. The advent of the kodak and other easily operated cameras gave an impetus to amateur photography that sounded the death knell of the view photographers. During the ascendancy of the latter business rivalry and self interest prompted

photographing all interesting and important buildings and events. Watkins, who traveled extensively over the Pacific Coast and assembled several thousand negatives soon had rivals in his pioneer field. Fardon, in San Francisco, made several most important local views and also copied the same Englishman's photograph of Mission Dolores which Watkins had copied. His work does not seem to have extended beyond San Francisco.

An optical firm, Lawrence & Houseworth, which dealt extensively in stereoscopes, then popular, and in European stereoscopic views, having failed to induce Watkins to accept a sum of five hundred dollars for making for their exclusive use an hundred stereoscopic negatives, hired some one else to do the job and began an active opposition in the view business which was developed to considerable proportions by Houseworth, who subsequently carried on the business. The sale of Watkins' pictures reached such profitable proportions that Houseworth sent men through the State to make similar views. Thus, among Mission pictures, we have a most important view of Mission San Jose.

E. J. Muybridge, who gained celebrity by photographing for Governor Stanford "The Horse in Motion" and thus became the father of the now popular motion picture, entered the photographic field in the early '60s. He traveled extensively through the State and made a photographic trip for the Pacific Mail Steamship Company to the ports of Mexico and Central America. As a part of his endeavors he has left us a few important Mission views. As his work necessitated frequent absences from San Francisco he established headquarters first with Bradley & Rulofson, portrait photographers, who advertised his views and whose mounts bore the now interesting legend, "The only photographic gallery in the World with an elevator". They were then located on Montgomery street, between California and Sacramento streets, on the top, or third story of a brick building and the primitive elevator consumed about the same time in an ascent as an active man would need in using the stairs. Later Muybridge made his headquarters with Henry W. Bradley (also of the firm of Bradley and Rulofson) who had a stock house for photographic supplies on Washington street below Kearny. Still later Muybridge conducted a gallery in his own name on the first block on Montgomery street.

Taber, who was primarily a portrait photographer, entered the field as a view photographer through a chance of fortune which placed in his possession the entire collection of negatives that Watkins had devoted some twenty years in making. During the latter's absence from San Francisco on one of his annual photographing expeditions an undue advantage was taken of him and his entire collections were sold to a party who turned them over to Taber. With such an important foundation the latter sought to build up his view busi-

ness and sent operators around to make additional negatives. But few of the Taber Mission photographs are others than those made from original Watkins plates.

When Watkins returned home and found how he had been treated he manfully started out and made an entirely new set of the most saleable views as soon as possible and made new negatives of his original Mission prints. All his later mounts bore the words, "Watkins' New Series". Not only did he replace the important subjects which had unjustly been filched from him but also added several thousand most important, historically, new subjects.

About 1876 J. J. Riley opened a tent studio in Yosemite Valley and made an important series of views as well as many group-pictures of tourists. During the winters he stayed in San Francisco, photographed Dolores, and made a visit to the new popular Del Monte and San Carlos.

Another well-known Yosemite photographer was George Fiske who became enamored with the scenic charm of the Valley shortly after leaving school and serving a short apprenticeship in a San Francisco portrait gallery. Fiske, during his earlier Yosemite career, spent the winters around the Bay and has left us an important view of San Carlos.

The period of the '70s and early '80s, was the time of several "Tramp Photographers" whose names and work are almost unknown to this generation.

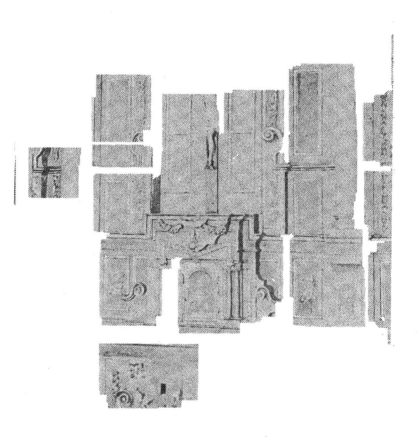

Search has thus far disclosed no Mission photographs as their work, though some important views of the old St. Ignatius Church are a heritage from one or two of this tribe.

The work of the photographers located in smaller towns has been almost entirely destroyed. Their collections of negatives were usually dumped out as soon as they died or moved away. Much important historically illustrative matter is thus lost, though in a few cases wood cuts made from such photographs survive in a few specimens. It may be mentioned that probably only one Mission photograph thus made survives in an extremely rare and interesting view at San Luis Obispo.

Special prominence has been given to the photographers having their headquarters in San Francisco. The undeveloped condition of our southern regions had not been conducive to sales of "views" and little attention was given to such outside of Santa Barbara and San Diego which were reached by boat. Some important stereoscopic views of Mission San Diego, probably the work of a local man, are preserved and a few scattered views of Santa Barbara practically complete the list of earlier efforts in this direction.

Somewhat later, after the railroad had been extended to Los Angeles and the tourist tide turned thither, a few loyal local photographers took advantage of their opportunities and have done good work.

Herve Friend who commenced his photographic career in Southern California in the latter '80s, did excellent service. He tried to do for the Missions of the south what Watkins had begun and has left most interesting specimens of his skill. It is recorded by Mr. Geo. Watson Cole* in his interesting and important paper, that Friend sold his negatives to Geo. Wharton James, who only used a few of them in his "In and Out of the Old Missions", a book which would be useful had its author cared to try to be accurate.

C. C. Pierce and Company of Los Angeles have done much to preserve a photographic history of the southern Missions during the last thirty years. Putnam and Valentine, also of Los Angeles, have assembled many most interesting Mission views. So did Harold A. Taylor, of Coronado, whom Mr. Cole credits with an hundred negatives. N. H. Reed has done loyal work around Santa Barbara. Amateur photographers in the South, have done much to assemble and add to the views of Missions. Mr. Cole especially mentions A. C. Vroman of Pasadena and that Nestor

*"Missions and Mission Pictures: a Contribution towards an Iconography of the Franciscan Missions of California", by George Watson Cole, read before the California Library Association at its meeting, Long Beach, April, 1910, and printed in "News Notes of California Libraries, Vol. 5, No. 3, July, 1910. It is most unfortunate that this, the only monograph on this important subject, has not been issued in a more popular and generally obtainable shape. It should be separately printed with Mr. Cole's subsequent additions which exist only in MSS.

of Southwestern lore, Charles F. Lummis.

Remembering the remoteness of Southern California from the routes of tourists until a comparatively recent date, we can understand why the most of the early Mission photographs were made by Watkins, whose prints have been copied and added to the sets sold by progressive photographers now doing business in Los Angeles and elsewhere.

The writer is glad that, as an amateur photographer, he visited San Diego Mission in 1887 and secured a dozen important views. It is a matter of regret now that other affairs interfered with his photographing more Missions at the same period. These are the only dated views of any of the Missions and several details are shown which have entirely disappeared through the lack of local interest to preserve. This is written as an incentive to induce others to make use of some of their photographic material and a little time and thus record by pictures historic conditions ere they are lost.

It is perhaps well to include in this paper, though foreign to its scope, a mention of Ford's Paintings and Etchings. These were made by Henry Chapman Ford of Santa Barbara. By thoughtless investigators too much importance is given these which, while meritorious in themselves and a pleasing addition to the pictorial record of the Missions, were, in but few cases, made from original sketches. Mr. Ford

in publishing his series of Etchings did important work in calling attention to the charm of the Missions. He sought little else beside the selling of his work. As it was expensive and took considerable time to visit and sketch many of the Missions he availed himself of Watkins' photographs as will clearly appear by a comparison where the Etching follows line by line the Photograph.

A careful classification of the various Mission photographs and the elimination of the copies made by present day men shows that we owe the greatest debt of gratitude to Carlton E. Watkins, whose views supplemented by certain work of Muybridge, Houseworth, Fiske, and the Southern California photographers named, practically complete the list of original views. So many errors have been made in copying and naming certain pictures that most careful collocation is necessary.

We must admit to the photographic list the sketches of Vischer owing to their photographic detail. He sought to render correct delineations rather than fancy pictures. We may justly add to his sketches another that has disappeared, made by an unknown hand, but which was photographed by Father Cichi, and which is the earliest sketch of Santa Clara.

In concluding this necessarily hastily prepared paper, the author wishes to state that the information is that gleaned mostly through personal knowledge of the several artists and their work and through personal acquaintance with many of them. No such sketch can be complete as constant search amid the dust of the past unexpectedly brings to light important evidence and occasionally an historically priceless picture. The earlier Daguerreotype of Santa Clara is but a single instance.

Much trash has been written regarding the Missions and much good paper and canvas have been wasted in reproducing unauthentic views of them. Ere it is too late every effort should be made to arrive at accuracy and publish the results of such search. Mr. Cole's admirable paper referred to is at present our only guide. He was the first to carefully investigate and record the results of his searchings. He dealt not only with photographs but all illustrations and paintings. His work was as exhaustive as time would permit to a man of most careful research and analytical determination. It is the writer's hope that the pioneer in writing on this subject may yet ere long give us the benefits of his fuller investigations.

Concepcion de Arguello

ALIFORNIA Romantic and Resourceful''; thus reads the title of the little volume in which Judge John F. Davis has given us the true facts of that sweetest of love-tales—the story of Concepcion de Arguello and Count von Rezanov. Prior to Judge Davis' researches, many of us, if we knew this story at all, knew it only as the fanciful imagining of Bret Harte's poetic soul. As had those of other lands, so too had we heard and, mayhap, admired the loves of Alexander and Thais, of Abelard and Heloise. nor did we dream that here on our own golden shores, beneath our own blue skies, a romance sadder, nobler, purer far than these had had its being. It is not our intention to recount that romance in the ''Redwood'' in all the fulness of the details that Judge Davis has made known. We reprint his version of Bret Harte's charming poem, for the reason that it is among the few pieces of literature in which the spirit and atmosphere of chivalric California of by-gone days are realistically and faithfully portrayed. It is our one hope that this ''Mission Redwood'' may aid in some degree in the preservation of that spirit and atmosphere in the people of California to-day.

It will prove of interest, we are sure, to most of our readers, to learn that to one, at least, still on earth, the name ''Concepcion de Arguello'' is vital with fondest memories. When A. M. Robertson published Judge Davis' book a copy was sent to the historian Zoeth S. Eldredge, who was very much interested in the history of Concepcion Arguello, concerning whom he had been corresponding with Mrs. Katherine Den Bell, of 234 West Islay street, Santa Barbara, a member of one of the oldest Spanish families of California, who, in her childhood personally knew ''the Beata'', as she was called for some time before she entered the Dominican Sisterhood. Mr. Eldredge immediately wrote Judge Davis, suggesting that he also send Mrs. Bell a copy of his book.

Judge Davis says that he felt more than repaid for all the labor of love he had bestowed on the story when he received a warm letter of appreciation from Mrs. Bell, in which, among other things, she said:

''The Treasure House of my childhood memories holds nothing lovelier than those that twine around the 'Beata's' historic name. They bring bursts of Spring into my heart! I learned my prayers at her knees; have cried and laughed in her arms; threaded her needles, fixed and unfixed her

194

COURTESY ARCHITECT AND ENGINEER, SAN FRANCISCO

sewing-box. And many a time, I remember waking, as the Mission bells rang the "Alba" (Dawn of day), to find her sweet pale face bending over me, signing my forehead with the Cross, and whispering her oft repeated blessing: "Dios te haga una Santita!" (God make you a little saint!). How memory is crowding me! I shall know her in Heaven by her tender, caressing voice.

"God's angels can not teach a purer love standard, nor bring us a brighter, sweeter fancy than that of Concepcion's life-long faithfulness to her girlhood's lover.

"Let me thank you in the Beata's name that, almost at the eleventh hour, it has been given me to hear another 'voice crying in the wilderness'."

And so, the author, who had started to try to find something substantial to what at first might have been supposed to be nothing more than a poet's fancy, ended by finding a living, loving human being, with a wonderful personal memory of the actual existence of one of the first nuns to join the Dominican order of California, of the woman who, in her radiant girlhood and tender womanhood had given California and the world the immortal love-story of the Presidio of San Francisco.

Concepcion de Arguello

(Presidio de San Francisco, 1806.)

By BRET HARTE.

Courtesy A. M. Robertson Co., San Francisco, Cal.

I.

Looking seaward, o'er the sand-hills stands the fortress, old and quaint,
By the San Francisco friars lifted to their patron saint,—
Sponsor to that wondrous city, now apostate to the creed,
On whose youthful walls the padre saw the angel's golden reed;
All its trophies long since scattered, all its blazon brushed away;
And the flag that flies above it but a triumph of to-day.
Never scar of siege or battle challenges the wandering eye.
Never breath of warlike onset holds the curious passer-by;

THE REDWOOD

)nly one sweet human fancy interweaves its threads of gold
With the plain and homespun present, and a love that ne'er grows old;
)nly one thing holds its crumbling walls above the meaner dust;
;isten to the simple story of a woman's love and trust.

II

)ount von Resanoff*, the Russian, envoy of the mighty Czar,
itood beside the deep embrasures, where the brazen cannon are.
He with grave provincial magnates long had held serene debate
)n the Treaty of Alliance and the high affairs of state;
He from grave provincial magnates oft had turned to talk apart
With the Commandante's daughter on the questions of the heart.
Jntil points of gravest import yielded slowly one by one,
And by Love was consummated what Diplomacy begun;
Fill beside the deep embrasures, where the brazen cannon are,
He received the two-fold contract for approval of the Czar;
Fill beside the brazen cannon the betrothed bade adieu,
And from sallyport and gateway north the Russian eagles flew.

III

Long beside the deep embrasures, where the brazen cannon are,
Did they wait the promised bridegroom and the answer of the Czar;
Day by day on wall and bastion beat the hollow, empty breeze,—
Day by day the sunlight glittered on the vacant, smiling seas;
Week by week the near hills whitened in their dusty leather cloaks,—
Week by week the far hills darkened from the fringing plain of oaks;
Fill the rains came, and far breaking, on the fierce southwester tost,
Dashed the whole long coast with color, and then vanished and were lost.
io each year the seasons shifted,—wet and warm and drear and dry;
Half a year of clouds and flowers, half a year of dust and sky.

---

*If the alleged facsimile of the chamberlain's signature, when written in
Roman alphabetical character, is as set forth in part 2 of the Russian publication,
"Istoritcheskoé Obosrénié Obrasovania Rossiisko-Amérikanskoi Kompanii", by P.
Tikhmenef, published, part 1 in 1861, and part 2 in 1863, by Edward Weimar, in
St. Petersburg, then the proper spelling is "Rezanov", the accent on the penult,
and the "v" pronounced like "ff".

For metrical purposes Bret Harte has here taken the same kind of liberty
with "Resanoff", and in another poem with Portola, as Byron took with Trafalgar,
in Childe Harold.

Still it brought no ship nor message,—brought no tidings, ill or meet,
For the statesmanlike Commander, for the daughter fair and sweet.
Yet she heard the varying message, voiceless to all ears beside; .
"He will come," the flowers whispered; "Come no more," the dry hills
  sighed.
Still she found him with the waters lifted by the morning breeze,—
Still she lost him with the folding of the great white-tented seas;
Until hollows chased the dimples from her cheeks of olive brown,
And at times a swift, shy moisture dragged the long sweet lashes down;
Or the small mouth curved and quivered as for some denied caress,
And the fair young brow was knitted in an infantine distress.
Then the grim Commander, pacing where the brazen cannon are,
Comforted the maid with proverbs, wisdom gathered from afar;
Bits of ancient observation by his fathers garnered, each
As a pebble worn and polished in the current of his speech;
" 'Those who wait the coming rider travel twice as far as he;'
'Tired wench and coming butter never did in time agree;'
" 'He that getteth himself honey, though a clown, he shall have flies;'
'In the end God grinds the miller;' 'In the dark the mole has eyes;'
" 'He whose father is Alcalde of his trial hath no fear.'—
And sure the Count has reasons that will make his conduct clear."
Then the voice sententious faltered, and the wisdom it would teach
Lost itself in fondest trifles of his soft Castilian speech;
And on "Concha", "Conchitita", and "Conchita" he would dwell
With the fond reiteration that the Spaniard knows so well.
So with proverbs and caresses, half in faith and half in doubt
Every day some hope was kindled, flickered, faded, and went out.

IV

Yearly, down the hill-side sweeping, came the stately cavalcade,
Bringing revel to vaquero, joy and comfort to each maid;
Bringing days of formal visit, social feast and rustic sport,
Of bull-baiting on the plaza, of love-making in the court.
Vainly then at Concha's lattice, vainly as the idle wind,
Rose the thin high Spanish tenor that bespoke the youth too kind;
Vainly, leaning from their saddles, caballeros, bold and fleet,
Plucked for her the buried chicken from beneath their mustang's feet;

So in vain the barren hillsides with their gay serapes blazed—
Blazed and vanished in the dust-cloud that their flying hoofs had raised.
Then the drum called from the rampart, and once more, with patient mien,
The Commander and his daughter each took up the dull routine,—
Each took up the petty duties of a life apart and lone,
Till the slow years wrought a music in its dreary monotone.

V

Forty years on wall and bastion swept the hollow idle breeze,
Since the Russian eagle fluttered from the California seas;
Forty years on wall and bastion wrought its slow but sure decay,
And St. George's cross was lifted in the port of Monterey;
And the citadel was lighted, and the hall was gayly drest,
All to honor Sir George Simpson, famous traveler and guest.†
Far and near the people gathered to the costly banquet set,
And exchanged congratulations with the English baronet;
Till, the formal speeches ended, and amidst the laugh and wine,
Some one spoke of Concha's lover,—heedless of the warning sign.
Quickly then cried Sir George Simpson: "Speak no ill of him, I pray!
He is dead. He died, poor fellow, forty years ago this day,—
"Died while speeding home to Russia, falling from a fractious horse.
Left a sweetheart, too, they tell me. Married, I suppose, of course!
"Lives she yet?" A deathlike silence fell on banquet, guests, and hall,
And a trembling figure rising fixed the awe-struck gaze of all.

---

†The mention of Monterey is a poetic license. Sir George Simpson actually met her and acquainted her for the first time with the immediate cause of her lover's death, while she was living with the De la Guerra family, after the death of her parents, at Santa Barbara, January 24, 1842. "Though Donna Concepcion," wrote Sir George Simpson, in 1847, "apparently loved to dwell on the story of her blighted affections, yet, strange to say, she knew not, till we mentioned it to her, the immediate cause of the chancellor's sudden death. This circumstance might in some measure, be explained by the fact that Langsdorff's work was not published before 1814; but even then, in any other country than California, a lady, who was still young, would surely have seen a book, which, besides detailing the grand incident of her life, presented so gratifying a portrait of her charms." (An Overland Journey Round the World, during the years 1841 and 1842, by Sir George Simpson, Governor-in-chief of the Hudson's Bay Company's Territories, published by Lea and Blanchard, Philadelphia, in 1847, page 207).

Two black eyes in darkened orbits gleamed beneath the nun's white hood;
Black serge hid the wasted figure bowed and stricken where it stood.
"Lives she yet," Sir George requested. All were hushed as Concha drew
Closer yet her nun's attire‡. "Senor, pardon, she died too!"

‡She did not actually receive the white habit till she was received into the
Dominican Sisterhood, April 11, 1851, by Padre F. Sadoc Vilarrasa, in the convent
of Santa Catalina de Sena (Convent of St. Catherine of Siena), at Monterey,
where she took the perpetual vow April 13, 1852, and where she remained continu-
ously till the convent was transferred to Benicia, August 26, 1854 (Original records,
Book of Clothings and Professions, page 1, now at Dominican College, at San
Rafael, Cal.) There being no religious order for women in California until the
Dominican Sisterhood was founded at Monterey, March 13, 1851, she had at first
to content herself with joining the Third Order of St. Francis "in the world", and
it was the dark habit of this secular order which constituted the "nun's attire" at
the time Sir George Simpson met her in 1842.

a e

A Tale of the California Seas.

A. J. Steiss, Jr.

S if a cold flurry of wind had suddenly puffed out the last flame of the sunset, the day died down in the West and with the long black shadow of the night there fell a . stillness, as though the sea were holding its breath. Only the slap of the wavelets and the sad mew of the sea-gulls about the masthead broke the intense and expectant silence that wrapped the "Aurora", rolling gently in the waves, just outside the harbor of San Francisco. The dim hills to the North of the bay had long since been enveloped in fog, as had the Presidio's ramparts, vanishing both, as a dream dies with the dawn. Theresa de Orea, standing in the doorway of her cabin, sighed. She was impatient. She had desired to reach San Francisco that evening, but the Captain would not dare the narrows in the fog, and so the ship lay motionless in the clammy grey solitude. In the next cabin, Theresa's guardian, the good Senora Ibanez, was reading, the light from her cabin falling in a yellow pool upon the oily depths of the water.. The lanterns fore and aft were but a dim blur in the mist.

Aside from these the deck was invisible.

Making her way to one of the lanterns, Theresa drew forth from somewhere beneath the black folds of her mantilla a tiny portrait at which she gazed long and earnestly. It was that of a youth, slim, dark, gallantly arrogant in appearance, and pleasing in countenance, with clear, lucid eyes. His hair was jet black. Something in his features bespoke the dominating force of his nature—a dreamer of lofty dreams. Beneath the painting were inscribed the words, Rafael Gonzales. Theresa was betrothed to Rafael and here in the land of promise she was at last to become his wife. Many years ago, so many in fact that her recollection of the event was a trifle uncertain the arrangements had been conducted by their parents in Madrid. Then she had received the announcement of the betrothal with indifference. But with months of companionship, her heart had opened, as the rose does, petal by petal, to the warm sunshine of Rafael's ardent nature. Then the lust of adventure had seized him and he had departed for California, little realizing the sorrow his going caused.

COURTESY THE OLYMPIAN. SAN FRANCISCO

CCURTESY THE OLYMPIAN. SAN FRANCISCO

COURTESY THE OLYMPIAN. SAN FRANCISCO

The weeks lengthened into months, the months into years, till Theresa became a woman, with all a woman's hopes and fears and all a woman's love. One day a letter came. Rafael had fared well he told her and was ready now to wed his 'Carissima''. Accordingly, though there were many delays, she had set sail, a queer choking in her throat as she watched the shores of her native land fade in the East, but a bright gleam in her eye for the fulfillment that was at last to come. Even yet it all felt fascinatingly strange and romantic.

Slowly she replaced the portrait in the folds of the mantilla. As she did so, her fingers came in contact with an envelope which her father, an official of the government, had entrusted to her for delivery at San Francisco, Curiosity in regard to its contents had been restrained only by tremendous effort, for Theresa was but human. Tonight, she knew, would be her final opportunity to peruse its contents. Returning to her cabin, she closed the door and with trembling fingers unloosed the cord which bound the packet. Within was a paper, sealed with the seal of Spain. She read it slowly, then re-read it again and again. Returning it to its place, she went out again to the deck.

Fog covered the lone wastes of water like a heavy pall. Black wavelets lapped the rolling sides of the "Aurora", while from an invisible somewhere the dull peals of a warning bell came solemnly. Suddenly in the darkness of the ocean she heard a sound as of a vessel parting the ripples. She stood for a moment shuddering in terror. Aft there was a jolt and a dark form leaped over the side in the mist. Another followed, and another, till softly, one by one, the pirates had gained the deck. Theresa, unperceived, darted to her cabin and bolted the stout door.

During the next few breathless minutes, she stood tense by the portal, listening to the sounds of the struggle, for by this time the crew had been aroused. After a time, things once more became quiet and footsteps were heard drawing near to where she was. She shrank instinctively into a corner. The footsteps paused and she heard in low tones, almost in a whisper, the words: "Senorita de Orea, do not be alarmed. No harm shall come to you."

Soon the straining of the cables, and the tossing, told her that the ship was in motion.

* * * *

When the dawn came, Theresa and her placid guardian were gazing from the small window in the cabin of the Senora. The golden lances of the rising sun pierced the dark green embroidery of an island, whither they now realized the ship's course was directed. Before long they heard the chains clank about the capstan as the anchor plunged in a beautiful little cove, set like an emerald in the glistening white sand.

A knock came at the door and the same voice that had addressed Theresa on the night previous, spoke: "Pardon,

Senoras, but you are captives for the present and shall be forced to remain here for some weeks. In the meantime the island is yours completely. You need have no fear.''

The Senora crossed over and opened the door. Before her stood a tall, bearded Castilian, his dark hair brushed by the wind across the bronze of his brow. His gaze met and held that of the Senora for a moment, but then turned and fastened inself upon the graceful figure by the casement. He regarded her with what seemed extraordinary interest. The Senora spoke: ''Thank you for your kindness,'' and closing the door, continued, ''Theresa, we need not worry, for the pirate is a true caballero. He will send to San Francisco for money and in a few weeks we shall be freed.''

Theresa was looking out at the sea.

* * * *

Theresa and her guardian spent most of their time wandering about the island. Days faded into nights of infinite quietude there in that lovely spot, and as the rosy, tapering fingers of the dawn loosed the violet mantle from the wide shoulders of the sky till days had become weeks, Theresa dreamed of her waiting lover.

One grey evening, when the low somber sky seemed to be swept by the lofty tops of the pines, and all the sweet choir of warblers was hushed, she emerged from the dark fringe of bushes onto the white slope of the beach. Half hidden by the purple shadows of the wood, she rested for a moment, her eyes searching the cove. On the opposite beach stood the pirate, barely discernible through the dusk. He was singing. A pretty song it was—scarcely such as one would expect to hear in a pirate's lair. Theresa straightened suddenly, her whole form quivering, for the notes were those of ''Maria Consolatrix'', the hymn her own Rafael had been wont to sing when his youthful dreams had been disturbed.

The next morning she did not wander on the island. All the night long she had lain sleepless, weeping and wondering in her heart. It was too strange, too unhappy. The days wore on and still she did not go ashore. Now her soft eyes attempted to fathom the still, dark depths of the water as though seeking there the answer to the riddle; now her graceful figure could be seen by the window, her gaze upturned to the stars as if in silent prayer.

One evening, just as the golden moon was rising behind the black fringe of the pines on the island she was roused from her abstraction by the sound of a soft voice beside her. Turning, she beheld the pirate. He drew closer to her. ''Senorita, pardon me,'' he said, ''the weeks have passed and I have not had the courage to tell you this tale before. May I trouble you to listen? I think that this story will be of interest to the Senorita. It is a tale of love.''

Theresa's countenance became rigid.

''In Spain, Senorita, there once lived a boy and a girl, who loved each other with a deep and tender love. One day the youth left Spain and set out for a far new land in the West. It was a sad parting, Senorita, but deep in their hearts there burned the hope of reunion. They had planned that when the youth had made his fortune, his 'Carissima' would join him in the distant land whither he was to sail. And, Senorita, the girl did sail from the shores of Spain, for her lover had written that he was ready. He told her that he had made his fortune. But, Senorita, he did not tell her that he had gained it by piracy, when all other means had failel —but it was so. He determined that when he wedded he would give up his wild ways forever, and indeed he purchased a "Hacienda" for their estate. Soon after he had written for the girl his guilt was discovered, and he was sought for his many crimes. Offering restitution, he petitioned the King of Spain for his pardon, praying for its early arrival. But it did not come, and his love was now on the ocean. For obvious reasons, neither he nor his band could appear in the harbor to meet the ship. He saw but one way out of his difficulty—he determined to seize the ship before she entered the harbor. In a few weeks a companion would bring him and his sweetheart to the "Hacienda" farther South. But in the meantime, he realized that it would be necessary to hold the ship's crew in captivity, lest they spread the alarm among the soldiers of the Presidio. One foggy night he accomplished his purpose, and guided the ship to his lair—an island. Weeks passed. Then on the day that the comrade was to bear them south-

ward to the "Hacienda" the youth pondered deeply over it all. Senorita, he saw then how foolish he had been— he saw how unworthy he was of the maid whom he had planned to wed. And Senorita, he resolved to free her."

Theresa gasped.

"He but asks forgiveness for his presumption," said the tall pirate, averting his eyes.

"Did you believe that I would be unfaithful?" asked Theresa.

"No, Theresa. But you must go. You could not marry a pirate. And now, you do not bid farewell to your lover of old Spain but to someone else who has arisen in his stead."

"And who is he?"

"It does not matter, Senorita.'

"Please—"

"He is the pirate, Pablo Ruiz, Senorita."

The girl's hand, resting on the man's shoulder, trembled.

"What was the name, Rafael?"

"Pablo Ruiz."

"Madre Maria! we are saved. For here is the pardon for Pablo Ruiz, come from the King of Spain!" Fumbling in her mantilla, Theresa had produced a long packet—the document she had opened on the "Aurora" the night that Rafael had seized the ship.

* * * *

And when the moon's silvery rays fell full upon the lagoon, no ship rolled in the gold lane of the waters. And on the island, the night wind whispered of Romance, with only the birds to hear.

The Palo Alto Big Tree

H. C. Peterson.

HE Palo Alto Big Tree was in 1769 the objective point of that first little band of tourists under Portola, immediately after visiting the vicinity of San Francisco, as today it is the objective point of thousands of Eastern tourists after their visit to the greatest city on the Pacific Coast. One hundred and fifty years ago—but what a marvellous change.. A marvellous change in all but the Big Tree, that tall, silent sentinel at the entrance to the Santa Clara Valley, defiant alike to time and the elements, though having a hard struggle against the inroads of man.

More questions have been asked concerning this tree, and, I must confess, not always satisfactorily answered, than about any landmark in this section of the state.

The first historical entry concerning it was made by Portola, Nov. 6th, 1769 —"We travelled, skirting this arm of the sea or port (S. F. Bay) and halted in a level place thickly overgrown with oak trees and surrounded by many villages, from which there came out to meet us one hundred and twenty natives. Here we had much water and pasture."*

Portola's men were tired, they were hungry, and so were their mules. This was an ideal place to camp, at the foot of the Big Tree. So they camped. For four days Portola and his men enjoyed their rest, all except Sergeant Ortega and eight men, who were ordered to make a trip around the bay, via what is now Mountain View and Santa Clara, and up the East side as far as they could go. Berkeley Hills was the limit reached by Ortega. On their return, they reported the results of their observations, camp was broken, and the whole party returned to San Diego.

The next party of explorers camping here that has particular interest for us, was headed by Captain Rivera and Father Palou. Rivera had been with Portola on his first trip and was very enthusiastic about the Palo Alto tree and the vicinity. They arrived about noon, Nov. 28th, 1774.

Immediately after camp was made, Rivera and Father Palou took a trip around through the trees and along the

*That this entry relates to the Palo Alto Big Tree is verified in the records of the later exploring expeditions.

COURTESY THE MONITOR, SAN FRANCISCO

COURTESY THE MONITOR, SAN FRANCISCO

bank of the creek. Father Palou writes in his diary—"At two o'clock this afternoon six unarmed gentiles visited the camp and stayed till evening. They behaved themselves very gently, had good faces, and most of them wore beards. I made the sign of the cross upon them all. They paid good attention to the ceremony, which they did not understand, nor its purpose. . . . Inasmuch as this place is very near the estuary which runs into the arm of the sea, and that it possesses everything for a mission, it appeared good to the commander and to me to mark it with the standard of the Holy Cross. We constructed the cross of strong timber and planted it on the bank of the arroya near the ford where we camped. We added our good wishes that on the same spot a church might be erected in honor of my Seraphic Father, St. Francis, whom I named as my intercessor, in order that His Divine Majesty might grant me to see it in my days, and to see all the numerous pagans that inhabit the surrounding country subject to our Faith."

It appeared to Father Palou that here was everything that could be desired for a mission. He lost no time but immediately ordered a cross to be made of oak. This was whitened and erected near the Big Tree. All that was necessary now to secure the mission was the approval of Father Serra.

"Mission Palo Alto!" Why was Father Palou's dream never realized? I have heard different explanations of why the idea was abandoned. When the report was made to Father Serra he arranged for an expedition to go and investigate the site. Father Palou had been there in late November after the early rains had started the grass and the creek was running full with water, for in those days the creek was comparatively shallow and the forestation on the mountain sides kept full the many springs that fed the San Francisquito creek.

When Father Serra's expedition arrived it was late summer, everything was brown and but little water was in evidence. They made an adverse report. I had many talks with Estocquio Valencia before he died and he told me that his uncle, Francisco Guerrero, for many years Alcalde of Yerba Buena, maintained that the real reason was a strategic one. It was too close to the Dolores site, and would be too close to one that must of necessity be established near the end of the bay, where the roads would diverge, one to Dolores and the other to the missions that were to be located on the East side of the bay. Hence, Santa Clara was chosen instead as the location for a mission and school. Thus we behold a peculiar chain of circumstances that came to fruition a century later—Portola camps at Stanford, sends Ortega around the bay until he reaches Berkeley, Father Palou chooses Palo Alto as the mission site, Father Serra decides on Santa Clara. Today, all three places contain the greatest educational centers of the Pacific Coast.

In 1775-76, Father Serra desired to start a colony at the Port of St. Francis. Anza and Father Pedro Font headed the party bound for the Golden Gate. Pedro Font went along as chaplain and map-maker, that future expeditions might have the benefit of reliable guidance through unknown trails.

It was while examining copies of the two maps made by Font, now in the John Carter library at Providence, R. I., that I discovered something that has since been of great interest to all of us, something absolutely unique—a picture of the Palo Alto Big Tree, drawn in its proper location on both the 1776 and 1777 maps, the latter taking in but part of Central California. The trails are clearly shown as is also the ford, practically where the County Road crosses now. Thus the Big Tree has the honor of being the first organic landmark to be shown upon the first detail maps of California. From that time to this, the tree has been of the keenest interest to all of us.

"Why did the tree grow there all alone?. I always thought they grew only in the canyons of the mountains." Thousands of times, while at the Stanford museum, has that question been put me.

The answer is furnished by Professor Geo. B. Pierce, of the department of Botany at Stanford. "Centuries ago, the site of Palo Alto was the mouth or delta of the San Francisquito creek. As it entered the lowlands, say at Camp Fremont, it spread out over the land fanwise, depositing the silt from the mountains. Some time during a heavy freshet, a few Redwood seeds were washed down from the hills and took root.. The strongest survived and in time became the Big Tree. The strange part of it all is, that it should have ever grown down here in the valley, far from the deep, shady, moist canyons where lies its true habitat. Its growth on the barren bank of the creek is remarkable when we take into consideration the heat of the summer and the cold, frosty days of winter. It needs a great deal of water, a tree the size of this one taking up through its small roots literally hundreds of tons of water annually. Part of this water must be taken to the extreme top of the tree. It needs a great deal of nourishment. Without it, it will die." And this brings us down to a very serious question: What are we going to do to preserve our Big Tree? Berkeley is worrying over her famous oak, Oakland has an old oak tree in the center of the city. It is also dying. We are all working for a solution of the same trouble.

Originally we had two trees, virtually twin trees. During a heavy winter storm some forty years ago, the one nearest the creek broke off. Governor Stanford immediately ordered a wooden bulkhead to be built against the creek bank to protect the other tree. Later a concrete bulkhead, about fifteen feet high was put in. Above this, in 1909, the railroad company built another concrete wall of fifteen feet. Owing to the constant removal of gravel through many years, the creek bed is now nearly thirty feet below the trunk of the tree. This simply means that in addition to the battling against the effects of a hot sun and of coal-smoke, the tree must send its roots thirty feet farther down inasmuch as the soil above has become thoroughly drained by the end of summer.

The tree stands on an elevation of 70.5 ft. It rises 137.7 ft. above the ground. It is 23.1 ft. in circumference at a height of four feet. Its age? Well, that it is a matter that has not, as yet been definitely determined, though it is probably between 750 and 1000 years old. This old redwood tree, living under such unfavorable conditions, fighting a grim fight with time, has become so tough and hard that ordinary rules of time measurement as applied to Redwoods cannot apply here.

As the years go by we notice a gradual thinning out in the foliage of the tree, while the dead limbs are becoming more and more visible. For several months a few of us have been making a careful study of the problem and hope to be able, very shortly, to make a report to the City Council which will enable them, with the co-operation of the Southern Pacific, to arrest the process of decay and once more restore the tree to its former healthy beauty.

This will mean the transportation from the mountain canyons of tons of leafy mold and rich soil, the installation of a thorough watering system, the erection of a still higher retaining wall and—protection from souvenir vandals.

The Palo Alto Historical Society, in conjunction with the D. A. R. and the Native Sons and Daughters, plans to appropriately mark the spot with a bronze tablet. This movement was well under way when the war broke out, when it was put aside to be resumed about a month ago.

The Big Tree means very much to us. Since the day when Father Palou planted the cross at its foot it has been symbolic of education. It was the inspiration for the cover of the Stanford Palo Alto when Holbrook Blinn brought out the first issue on the day when the University was dedicated. It was the inspiration for the great seal of Stanford. In every history of this section it appears. It is pointed out to thousands in the passing trains: When you pass the Big Tree you will be in Santa Clara County. A County landmark, a State landmark, and, educationally, an International landmark, let us put forth every effort to preserve it for generations yet to come.

H. G. WANDERER   J. E. HEIN

UNIVERSITY ELECTRIC CO.

House Wiring and Motor Work
a Specialty

834 FRANKLIN STREET   SANTA CLARA, CA

If It's Made of Paper
We Have It !

The San Jose Paper Co

Phone San Jose 200
161-181 W. SANTA CLARA ST.

LOUIS CHABRE & JEAN MILLET, Props.   Phone San Jose 47

PARISIAN BAKERY
FRENCH AND AMERICAN BREAD
PIES AND CAKES

Pain de Luxe, French Rolls, Parisian, Richelieu, Rolls Fendu, Vienna Rolls, Etc.

Automobiles deliver to all parts of city   251 W. San Fernando St., San Jo

---

A. G. COL CO.
Wholesale Commission Merchant

Telephone San Jose 309

201-221 North Market Street   San Jose, Cal.

CONTENTS

VARSITY BASKETBALL TEAM

DIAZ, FERRARIO, MUTH, BAKER, COCHRAN, COMAN, MANELLI, CAPTAIN, O'NEIL, NEEDLES, PECAROVICH, BANNON, ARGENTI, O'CONNOR, MANAGER, HARMON, COACH

Entered Dec. 18, 1902, at Santa Clara, Cal., as second-class matter, under Act of Congress of March 3, 1879

VOL. XIX   SANTA CLARA, CAL., APRIL, 1920   NO. 5

Windings

OWN thro' the meadowlands robed in green,
Laughing so happily---joyous and gay,
Seizing the beams of a cloud-flecked sheen,
. Bearing them hurriedly far away---
Into the woodland hued · with Spring,
Kissing the lips of the buttercups there,
Making the stillness with music ring;
Wetting the wings of a butterfly fair,
The tinkling brook danced onward.

Down thro' a garden where song-birds call,
Catching the image of innocent eyes---
Dark as the pools where the wood shades fall
Clear as the depths that mirror the skies---
Farther along where the willows weep,
Low o'er a grave where the leaves have blown
And sad winds wail o'er a child asleep,
Lying so silent and so alone,
The brook stole softly onward.

A. J. STEISS, JR.

April Showers

Henry C. Veit.

April showers bring May flowers.—Proverb.

"ABIE! Vere are you goin'?" It was more of a command than a request. But Abraham Goldberg throughout his twenty-two years of life under the Goldberg roof had become accustomed to such curtness. More so of late since Ruth, the pretty little stenographer of his father's supposedly best friend Blair, had enshrined herself in the heart of Abie.

"Papa", as Abie was wont to call his parent, disapproved of the girl. He could not however, offer one sound argument why his son should discontinue his frequent calls at Ruth's home, or at Blair's office where he stopped frequently under the pretext of being about his father's business. There was a possibility of marriage and Nathan Goldberg could find in such a union no advantage, no increment to his worldly stores by reason of it. He would not admit it, even to himself, nevertheless this was his sole reason for objecting.

Now Blair's daughter he thought the real helpmate, the ideal wife for his boy, Abie. With her as a daughter-in-law, his business relations with Blair would be fortified. With her in the family the transfer of real estate down in Florida would be assured him. Blair had always been willing to expatiate upon its value as a factory site, how northern manufacturers were forced to seek southern fields in which to build, how he needed ready cash, but not quite so badly as to let such a valuable tract go until a very reasonable price had been paid him.

Nathan wanted to invest his hard earned capital in an investment which, in a few years, would net him handsome returns. Then he could retire. Blair's tract of five thousand acres was his air castle. With title to it in his own name, he could divide it and then subdivide it. Then northern manufacturers would come to him almost on bended knee and pay him a handsome profit for his land, for the privilege of starting factories on virgin soil. All this if Abie would only win the hand of Blair's daughter. She could induce her father to sell for a lower figure, Nathan's estimate.

Nathan Goldberg was doting on this as he watched the passing April shower from the window of his home. The pitter-patter of the rain without swallowed

210

up whatever slight noises Abie's surreptitious advance to the opposite and outer door made. Then a rustle of Abie's ulster awakened Nathan from his day dream.

"Vere are you goin', Abie;" repeated Nathan.

"To the club, papa," came the reply.

Then observing that Abie was dressed with a bit more ostentation than was his customary wont, except on such occasions as he chose to call upon Ruth, Nathan's eyes narrowed and he remarked: "Und do you alvays dress up like dot ven you go to the club?"

"Why papa, can't I dress up if I want to?" put in Abie.

"Most certainly Abie. But tell me why do you alvays buy dem orchards und vilets und candies? Do you take dem to the club too? Vhy you show all de stymtoms of bein' in luf wid dat Ruth goil."

Abie's silence gave his assent.

"Abie don't be foolish. She is no goil for you."

"But papa she is all right," remonstrated Abie.

"Did you heard vot I said, Abie," angrily put in Nathan, "she is no goil for you."

Nathan pondered a moment then his tone grew conciliatory. Experience had taught him that such was the best way to deal with his boy.

"Take dot Blair goil, Abie," continued Nathan, "Ah! She's a nice goil Abie. She's the goil I vant you to mar-

ry. Don't break papa's heart Abie, but marry the goil I vant."

His tone grew pleading.

"You marry the goil Abie und then Blair vill sell me the real estate und Abie, ve vill get rich."

Abie had heard the story before. How his father had started in life penniless, how he had earned a living as an umbrella mender, then the first little shop he had bought, then the larger one until finally he was permanently located with a bank account of some twenty odd thousands.

"All this Abie, I earned, und now you don't vant to help papa get rich."

Abie had listened to his father more out of politeness. His mind had been made up to see his own plan through, long before Nathan had begun his plea.

"Well, good-bye papa," he put in abruptly and with a somewhat nonchalant air he made for the door.

Nathan stood there blankly listening to Abie's footsteps become fainter and fainter as he hurried down the outer stairs. He heard the hall door slam, then he turned to the opposite corner of the room where hung a number of old umbrellas, the first of his stock in his first little umbrella store.

His eyes were moist as he removed the bundles from their peg on the wall. Fondling them, he recalled the many hours of anxiety he was wont to endure twenty-five years ago, ekeing out a meagre pittance at their expense. Then the familiar hum of his little motor came up to him from the street below.

Going to the window he hurriedly lifted the sash and espied Abie driving madly down the muddy avenue.

The rain beat in upon Nathan's face. "Abie! Abie!" he called after him, cupping his hands about his mouth that his son might better hear his command, "you'll spoil de new paint und gasoline is twenty-two cents a gallon, Abie."

But the car veered and careened on down the street.

Nathan closed the window and turned back to his treasured umbrellas, mumbling the while of the foolishness of Abie in taking out his repainted 1913 model Ford in such rainy weather. He wiped the rain from his face with a red bandana and blurted: "Dot Ruth goil vill ruin Abie und me yet."

He found some consolation in cutting loose a string of Yiddish invective and hurling it at Abie and the girl. The umbrellas seemed to jeer at him as if to say: "We've made you once and we'll have to make you again."

The mere possibility of it galled Nathan. He bundled them up and thrust them back upon their peg on the wall. Nathan did not realize that an April shower had begun in his life which soon was to bring forth a May flower.

A knock sounded upon the door. "Come in!" called Nathan with expectancy ringing in his tone.

The door opened and the huge proportions of Blair filled the doorway. He was a square-shouldered man with a rubicund face, a square jaw and a peculiarly keen piercing eye. Under his arm he carried a rolled up map and blue prints.

Brushing off the tiny beads of rain that bedecked his clothing, Blair entered and crossed over to the chair proffered by Nathan. He shook Goldberg's hand and made inquiries regarding his spirits.

"No, Mr. Blair," returned Nathan, "you're wrong. I never vas a drinking man und ven the country vent dry I didn't stock my cellar."

Blair burst into hearty laughter.

"No, no Nathan, you misunderstand me. I mean how are you?"

"Vell," he answered with a shrug of his shoulders, "so, so. Und may I ask Mr. Blair, vat brings you here so early in the day? Has the real estate raised?"

Nathan thought it likely as Blair had intimated but two days before that the eagerness of northern men to buy in the south, particularly Florida, would make the rise shortly forthcoming.

Blair's answer in the negative dispelled the anxious look on Nathan's face. He was all aglow presently as he watched Blair spread the blue prints and map on the table before him.

"This," began Blair, indicating by means of a pencil the exact spot neatly divided up into sections, "is the Loveall tract, Nathan. As fine a piece of land as ever anyone attempted to buy. It is particularly adaptable to excellent manufacturing sites. Here you are connected with a railroad and about three-quarters of a mile westward you have an incomparable water outlet. The advantage this tract has over others farther inland is readily apparent. Your railway and waterway facilities are second to none.''

Nathan could remember only up to this point. From here fancy took wings and fluttered off into a veritable manufacturing city, where the wheels of industry never ceased their turning and where the shekels eternally rolled into Goldberg's coffers, welling over their bulging sides in waves of gold. Nathan succumbed to the spell of money magic.

"Und vat is de price of dis land, Mr. Blair?''

Goldberg thought $30,000 a conservative estimate. He was willing to pay that much even if he had to mortgage the store, but Jew-like he wanted to angle about for a smaller sum.

"Well, Nathan, it's a shame to let it go for $30,000, but I guess I'll have to. I need the money.''

Goldberg threw up his hands as if it were an impossible price and began pacing the floor.

"Dat's an awful lot of money, Mr. Blair! Und me a poor man.''

He stopped a moment and posed as if in deep thought.

"Of course,'' he continued, "if you vill let it go for $20,000, $15,000 cash und a mortgage on my business, I vould buy villingly.''

"I don't think I could even consider it, Nathan. Greenbaum offered me $30,000 yesterday, but I was reluctant to sell it for this reason; he wanted two years in which to pay the price and I don't think I can afford to wait that long. It's ready cash I need and have to have. However, $30,000 even in two years time is better by far than your offer.''

Blair arose and began to roll up his map and blue prints. Nathan grew uneasy and made haste to offer him $25,000 with the mortgage on the store. After much apparent and mature deliberation Blair consented, offering as his reason for selling at such a remarkably low figure, the fact of their short though intimate friendship and the hope that the two families would be forever united through a marriage between their respective offsprings.

As Goldberg hastily made out his check for the amount, Blair smiled the smile of the victor. Nathan on the other hand experienced a recrudescence against Abie for not having followed his advice the sooner. Perhaps it would have saved him five or ten thousand.

As Blair took his leave Nathan took to dreaming once more. At any other time he might have asked Blair to stay for dinner, but too absorbed in his plans for a bright and a gold-bearing future, he quite forgot such a thing as etiquette ever existed. It mattered little to him in his present high frame of mind.

The chimes pealing forth from the ancient clock reminded him he was long overdue at the store. Hurriedly he donned a heavy raincoat, and in passing the old umbrellas suspended from their peg on the wall, he tossed toward them:

"Vell old pals, you go vid me to de new place even ven I do get rich."

Supper time came upon the jubilant Nathan ere he realized it. He had not even noticed Abie's absence from the store the entire day. Now, as he walked briskly along he wanted the companionship of the boy, to talk to him of his new plans and the riches that were soon to be theirs. He hoped Abie would be at home awaiting him.

A telegram instead greeted him as he pushed open the door. There it lay upon the floor directly at his feet. He always had an abhorrence of the yellow sheets. To him they could be nothing but purveyors of bad news. Opening it he read with startled eyes:

"Papa, Ruth and I were married this afternoon. Wire your blessings to Grand Hotel, Greenville. We leave tomorrow evening for South.

Abie."

Goldberg was speechless for the moment. Then a torrent of Yiddish, the epitome of his disapproval was all the parental encouragement Abie could hope to get in his new station in life from his father.

It took a deal of arguing with himself to finally persuade Nathan to send the following to Abie:

"You disobeyed papa and are no longer a son of mine.   Papa."

The morning paper precipitated another shower in Nathan Goldberg's life. He was reluctant to believe himself fully awake as he read it. Once, twice,

a dozen times, he perused the article and always the same.

"GIGANTIC REAL ESTATE SWINDLE DISCOVERED," were the glaring headlines. Then in smaller caption, "R. G. Blair & Co., a fraud."

Nathan found it some little effort to prevent himself from collapsing. Soon he mustered up sufficient courage to read in detail the lengthy article covering the entire page of the morning daily. He learned of how he had been swindled out of his entire store of worldly goods, how Blair had been selling swamp lands down in Florida for good tenantable acres.

By a single act Nathan had been sent back twenty-five years, penniless once more with nothing to call his own save the little bundle of umbrellas that had stood by him all these years.

After a period of long duration in which conflicting emotions surged within him, he picked his laboured steps over to the corner and removed the old treasures from their place on the wall.

"Ve did it vunce," he intoned, "and ve can do it again. Back to mending umbrellas, ve go. It vill take some little time but den ve'll buy a shop und start over again. Abie, I vant you. Come back und help papa."

An hour later Abie and his wife were reading this telegram at the Grand Hotel in Greenville:

"Abie. Papa bought 5000 gallons of real estate in Florida for $25,000 und gave his business to boot. Abie come back to papa quick.   Papa."

The afternoon train deposited the newlyweds in their native city, and a few minutes later they gained admittance to the Goldberg household.

"Abie," said Nathan, after the first greeting was over, "I'm a poor man. But ve're goin' to start over agáin, Abie. You und me is goin' to mend umbrellas, Abie. Und ven ve get fixed Abie, Papa don't buy any more real estate."

"No, papa," said Abie with much gusto, "we don't have to mend umbrellas." And, taking from Ruth's hand bag, the check and the mortgage deed passed them over to the dumbfounded Nathan. Another speechless period overcame him. But Abie observing the quizzical look in his father's eye hastened on to explain how Ruth was really the good girl Nathan had disliked to credit her with being, how she came to realize Blair's crookedness and seeing the check and mortgage in Blair's open safe but a few hours after he had received them, took both to make restitution to their rightful owner.

Nathan's happiness was profound. He crossed over to the window to observe the clear sunshine bringing to light the freshness the late April shower had wrought. And in his own Hebrew way he came to realize that May flowers are really the result of April showers be it humanly speaking or in the order of nature.

"Abie," he said after a moment, "vot became of the Ford?"

But Abie and Ruth did not hear.

Two Thousand

Frank Maloney.

CHARLEY WHITE was in sore distress. He was in love with a certain fair young lady—who wanted a pearl necklace. When she had hinted about this to him, he chivalrously favored—and promised—the purchase of the string of jewels. So one fine Sunday evening they went to the movies, stopping to gaze at the much-coveted stones on the way—and Charlie spied the price! Two thousand dollars! O boy. Two thousand dollars! How was he ever going to get it? And all the while his loved one ignorantly and blissfully gazed on, dreaming fondly of the treasure so soon to be her own.

They finally left the fascinating window and proceeded to the movies. During the entire show, she did little else but thank her "dear boy" for his present; to her "dear boy's" decided discomfort. It was a good thing for both of them, possibly, that the place was dark, otherwise——

When the entertainment was over they left and took a car home. On arriving at their destination, she invited him in, as young ladies should "dear boys" about to give a present. However, in the course of a couple of hours he was able to find a good excuse to leave.

She accompanied him to the door. "Now, dear, thanks awfully for your beautiful present. I never expected it, really I didn't. Oh, how could you be so kind! I'm sure I really will never be able to repay you!"

He mumbled something under his breath, which she took to be an answer. It was—but had she heard it, something might have happened!

As he walked down the street, the question uppermost in his mind was, "How in the world am I ever going to buy that for her? By the way she talks, you'd think I was J. P. Morgan himself. Good lord. What a pickle."

He got to the corner and waited for a car. When it finally came, he climbed dismally up the steps and dropped into the nearest seat. Having nothing else to do he picked up a discarded newspaper and glanced listlessly over it. Suddenly his eyes bulged from their sockets. He read an article in the sheet through several times as though his very life depended on it.

* * * * *

The Pleasanton grandstand was a

seething mass of humanity. The day was fair and all the people from the surrounding country had come to see the motorcycle races. The track itself could not have been in better condition. It had been sprinkled and rolled down that morning until there wasn't a bit of dust stirring. To be sure, the contestants had ridden around it several times, but they hadn't attained speed enough to cut it up a great deal.

At two-thirty, twelve cycles were sent off three at a time every two minutes. Thus it happened that the last man to leave was a little red-headed fellow on a Harley. With a roar he gave her the gas and shot off at a clip that was exceedingly hard on tires. But that didn't bother him; his idea it seemed, being to win the race, irrespective of tires or anything else for the matter of that.

"My God, he'll be killed." exclaimed a spectator as the racer took the lower turn at a forty mile clip. After what seemed an eternity he straightened out and opened his throttle. His machine jumped ahead by leaps and bounds, smoke shooting from its exhausts. Slackening a bit he took the upper curve. But once around it, he shot over the course at a rate of seventy miles an hour.

After fifty such miles of riding he had left all but three of the field hopelessly behind. Suddenly, the attention of the spectators was riveted on the two machines racing neck and neck toward the curve! The closer they came to it, the faster they seemed to go! They hit it at sixty per! There was a great cloud of dust; every heart was stilled! When the spectators could see again, they beheld one cycle coming like the wind—the other, was nowhere in sight! Instead, two ambulances were speeding toward the spot where the wreck lay.

"My, Lord," someone muttered, "I knew he'd get it at the clip he was traveling!"

The speaker turned toward the track again. He looked! No! It couldn't be true! Yes, it was! The man on the Harley was still coming! And he didn't seem to know when his machine was doing its best.

By the time the seventy-fifth mile was passed, he had moved up into second place. The man who had been there had been forced to stop at his pit on account of engine trouble. So now there were only two left on the track, Joe Miller, the state champion, and the Redhead.

The spectators drew their breaths. They know they were about to witness one of the greatest struggles between cycles ever seen in the West. Those who were acquainted with Joe Miller knew he would do all in his power to win the contest fairly. Furthermore, everybody felt that the other man was as great a dare-devil as his opponent. Many an onlooker, fully expected to see one of the two carried off the field in an ambulance.

Only ten miles to go! The champion was a length ahead of his opponent, but on his begoggled, grimy face there was a worried expression. Twice around the track again, and Miller was but half a length ahead! Thrice more they passed the stands—and six inches was all that kept the "dark horse" from evening things up.

By this time the stands were in an uproar. Every spectator was on his feet, cheering either or both of the contestants on to victory. Suddenly, every voice was stilled! The cyclists were again on the straightaway! The onlookers strained their eyes to see who was in the lead. And as the roaring, two-wheeled monsters shot past them, they saw that they were even!

And how they went! Smoke, dust, and dirt half-obscured them from the vision of the multitude.

"My God, they'll surely be killed!" someone yelled in agony.

And the words seemed true. Both riders took the curve at top speed! The machines seemed to hesitate, go straight ahead, to skid from under their guiders! A great cloud of dust arose, and it seemed as though the cycles had crashed! A woman screamed. Two ambulances set off toward the scene of the accident at top speed!

But lo! When the people looked again, they saw the racers going down the straightaway, neck and neck, and at top speed. They took the upper curve as they had taken the lower.

They passed the stands on their last mile. Not a sound was heard, except that of the roaring of their motors. Not a spectator dared to speak. When they took the lower curve inches seemed to separate them! They straightened out and headed toward the upper turn and —victory!

Now three hundred yards separated them from the finish!

Now two hundred!

Now, one hundred!!

Now fifty—still they were wheel and wheel!

Suddenly Miller's motor missed fire a couple of times—then it resumed its song! Yet in that short time, his opponent drew ahead six inches—and held the advantage! A moment more and they had crossed the line—the "sorrel-top" a winner by half a foot!!!

With that, bedlam broke loose. Both men were vociferously cheered, for both men had fought bravely and gamely.

When the winner arrived at his pit on the next lap, admirers nearly smothered him in an endeavor to shake his grimy hands. Suddenly, someone elbowed his way through the crowd and cried:

"Of all things! What in the world are you going to do next?"

The rider looked at the speaker and smiled wearily.

"Tom, old man," he said, "the next thing I'm going to do is to get that necklace."

Easter Lily

UPON the altar's snowy breast
　　Thou shrink'st in self-oblation,
As gentle as some prayerful nun
　　In breathless adoration.

Most fair of Nature's handiwork,
　　Bowed down in meek petition---
Most pure of Nature's virgin realm,
　　A-droop in soft contrition---

May our souls learn from thy sweet air
　　The glory of humility---
May our hearts draw from thy chaste mien
　　The secret of thy purity.

MARTIN M. MURPHY

Through the Pines

A. J. Steiss, Jr.

I.

HE breeze that blew in through the doorway of the Dead Pine Grocery was gratefully cool. It carried more of the pleasant aroma of the mountains, and less of their fine, red dust. Dead Pine was peacefully silent under the dusk; only the crickets chirped in the grass in the clearing; and the tall, black pines that frowned upon the low building, whispered softly among themselves.

Bulger, with his wrists bound behind him, sprawled in a chair in the grocery. His slouch hat shaded his large features from the dull rays of a lantern suspended from a rafter above him. When his glance turned from the contemplation of his large boots, to the two forms by the door, he was aware of Sheriff Foster's eyes, gleaming from out his bearded countenance, through the semi-darkness of the room. Bedloe, proprietor of Dead Pine Grocery, leaning lazily against the open door, seemed chiefly concerned with the upward progress of the moon.

Foster yawned. "Ef I'm going to take ye to Buckeye Station to-night," he said to Bulger, "I reckon it's time we moved. Get up." The outlaw stood. Foster slipped the noose of a rawhide lariat about Bulger's gaunt figure, and the end he knotted securely to his own arm. Then he ambled to the doorway. On the counter someone had inadvertently left a clasp-knife. Bulger edged toward it with his keen eyes fixed on the broad shoulders of Foster; his hand closed on it and he stepped into the moonlight. Bedloe followed their receding figures into the shadow of the pine-arched road, with characteristic listless abstraction. Suddenly his recumbent figure straightened, and he gazed earnestly into the darkness. "Cracky!" he said, "I fergot t' borry a smoke!" And the door of the Dead Pine Grocery slammed with a crash that startled the woods.

* * * * *

They had emerged from the pines and the moon shone full upon the roadway, when Foster and the outlaw saw the clustered buildings of Buckeye, clearly outlined against the shadowy hillside below them. Somewhere beneath a horse neighed loudly; and on the opposite mountain a wolf howled at the moon. Again the two figures approached the dark tunnel of the pines; Bulger turned and glanced at the sheriff; and the seamed face with the ragged mustache in the pale light filled Foster with an uneasy tremor. Then the shadows enfolded them, Bulger first, and the sheriff following with the lariat bound to his arm. . . . Foster noted that the lariat's length had slackened, and he stopped. At the same instant a fitful gust swayed the black bough of a pine, and as the white spotlight of the heavens cast its circle of brightness upon the stage of this strange drama, Foster saw the outlaw, crouched in his path, a knife gleaming in his hand.

In a trice Foster was upon him, and the weapon flew into the thicket. Foster wrapped his arms about Bulger's neck, as the man fell to his knees. With a mighty effort, Bulger rose, and the huge figure of his antagonist was projected over his shoulders, his head striking the road with stunning impact. The sheriff of Dead Pine Camp lay silent. Bulger plunged into the thicket. For a time the crackling of the underbrush gave index to his path, but soon there was no sound.

II.

In a stupor, Foster had walked in the night far beyond Buckeye Station, and when the morning breeze fluttered the tree-tops, and the blazing beams of the morning sun fell warmly over the pines, he was on a strange road. His long hair blew down into his eyes, and his beard was wet with dew. He looked about him with interest. Far below him in the valley a silver stream coursed among the green fields; behind him the forest rose, silent and austere in its majesty. To the westward the road sloped downward, losing itself in its own aimless meanderings.

Foster rubbed his chin. Strange, but for the life of him, he could not remember how he had come there. The locality puzzled him; he did not remember the valley or the river. . . . The sombre curtain of forgetfulness had dropped over the stage of his past existence, and had lifted upon a new drama under the guidance of the Great Director.

* * * * *

Foster wandered among the Sierras and into the distant valley till the snows passed, and a summer shone once more. But out of the flotsam and jetsam of the great Stream of Destiny, two figures emerged, and the hand of the Great Director brought them together once more at the mines in Dead Pine Camp. Bedloe leaned on the open door of the grocery as of old, when Foster emerged from the shade of the woods and strode into the burning dust of the clearing. But Foster's beard was white, white as the snows that had drifted deep in the winter, and Bedloe did not know him.

Bulger, too, had returned to Dead Pine Camp, and when he talked with Bedloe in the long evenings, he smiled to himself behind the beard he had grown for disguise. But the Director

gazed complacently on the actors, for
He knew how the play would end.

* * * * *

Gold! Foster brought up a handful
of mud from the bed of the stream, and
examined it, still upon his knees. He
rocked his hand gently under the water,
and the lighter particles of silt were
washed away. In the palm of his hand,
gleaming in the sun that streamed
through the foliage of the pines, a few
golden grains were embedded. Foster
had found a mine!

* * * * *

Foster stood in the doorway of his
cabin, with his hand upon his damp
forehead. His eyes swept over the buildings below him, their windows gleaming, the light smoke of their chimneys
trailing upwards into the sky, where
the first star had slowly appeared. The
wealth he had stored through the weary
months was gone, had been stolen, and
who, who was the thief who had stolen
it? He set off slowly down the slope
toward Dead Pine Grocery. A cabin
was in his path, and his suspicions were
aroused by the fact that a blanket on
the window concealed the view of the
interior. He applied his eye to a chink
in the logs, through which a feeble
stream of light shone forth.

A man, standing before a table, seemed ready to depart from the cabin. His
revolvers were at his hips, and his pack
lay upon the floor. But on the deal table before him stood the small pouch

that contained Foster's gold. Thrust-
ing this into a pocket of his trousers,
assuming the roll of blankets, and ex-
tinguishing the lantern, he entered into
the cool air of the night, and Foster,
crouching in the grass, watched the tall
figure disappear in the darkness, on the
road through the pines to Buckeye.
Then he swiftly glided away across the
clearing.

The man had passed the open space
above Buckeye now, and he was nervous as he hastened among the black
shadows of the pines. There were woodland rustlings in the underbrush, the
wind moaned in the tree-tops, and an
owl from his perch on a lofty limb
hoo-ed dismally through the night. Suddenly the thicket parted and a dark
figure stepped forth. The man turned
and his gun flashed in an instant. The
apparition reeled; then lunged forward. Cold fingers clutched the man's
throat, fingers like the talons of a
ghost. His eyes stared, and his mouth
hung open. Then his right arm swung
upward, colliding with his assailant's
jaw. The fingers loosened, and the
white-haired specter staggered. Then,
recovering, it caught the thief in its
arms, raised him over its head, and
dashed him to the ground. The man
had screamed wildly as he was lifted in
the air, but he lay limp and silent in
the dust. The bullet had pierced Foster's lung, and the agony had distorted
his features. But the keen shock of
the moment had rended the veil that

concealed his past, and he was again the Sheriff of Dead Pine.

"Ef - I'm - going - to - take - ye - to- Buckeye——," he murmured; but the dark blood welled to his lips that had formed another word, and he fell forward upon the body of Bulger.

And as the curtain dropped forever, and the Great Director, Who knows all things, beckoned Foster from the stage, the wind sighed over the two forms, motionless under the pines in the darkness.

"Oh Man!"

Martin M. Murphy.

H John! John! get up quick, there's a burglar downstairs."

From under the pile of blankets a disgusted grunt arose.

"Oh, John, do go down and see." ·

"It's only the cat," came the mumbled response, "go to sleep."

"Then I'll go down myself."

But to judge from her actions the woman had no intention of indulging in a nocturnal peregrination which she had reason for thinking might terminate in an unsolicited introduction to a lead pipe.

Instead, her drowsy spouse was soon sufficiently aroused to grasp the drift of her conversation.

"Do hurry, John before he gets away. John, if you don't hurry he'll escape."

Goaded to desperation John leaped to the floor. For a moment he wavered, undecided whether to return to the comfortable little berth he had vacated or to embark on a cold if not actually perilous tour of the lower regions of his home. Then, with a look toward his wife and a thought perhaps that it would be more gallant of him to die by the hands of a fullfledged assassin, than by the hand which he had once feverishly wooed and won, John groped his way toward the door.

Down the stairs he went, tripping, stumbling, muttering and grumbling in the inky blackness of the night. Below, a faint sound as of shuffling feet broke the ghostly silence. By the mantle back of the stairs a small flashlight played up and down on the wall. Behind it a burly figure crouched like a giant bear, his powerful shoulders stooped and his head half turned as if listening.

With sinking heart John tiptoed on. Now the massive figure loomed straight before him. The light had been extinguished, but to John the darkness only made the huge splotch over near the wall appear more bulky. Just then some slight object, probably falling from the mantle, crashed to the floor with a noise that sent John's heart to fluttering wildly in his manly breast.

"Something must be done now," he thought, driving from his mind the idea of a quick return to the sheets.

"Oh H——!" thought the burglar, "he's got me with the goods."

224

"Here, pussy, pussy," said John, in a tentative tone.

"Meow, meow," returned the burglar softly.

"I wonder if he thinks a cat would sound like that," thought John.

"Pretty clever for me," thought the burglar.

"Come, pussy, pussy," said John.

"Pur-r-r-r," said the burglar.

"That was pretty raw," thought John.

"I wonder if he thinks I'm a cat?" thought the burglar.

"Come, kitty, come kitty," said John more firmly.

"Meow," reiterated the cat in a surprisingly human voice.

"He's getting worse," thought John.

"That was rotten," thought the burglar.

"Bad old pussy," said John, "you woke us all up."

"Purr," repeated the burglar, tripping over a chair.

"Sounds like a tiger cat," thought John.

"I guess I'll make a break for the window," thought the burglar.

"Be quiet now, pussy," said John retreating up the stairs rather briskly.

"P-s-s-s-s-s," said the burglar, slipping toward his exit.

"I wonder if he thought I took him for a cat," thought John, passing through the bedroom door.

"I wonder if he thought, I thought he took me for a cat," thought the burglar, as he jumped into a group of hyacinths near the lawn.

Upstairs John tiptoed on in silence and soon the alluring covers had buried him within their snug and cozy depths.

"Oh John, what was it?" asked his bed mate excitedly as a huge sigh emaciated from the mass of quilts at her side.

"It was only the cat," came the mumbled response, "go to sleep."

Withered Leaves

AJESTIC crimson Rose-flow'r open blown!
  With sparkling dew-drops in thy flaming heart--
Bright hues of Sunset, gentle warmth of Art
  Commingled, blend their glory in thine own.

One dawning Grey hath softly blushed and gone,
  The sun-swords burst the gems of eve apart---
And now, alas! Thine own sad charms depart
  Dear Rose! Thy too frail, lovely life is flown.

But flow'r thy morn-kist leaves must yet retain
  Some ling'ring vestige of thy queenly air
God's love-beams must not light and burn in vain---
  The Rose's petals are not aught but fair,
Sweet-scented blisses in thy heart remain,
  Proud beauty's fondest memory hiding there.

A. J. STEISS, JR.

The Redwood

· PUBLISHED BY THE STUDENTS OF THE UNIVERSITY OF SANTA CLARA

The object of The Redwood is to gather together what is best in the literary work of the students, to record University doings and to knit closely the hearts of the boys of the present and the past

EDITORIAL STAFF

EDITOR-IN-CHIEF - - - - - - - HENRY C. VEIT
BUSINESS MANAGER - - - - - - TULLIO A. ARGENTI
ASSISTANT BUSINESS MANAGER - - - - - JACOB E. HEINTZ
CIRCULATION MANAGER - - - - - EDMUND. Z. COMAN

ASSOCIATE EDITORS

EXCHANGES - - - - - - - P . F. MORETTINI
ALUMNI - - - - - - - - - MARTIN M. MURPHY
UNIVERSITY NOTES - - - - - - - LOUIS F. BUTY / FRED J. MORAN
ATHLETICS - - - - - - - - JAMES E. NEARY

EXECUTIVE BOARD

EDITOR   BUSINESS MANAGER   EDITOR OF REVIEWS

Address all communications to THE REDWOOD, University of Santa Clara, Santa Clara, California.
Terms of subscription, $1.50 a year; single copies 25 cents

EDITORIAL

Student Control

When a mariner puts out to sea from his home port he depends upon a number of things to carry his ship safely to its destination. Chief among these are the pilot, a compass and a reliable crew. The first mentioned is dropped in the very early part of the journey; immediately that the shoals and rocks and unfamiliar passages of the harbor are safely left behind.

With the launching of Student Control in all affairs of the Student Body, Santa Clara has made a marked advance along the course of progress. Yesterday, this and that branch of student activity had its Faculty Moderator, its pilot. Today that same activity continues to course along the line mapped out for it long years since, with however this exception: the Student Body ship has dropped its pilot. The

227

wheels of athletics, of the book store and not infrequently,·. of disciplinary matters, have been turned over to their own men. Theirs to guide it safely by the shoals, the treacherous rocks, through the whirlpool of mistakes and out upon the placid bosom of safe waters, sounding deep of success.

Though the going be rough and the frail craft tossed mercilessly. about on strange seas it is the compass of the Faculty Board of Control that.· will guide and point out the best way. Down in the hold and up on deck the crew of associated students will feed the boilers and generally man the ship, that by collective effort every trip of the ship of state will not have been in vain.

Attaching to this is no little amount of responsibility. The Student Manager and the overseers of both stores must watch with wary eye for the shoals of error they must inevitably encounter. But responsibility such as has attached to these men will only tend to· make them guard more jealously the trust given them. We place every confidence in them, knowing that under their guidance, naught but success can result. Cooperation on the part of every student is the key-note to success. It will be the only true measure. Let's make good by each one contributing to the full his store of capabilities.

Save Paper

Did you ever notice the way Uncle Sam does his effective advertising? He uses the mails, and upon each parcel of mail he stamps the message he wants the people to hear.. So it was in time of war when he wished the conservation of food. So too it is now in matters of vital concern that otherwise would not reach half so many people if periodicals were to be solely depended upon as an advertising medium. It is his one way of reaching everybody.

We want to reach everybody but unfortunately we have not so convenient a system. We are going to inaugurate a campaign for the saving of paper to the financial benefit of the Student Body. No doubt you have all noticed the numerous placards about the campus telling of the plan. It is just one of the many little ways that funds can be added to the credit side of the Student Body ledger to offset the heavy debt that now threateningly hangs over us.

The paper need not be of any particular kind. All sorts are acceptable. The store, as it accumulates, will be sold by the ton to a local paper company and the shekels reaped therefrom poured into the coffers of the Student Body treasury.

It behooves us then to lay aside any and all paper which is of no further use to us. Thus will each do his little bit to clean the slate of our common debt.

The Thespian Art

After lying dormant for a period of many years, dramatics are once more to be revived. On our own stage in our time-honored auditorium, the thespian art is to wax again in all the eloquence and finesse that it enjoyed in years gone by when Clay M. Greene staged his Passion Play, Charles D. South his Constantine, and Martin V. Merle his Mission Play and The Light Eternal.

To those listed among Santa Clara's graduated sons, will come the reminiscences of a glorious day passed. Some, perhaps, will bask in the memory of having been a successful participant, others, the no less pleasant retrospection of viewing themselves once more as elated, enthralled spectators. To both classes will come a realization of what the revival of dramatics in the Santa Clara sense of the word will mean.

We of the present will appreciate to the full what golden opportunities present themselves, only after history has added to its numerous pages our present sincere endeavors, and after departing from these hallowed walls we can look back upon the emblazoned record and find therein a source of keen enjoyment. Then will come to him who reads between the lines a knowledge that hard work, sincere endeavor and steadfast loyalty to the task at hand, were the milestones dotting the course to the goal of success.

We've hinted at the future. We know full well the past. Ours it is therefore to act in the living present. Acting with the determination to better yesterday's attainments insures the future with its pregnant possibilities. Now that dramatics have been once more revived let us be minded to give our best. The past was good, the present should be made better, and to the future generations will fall the task of establishing the superlative degree.

University Notes

Retreat Three days and four nights of silence and meditation border on the impossible if applied to three hundred or more College Students filled with the pep of youth, but that word "impossible" is more a stranger to the fellows of Santa Clara than are the frail poppies of California to snowbound Nome. Sunday evening, February first, the Student Body assembled in the Chapel for the purpose of giving themselves the "once-over" spiritually. Father Maher, S. J., of Los Gatos, conducted the retreat and mere words cannot begin to enumerate the graces bestowed on the retreatants through his efforts, coupled with the earnest co-operation of the students. A machine in need of an overhauling must temporarily be disabled while the mechanic works and similarly the man endeavoring to improve his inner self must retreat from worldly manifestations and distractions if that end is to be thoroughly accomplished.

So vividly did Fr. Maher bring home to us our purpose in this life and the means by which that purpose might be attained that his words will be our constant thought. The evident sincerity of each member of the student body was ample proof of our gratification for such a rare opportunity.

House of Philhistorians With a membership of no less than sixty-five, the accustomed progress of the House was somewhat retarded and quantity became more prominent than quality. Since the beginning of the second semester legislation has restored the Society to its old practice, limiting the number of representatives to thirty.

With the resuming of its former status a more keen interest has taken hold of the debaters, as was made manifest at the last session. The question of open shop versus closed shop being the subject of the debate, caused considerable excitement. Representatives Haneberg and O'Shea upheld the side advocating open shop, while Representatives Cashin and Moran argued for the closed shop. The opinion of the House which was taken in ballot, favored the closed shop by a margin of two votes.

Representatives Copeland, Daly and Damrell have been selected to represent the House in its debate against the Senate to be held next month. Last year the House was victorious over the Senate in the Ryland Debate, and a similar outcome this year is expected by the team of under-classmen.

Ole Hanson

The enemy of the Bolsheviks, Ole Hanson, brought his message to us with the fervor of an old friend. He granted us the opportunity of hearing from his own lips the appeal he has spread throughout the United States, urging the people to curb the "Reds" with more stringent laws, and commanding a revival of the ebbing American spirit. Through the efforts of Father President, the ex-Mayor of Seattle addressed the Student Body in the Auditorium, and the welcome that was extended him showed our loyal support of his principles.

Junior Dramatic Society

At the last meeting of the Junior Dramatic Society the question of Universal Military Training was debated. Practically all the youthful members have tasted of army routine, hence the viewpoint of the subject was elucidated after a fashion characteristic of Young America. Fr. Regan, the Director, is justly proud of the interest the future members of the House and Senate have demonstrated in their recent

meetings. Among the promising debaters of the Society are Halloran, Burns, White, Haviside and Del Mutolo, not to mention the gifted orator Albert Duffill.

Freshman Letters

"Prexy." Neary and company are highly elated over the prominence attached to this year's Frosh. In every undertaking, whether dramatics or athletics, the Frosh are at the front.

"Herbie" Garcia was elected Treasurer at the last meeting, to succeed Burke Curley, and there is no fear but that the present cutsodian of the "shekels" will bulge the till.

Fr. Egan and his Mineralogy Class have been doing some research work in the Valley, Santa Cruz mountains and Manresa. With the versatile Padre as its guide, the class is expected to return any day with the news of a gold mine discovery.

Sophomore Letters

The last session of the Sophomore Class completed the plans for the picnic in April. The committee in charge of the "eats" is composed of Pecarovich, Gassett and Argenti, while those in charge of transportation are "Pop" Rethers, Cassin and Trabucco. With that corps of hustlers the success of the outing is assured. Spring has got us and we're 'rarin' to go! .

Fred J. Moran.

Class '20

A lively session of the Senior Class took place on February 20, when plans were discussed for the Senior Ball and other things. Arrangements are already under way to make the graduating functions this year the most brilliant in the history of the University.

Committees in charge of the various affairs were appointed, among them the committee which will arrange for the Ball. It consists of Mr. Savage, Mr. Bricca, and Mr. Sullivan.

It was also decided to establish a permanent Senior ring, which will be adopted by future graduating classes. The choice of this ring was put in the hands of a committee consisting of Mr. Di Fiore, chairman, Mr. Buty, and Mr. Dieringer.

General Azgapetain

On February 14, the student body was privileged to hear a distinguished character of the great war, General Mesrop Nefton Azgapetain, of the Armenian army, in a lecture on "Distressed Armenia." General Azgapetain deeply impresses his hearers with an intimate recounting of the history, aims, achievements, and sufferings of a nation exposed to the merciless atrocities of the unrestrained Turk.

Accompanying the General in his lecture tour of the United States, in the interests of his country, is his charming wife, Lady Mary, who served as a Red Cross nurse with the Armenian Army throughout the war.

General Azgapetain is an accomplished linguist, speaking no less than ten languages fluently. He is a graduate of Roberts College, Constantinople, the University of Geneva, Switzerland, and holds a degree from Columbia University.

Student Control

"The world do move." Times, like styles, change. As evidence of the truth of the above statements, witness the change wrought by the action of Father President. For aeons and aeons, for a long, long time, Santa Clara athletics were under the guidance of the Moderator of Athletics, a member of the Faculty.

But on February 14, a radical change was effected. Father Murphy, believing in student control, abolished the office of Faculty Moderator, and placed the entire control of athletics in the hands of the Student Manager, which position continues to be held by James B. O'Connor. By the same act, the Faculty Board of Control, to which alone the Student Manager is accountable, was created. It consists of Father Sullivan, chairman, Father Buckley, and Father Oliver, in their respective offices of Vice-President, Dean of the Faculties, and Treasurer.

As incidental to the general policy of student control, the Book Store and the Co-Op, the Student Body's two great financial assets, were placed in charge of student managers.

Mike Pecarovich now presides over the popular sweets dispensary, and by the most up-to-date methods of profiteering, has already added many dollars of profits to the Student Body treasury.

Father Kennedy has been relieved of the management of the Book Store, and John J. McGuire now fills that position, with the able assistance of Roy Fowler.

Student Body The all-important question of awarding football blocks, which had occupied many hours of wrangling throughout the Student Body meetings of last semester, has been finally, and likewise satisfactorily, disposed of.

By a vote of the Student Body, it was decided that a committee be appointed to draft an amendment to the Constitution which would prescribe the conditions for winning the block S-C for participation in football games, which amendment would be retroactive, so as to take effect in September, 1919. The committee appointed by President Veit for this purpose consisted of Mr. Bricca, chairman, Mr. Moroney, and Mr. Trabucco.

The amendment submitted by this committee, which was passed by the requisite two-third vote of the Student Body, at a subsequent meeting, and which is now a part of the Constitution, provides: "One deemed eligible to be awarded the block S-C, must partici-

pate in the whole or any fraction thereof, of the game against our logical opponent; and in the whole or in any two-quarters or fractions thereof, in each of three intercollegiate games, or their equivalent. The logical opponent, and the equivalent of intercollegiate games, will be chosen by the Executive Committee at the beginning of each scholastic year."

At a meeting of the Executive Committee, the logical opponent chosen for the season just past was Stanford. The three other games upon which the awarding of blocks were based were the Nevada game, and the two games with the Olympic Club.

Those men who had fulfilled the requirements entitling them to block S-Cs were determined by the Executive Committee to be: Caesar Manelli, Harold Cochrane, Tom Whelan, Roy Baker, Jim Needles, Norbert Korte, and Rudy Scholz. The last two men named, however, having already won their four-star sweaters in football, the Committee recommended that they be awarded gold football charms for the distinction which they have won. This recommendation was approved by the faculty.

However, there were many who had almost fulfilled the conditions set down in the amendment, and in view of the changes which the Constitution had undergone, the Executive Committee considered them entitled to blocks. These men were recommended to the faculty, and approved as being worthy of receiving the emblems. They were:

George Noll, Mike Pecarovich, Ray Schall, Capt. Ferrario, Tom Bannon, John Muldoon, and Bill Muldoon.

At a special meeting of the Student Body these men were formally voted their blocks.

Philalethic Senate

With the opening of the new semester, interest in debating which had been in a state of depression with the weight of impending examinations, was once more revived. The initial meeting of the Philalethic Senate was opened with the election of officers for the ensuing semester. Henry C. Veit was re-elected to the office of Vice-President. The new officers are: Recording Secretary, W. Ward Sullivan; Treasurer, Tobias J. Bricca; Corresponding Secretary, Louis F. Buty; Sergeant-at-Arms, Louis J. Trabucco; Reporter, Eugene R. Jaeger; Librarian, William G. Koch.

The ranks of the Senators were depleted somewhat by the failure of several of the former members to return, and to fill this vacancy it was decided to draw upon the House for new members. Accordingly the following Representatives were voted admittance into the higher body of the Literary Congress: Casimir A. Antonioli, Donald R. Burke, Capelle H. Damrell, Joaquin Fields, Aloysius C. McCarthy, Martin M. Murphy, Chester Moore, Michael Pecarovich, and Ralph Purdy. They were later duly received, and in response to

the address of welcome extended by the President, Father N. Bell, an eloquent expression of gratitude was delivered by Capelle Damrell, on behalf of the newly elected members.

Several important questions were presented by the President, in the nature of challenges for intercollegiate debates. The first was an offer from the University of Southern California for a dual debate, but as the date proposed would conflict with the Ryland Debate, it was found necessary to reject it.

The second challenge was received from the College of the Pacific, and the date being satisfactory, it was voted to accept it. For unknown reasons, however, the worthy gentlemen from our neighboring college, when notified of the decision of the Senate, failed to comply with their own request.

However, an invitation was received from the San Jose Council of the Knights of Columbus to have two teams from the Senate debate the question of The Open vs. The Closed Shop before the Council. This was accepted, and the two teams were picked by the President. The affirmative was upheld by Senators Jaeger and O'Neill, the negative by Senators Damrell and Heafey. The question was ably debated to the edification of the Council, and also to the satisfaction of the members of the Faculty who were present as guests.

The proximity of the Ryland debate was also a matter of concern to the Senate, and in order not to be handicapped by lack of time for preparation, the choice of the members who will endeavor to regain the lost laurels of the Senators in this annual event of events in Santa Clara debating was imperative. The return of the ballots showed Senators Damrell, Heafey, and Jaeger, all of whom have taken part in Ryland debates of the past.

According to custom, the privilege of submitting the question alternates from year to year, so that the question was proposed this year by the House, according the Senate the privilege of either defending or opposing the question. The following question was accepted as satisfactory, the Senate debaters choosing the affirmative side: Resolved: That one of the great reconstruction measures that should be adopted to meet the present conditions of social unrest is the enactment by Congress of more stringent and comprehensive immigration laws.

Although the custom of past years has been to hold the Ryland debate on March 19, the Feast of St. Joseph, by mutual agreement the date has been postponed this year to April 6th.

Senior Sodality

The Senior Sodality reconvened once more to continue its weekly meetings, under the leadership of Director Father Boland. The faces of new members were noted, and the number in attendance was most gratifying, so that nothing but a semester of devotion to the Blessed Mother can be anticipated.

Officers for the new term were elected with the following results: Prefect, William G. de Koch; First Assistant, Jean Paul Reddy; Second Assistant, Emmett W. Gleeson; Secretary, Frank A. Camarillo; Treasurer, Louis F. Buty; Vestry Prefects, Frank A. Rethers and Louis J. Trabucco; Guardian of Candidates, Edmund Z. Coman; Organist, Ernest D. Bedolla.

The following were chosen as Consultors: Henry C. Veit, John J. Savage, Rudolph J. Scholz, James B. O'Connor, Thomas McV. Crowe, and Thomas Bannon.

Olympic Games

The decision of the A. A. A. officials to have a representative Rugby team from the United States at the 1920 Olympic games, to be held at Antwerp during the latter part of the year, resulted in a summons being issued to Santa Clara Rugby stars of both the past and present, to appear for the tryouts.

The pick of the last ten years of Rugby—stars from California, Stanford, Olympic Club, Santa Clara, St. Mary's, St. Ignatius, College of the Pacific, and Davis Farm—are given a stiff workout every Saturday on the Stanford turf, and competition for berths to Antwerp is very keen. For the purpose of aiding in the selection the contestants are divided into two clubs—the All-

American and the All-British. The former is captained by none other than "Jawn" Muldoon, of '16 and '17 fame, who is now attached to the Olympic Club. Others from amongst us, who are competing to have Santa Clara represented on the team which will travel to Antwerp are: "Dumpy" Diaz, "Rudy" Scholz, Bill Muldoon, Roy Fowler, Caesar Manelli and "Phat" Ferrario. Jimmy Winston, of '16 fame, is also trying out under the California colors.

The Irish Bond Drive

On the evening of March 4th, the cause of a free Ireland was promoted by an enthusiastic rally held in the Auditorium under the auspices of the Santa Clara County branch of the American Commission on Irish Independence. The purpose of the rally was to aid in the nation-wide sale of Irish Bonds, and to this end the talent and support of the University were contributed. The address of the evening was delivered by Father Timothy L. Murphy, our President, who measured up to his appeal for "the right that Ireland asks, the right to live, and be free," by subscribing for a $1000 bond certificate of the Republic of Ireland, in the name of the University.

He was followed by Father Richard Collins, pastor of St. Patrick's church, San Jose, who, in a spirited appeal, showed that the people of the United States are in gratitude bound to repay Ireland for the aid which she rendered us during the Revolution.

RESOLUTIONS.

WHEREAS, God in His Infinite wisdom has seen fit to call to Himself the beloved uncle of our dear friend and college fellow, James B. O'Connor, in a manner sudden, and humanly speaking, at a time when his goodness and charity would be most felt and appreciated by his devoted nephew, and

WHEREAS, our duty towards the departed uncle and our sincerest sympathies towards his sorrow-stricken nephew, our fellow student, demand that we be mindful of this, his great loss and sorrow;

BE IT RESOLVED that a heartfelt expression of profoundest regret and deepest sorrow over the loss of the beloved uncle of our esteemed fellow student, be conveyed to him and his sorrowing relatives;

BE IT FURTHER RERSOLVED, that a copy of these resolutions be forwarded to our college fellow and that they be printed in the next issue of the official organ of the Student Body, "The Redwood".

(Signed)
HENRY C. VEIT, Pres.
LOUIS F. BUTY, Sec.
EDMUND Z. COMAN, Treas.
THOMAS E. WHELAN,
Sgt.-at-Arms.
MR. J. P. O'CONNELL, S. J.,
Moderator.

The event which is to have social precedence over University doings this semester, and bids fair to surpass any activity of the year, will take place on the seventeenth of April. It will be known as the Engineers' Dance.

For two months the Entertainment Committee has been tirelessly laboring to make the dance a success—and now it seems that their desires are to be realized. The exclusiveness of the affair is assured. Only alumni, active, and honorary members, together with their close friends, will be invited. The dance itself will be held in the spacious Rose Room of the Vendome Hotel in San Jose. The Y. M. I. orchestra is to furnish the syncopation. Every feature of the dance, even the design of the programs, has been carefully studied; every item should prove interesting and delightful to those privileged to attend. The Society thanks the wives of the Engineering professors for their gracious consent to act as patronesses. Moreover, we congratulate Mr. Di Fiori, as chairman, and each member of his committee, for the results they have obtained, and thank them for their work in connection with the Engineering Dance.

Last month we had a picnic. Here the account.

At nine-thirty on the sunniest of this year, the crowd left the camp and it wasn't long before the high-p ered motors, followed by the Li with the ''eats'', had transported fellows to Villa Maria. Everybo knows how the gang piled out of cars, filled their lungs with a flood California's oxygen and expelled it a shout; then, failing to frustrate Sergeant-at-arms' careful watch, o the food, grabbed bat and ball a started that king of picnic sports— indoor game. And after the game— feed.

First of all, the Engineers thank University for that feed. Needless say, there was an overabundance of and its deliciousness was fully prov in the manly attempt to make it dis pear. Then there is Fr. Egan to thar Perhaps he would rather we think thanks, but the way in which he work in the preparation of the meal, and the doing of everything to make the fair a success, forces us to outward show our appreciation. The aroma broiled steaks mingled with the p fume of freshly cooked coffee, was

237

most enough to remove one's appetite for the more important items of cookies, jam, cake, and other dainties, created for the sole purpose of ruining a temperately regulated eating habit. The festive board took the appearance of a regular banquet as the celebrities in attendance were introduced. After Leo Martin, our past-president and departing professor, was given a little remembrance and appreciation for past services in the form of a blue-printed resolution, and we had listened to his thanks, we settled down on the rough benches to enjoy the words of the other guests. To start the talks, Mr. Di Fiore was called upon to acknowledge the thanks given to his committee on arrangement. Then followed a few words by Fr. Egan, and after him, the gladly received speeches of Colonel Donovan, whom every Engineer here knows; of Professors Evans and Lotz; and of our own Dean, Professor Sullivan. Our president seemed to have had more than enough of good cheer for the occasion, and called on a few "nuts" from each class to lend gayety to the gathering. Mr. Tuttle represented the Seniors; Mr. Jones orated for the Freshmen, Mr. Sullivan portrayed the "nutty" side of the Sophomore class; and for the Juniors, Messrs. Ford, Abrahamsen, Heaney and

Koch, spread oil over the audience. After this "dessert" the bunch split into groups: some enjoyed a hike over the hills, others indulged in a game of "nigger-baby", but most watched the Soph-Frosh game, or the Junior-Senior scuffle. The former was a fifteen inning victory for the Sophs, while the latter ended in a predestined triumph for the Juniors at the end of twelve long-debated and much argued innings. Little did Colonel Donovan realize the task he had attempted in assenting to keep track of the 40 or more tallys.

When the evening was drawing to a close, the party started back; and all along the way the singing and shouting was evidence enough that the picnic of the Engineers was a supreme success.

It is fitting in closing this month's notes, to mention our new professor. He is Mr. Alvin Evans, E. E. '17, of Arkansas University. As superintendent of a Light and Power Co. in South Dakota, he has gained considerable experience. The Engineers have elected him an honorary member of their Society, and assure him of their support as fellow-members. We trust that his stay with us will be pleasing and long.

Alfred J. Abrahamsen.

89

Judge Trabucco, of Mariposa County, is an alumnus who has ever had the best interests of Santa Clara at heart. The Judge was on the campus last month revisiting the scenes of his college days, and renewing old acquaintances among the faculty.

'01

Among the prominent victims of the influenza in San Francisco last month was Tito Corcoran, of the class of '01. Tito possessed a genial and happy disposition which endeared him to everyone with whom he came in contact, and his death came as a severe shock to his many friends. Needless to say, our hearts go out in sympathy to those who were near and dear to him.

'06

Another old boy to succumb to this dreaded disease was William J. McKagney, a collegian of the '06 class. While at school Mr. McKagney made quite a name for himself on the stage, having been one of the leading characters in the "Passion Play", besides appearing in several lesser entertainments of the Senior Dramatic Society. To his bereaved friends and afflicted loved ones we extended our most heartfelt condolences.

Johnny Jones is chairman of the Irish Bond committee in Santa Clara County. So far, quite a number of bonds have been sold, and with this ever loyal son of Santa Clara at the helm, the drive is doubly certain of success.

The Seattle North Pacific Company last month turned out in record time the last of a series of ten steel steamships which it had contracted with the government to build. In fulfilling the contract a world's record was set by the company when the steamer Chicomico was delivered last November within five working days from the launching. The men responsible for this remarkable feat are both former students of Santa Clara, John D. Twohy and James F. Twohy, general manager and treasurer, respectively, of the shipbuilding firm.

To quote one of the leading experts

of the shipbuilding industry, "they are one of the greatest teams of Industrial leadership in the west," and "their tremendous shipbuilding record for speed and efficiency is unparalleled in any port of the world." The two brothers intend to retire from shipbuilding to resume their "own game", of railroad construction and similar activities in which they were engaged before the war. These distinguished sons, by their great achievements in the industrial world, are bringing honor to their Alma Mater as well as themselves and every Santa Claran wishes them the greatest success in their undertakings.

'09 Felix Galtes, a brother of Father Galtes, S. J., was another welcome visitor. He is now a prominent banker in Bakersfield, but in his college days he bore the reputation of being the fastest base runner that ever attended Santa Clara.

'10 Vic Salsberg came down from far-off Bellingham, Washington, lately to visit his Alma Mater. Vic was in business in the northern state and met with much success.

'10 Edmund S. Lowe recently appeared at a local theatre in the leading male role in the picture play, "The Eyes of Youth," starring the famous actress Clara Kimball Young. For several seasons Ed

was on the legitimate stage, where he achieved notable success in such plays as "The Brat", and others, but last year he accepted a flattering offer to enter the movies, where his extraordinary talents have already won him a high reputation.

'11 Word has reached us from Sacramento that another old boy has fallen victim to Cupid's snares. A few months ago Ralph Weyland resolved to start the new year aright, so on the first of January he made a promise to "love and protect" a charming Sacramento girl, Miss Gazenia Gibson. The Redwood wishes Mr. and Mrs. Weyland a long and happy married life.

'13 Conspicuous among those who have ever taken a sincere interest in Santa Clara is Constantine Castruccio of the class of '13. He is already making arrangements for a football game between the Varsity and the University of Southern California, to be played next year in Los Angeles.

'14 Chauncey Tramutolo is creating quite a stir in legal circles around the bay section, where he has acquired a large practice. He figured prominently in a sensational murder trial recently held in San Francisco and succeeded in winning the case for his client.

'14 Dr. Rodney Yoell, once editor of "The Redwood", and recently graduated from the College of Medicine at St. Louis, has returned to California to practice his profession. He will be associated with Dr. Gallwey of San Francisco and has already been notified of his appointment as resident physician of St. Francis Hospital.

———

'15 Jimmy Curtin spent a pleasant afternoon last month revisiting his old haunts about the campus. Jimmy is practicing law in Tonopah, Nevada, and though too modest to talk about himself we venture to state that if he can handle himself as well in a courtroom as he could on a football field he need have no fear for the future.

———

16' William Herrin, who still keeps in touch with the old school through an occasional letter, is associated in the practice of law with his father, the noted Southern Pacific attorney. Bill was a good student while at school and we look to see him closely follow the paternal footsteps.

———

'16 A little baby girl has arrived to brighten the home of Orvis Speciale. We send the happy parents our warmest felicitations.

Thomas (Tony) Boone is reestablish- ed in his uncle's law firm in Modesto. Before the war called him to the colors Tony was one of the most prominent citizens in the "hum town". In his collegiate days Tony was Student Body Manager and president of the Student Body and won more honors and distinctions, perhaps, than any other student at college. He won the famous "Cyc" Prize in his Senior year besides meriting the first honors in the Ryland Debate.

———

'17 Mike Leonard dropped in a few weeks ago to shake hands with his old friends on the campus. Mike will be remembered as the pitcher who beat the White Sox when the latter were training in California. While in the army the "Idol of the Engineers", as he was known in France, pitched and won a game in Paris with an audience of eighty thousand wild Frenchmen looking on. Rumor has it that the crowd, especially that part which wore skirts, was pulling hard for Mike all the time.

———

Ex '17 The southern papers recently contained a full account of the wedding of Frank Spearman and Miss Elizabeth Fife. The ceremony was performed in the Church of the Blessed Sacrament in Hollywood by Fr. Villa, and the honeymoon spent in the San Bernardino Mountains. The newlyweds have returned to their home in Hollywood, where they intend to

242 THE REDWOOD

make their permanent residence. Congratulations, and may you live long and prosper!

C'l '17 DeWitt Le Bourveau was with us long enough a few weeks ago to state that he was leaving in March for the Philly training camp in Alabama to report for spring practice. "Liver" had a successful season last year and will undoubtedly "clout 'em" harder than ever this year as he now is a veteran with good experience behind him.

'18 Bob Tremaine has just recovered from a long siege of sickness at O'Connor's Sanitarium. Bob was known as one of the most cheerful fellows in the yard in his undergraduate days, and his many friends here will be glad to know that he is in good health again.

Ex '18 Al Quill was awarded a degree from California last year and is now taking a P. G. course in law. He expects to take his bar examinations shortly and if successful he will probably hang out a shingle on his own account.

'18 Ed Nicholson has entered the law office of his uncle, Mr. Lorigan. With brother George to initiate him into the finer points of the game, Ed should become a "counsel learned in the law" in short order.

We read with pleasure in the local papers that Joe McKiernan has made a contract with the Joseph Remick Company to write popular songs. Joe has already met with considerable success in this work, several of the latest "hits" being of his composition. His new position affords him the opportunity of association with the most experienced and best known song writers of the country, so we look to see him soon establish a wonderful reputation for himself.

Ex '19 Jimmy Winston and John Muldoon, both of the class of '19, are looming up as strong candidates for the Rugby team which is to represent America in the Olympic games. Jimmy is a mighty fast man on his feet and Bag,—but we will not attempt to tell what Bag can really do in a Rugby game. Suffice it that both are worthy representatives of Santa Clara and that every fellow in the yard is pulling for them to make the team.

Ex '19 John Bradley, so we hear, is leading the Senior Class at Georgetown by several laps in the race for scholastic honors. John was a good student while here and in athletics showed a lot of form on the track.

Tom Casey, another of our star athletes, has signed with the Cincy Reds as a catcher. He will meet with keen competition there, but his wonderful ability should assure him of a place on the team. His many friends wish him success.

Chester Palmtag, once a frequent and able contributor to the pages of the Redwood is now representing a big San Francisco hardware firm. Besides possessing much literary ability he was an excellent Rugby player and track man. Why not drop in when you're down this way, Chet, and look the old place over?

Mel Pratt, who caught for the Varsity in 1917, has signed up with the Oakland Coast League team. Mel is a snappy little backstop and should make good from the start.

'22 Jim Cunningham has been appointed deputy sheriff in Los Angeles. Jimmy has all the qualifications for a first class upholder of the law, and were there such an office we would predict without hesitation that Jimmy would soon be the sheriff of the United States.

Ex '22 John Murphy is making a success of rice raising in Chico. "Spud" was on the campus a short time ago and had many interesting tales to relate of a trip he recently made to Alaska.

"Les" Perasso is playing a star game with the St. Mary's Varsity this year, being one of the heaviest hitters on the team and the mainstay of the infield. Go get 'em Les, and watch that old average.

Summer Retreats Just as a reminder to those who are already planning their summer vacations we would like to insert a word about the Summer Retreats. The retreats this year will begin on June 17 and 24; July 1 and 8, and will last three days. They will be held here at the college; all applications and correspondence should be directed to Father William Boland.

The Fathers in charge of these retreats wish to have even a larger attendance than last year and extend their warmest invitation to all those who wish to utilize their vacation period to the very best advantage.

Martin M. Murphy.

EXCHANGES

The Tattler

Out of the East, across the Rockies, and even to the slopes of the Pacific, this dainty piece of college literature finds its way; and once again we feel assured that our Virginia friend has not forsaken us. The verses of this number have a pleasing picturesqueness, and even a slight tinge of Wordsworthian appreciation of nature's beauties. "Memory" is portrayed with a deft artistic touch; something quite good. But in "Evening", besides the sketching of the sea, which is quite Tennysonian, there is the sympathetic thought of a hero dead, for whom love is kindled by the Evening Star. Turning from verses to the study of poetry we meet "The Door of Dreams," a critical analysis of the latest work of one of our contemporary litterati. It displays knowledge, poetic instinct, and honest appreciation for the efforts of others that argues no hastily drawn conclusions. "K-a-j-a-h" is a story, which, like its title, has a rather queer plot with ingenious workings. But we did not care so much for the plot as for the amiable character of the bewitching heroine of eighteen, Bessie, with her re-sourceful and enthusiastic schemings, and who evidently dislikes anything or anybody that is gloriously monotonous. And we may add that there is more than one Bessie in this world. "A Matter of Gloves" leads us to believe that it is the same old rivalry between two gallants strategizing after the same object of their affections. but it turns out unexpectedly that there is really only one—and he lost.

As a suggestion to the Exchange Editor, we would like to see that department more amplified, and each magazine more fully treated.

The Academia

The fall number of this neat harbinger from the Northwest has made its appearance, and its contents display a goodly set of verses and an apt selection of essays and stories.

Of the verses, "Queen of the Holy Rosary" expresses a beautiful religious sentiment; while, with a decided taste for the aesthetic, we noted "A Summer's Evening" and "Autumn in Oregon". The latter to us appeared as the best bit of verse in the number, although "The Artist" is not far behind in charm of expression. The editor is quite prominent with a majority of the verses to her credit, and also a prize-winner short story, "Winning the Kenyon". What is most noticeable in this tale is the evidence of local color; but we were willing to overlook any domesticity for the clever portrayal of character. Indeed, character study is one of the essentials, if not the most important part, of story telling.

The second prize winner is not so happy in its choice of incidents, some of which seem to us somewhat improbable, although not quite so much as in "The Appetite of Laura Jane". The incident and dialogue of the two immigrants, moreover, is palpably unnatural. The theme of this story, however, is not as common as the former.

The several articles on the works of John Ayscough by the different authoresses are quite commendable, and manifest a scholarly appreciation for the efforts of one of our leading contemporary Catholic writers.

"The woods are mad with minstrelsy,
    The air is touched with witchery,
The soul responds in ecstasy,
    In the Autumn tide."
            This is the ending of a
The Solarian   neat bit of verse that met us as we first opened the October number of this Illinois literary product.

Revelling in the same atmosphere, but with a religious garb reminding us of the souls of our departed we read "In November". The pithy lines, however, did not do justice to the excellent thought struggling for its proper expression. The diction in "Concerning Strikes" is at times labored and unpolished, and we further register a dissenting opinion with the writer of this topic on some of his remarks. With a better understanding of the subject, and with a clear and logical exposition of the advantages of good selective reading, the author makes a fine impression in "Desultory Reading"; while, following a different strain, but displaying an accurate insight into the real causes of the present day unrest and demoralization, the author of "Christianity and Civilization" points out the road to true Christian peace and prosperity. The essays, on the whole, advance the standard of this number, which from the verses would indicate slightly mediocre tendencies.

The St. Louis Collegian From the land of pineapples and ukeleles, and coming with an air and dignity of a South Sea romancer, this youthful magazine makes its appearance within our sanctum as the second number of its first year in college literary circles. As this is, therefore, only the second effort along literary lines, we are wont to overlook its youthful discrepancies; and so it is our endeavor, not in the spirit of egotism, however, to counsel it along certain well defined lines of college literary form.

On the whole the stories and articles are rather below the standard; but, taking into consideration the circumstances we are apt to make less of it. Still, we are inclined to expect some real up-to-date short stories, with real live plots and character study, from such a well-known institution of learning; and we look forward to marked improvement in this department of the magazine.

The debate on the Monroe Doctrine, on the other hand, is a good example of a thorough study of the question and a clear grasp of the subject. In the arguments of the affirmative we find very little convincing force—only statements in lieu of arguments. Consequently, we are forced to disagree with the learned judges in their opinion rendered. Still, what do we know about conditions and the Monroe Doctrine away across the Pacific in a land of perpetual optimism and sunshine?

Conspicuous by its absence we failed to notice any verse; something, that leads us to suspect, quite uncharitably, that our Islanders do not read or appreciate poetry. With improvements in the stories and essays, and with the appearance of some verse, the Collegian will, indeed, make a very creditable impression.

The Mountaineer

After the silence imposed by the unholy arm of Mars this natty messenger from its cradle among the historic mountains of Maryland makes its debut again with its appealing blue cover; and we hasten to welcome it most cordially.

In both the October and November numbers the matter is creditably presented; for this exchange, however, we noted in particular the contents of the November issue. "Ruskin" is a scholarly essay in a clear and convincing style on the principle works of this English author. The matter is well presented, and the writer seems to have taken especial pains to unfold to his readers the remarkable character of this great man through an insight of his aims and struggles. Some new side lights, also, on the character of the great war hero are skillfully portrayed in "Cardinal Mercier". "Is There a Doctor Present?" is a story with a rather common plot, although the details suffer little from this defect. The main objection is that the end is too plainly evident, and thus largely spoils the effect intended. To us the last paragraph should have been omitted, as the action had already terminated, and so this addition appears rather as an after-thought. The other story stands well under a more favorable arrangement and action.

On the whole, the verse does not reach the sublime heights attained by some of the contemporary college magazines; still, we could not help but feel compensated and refreshed in reading "My Old Plantation Home", expressing, as it does, a quaint inward feeling in unadorned but impressive language. The superior quality of the editorials is something that we cannot fail to remark: well written, thoughtful, and clear.

The Creighton Chronicle

After what seemed interminable time we are again accorded the opportunity of exchanging with our friend from Nebraska. And what a change! If memory still functions within us, it was our unpleasant duty to criticize your monthly about a year ago; and some unpalatable remarks were registered. Yet they were offered as honest and helpful observations in an effort to form a truly representative college magazine. Our surprise and pleasure, therefore, may be imagined when the December and, later, the February issues of the Chronicle made their appearance at our sanctum with an astonishing absence of stately legal, med-

ical, or religious disquisitions, and in their places real refreshing short stories, college verses, and essays.

May we not record such a pleasing innovation as one of the blessings of the war? Among the verses "Only a Star" almost succeeded in tempting us to quote it at large, while "Sic transit" is something more than an ordinary thought; but in "In Memory" there is an effort, prevalent in other college monthlies, to plagiarize the popular war ode. In the realm of short stories "The Angel in the Case" unfolds a remarkably beautiful sentiment that like a golden thread of a mother's love, glistens through the pages in a noteworthy character portrayal. In reading "The Return of Harry Roe" we were involuntarily reminded of a similar story by O. Henry. Perhaps it is a case of "all great minds running along the same channel."

Aside, however, it is indeed with genuine interest that we remark the success of the Chronicle in college literary circles, and we feel certain that its standards will never be lowered.

ATHLETICS

BASKETBALL.

Stanford 31.   **Varsity 25.**

The spacious court of the San Jose High School was the scene of Santa Clara's first intercollegiate battle. Four minutes after Referee Harris had opened the game, the figures told of an eleven to three count, with the Varsity claiming the former. Pelouze, the Marcel wave from Medford, soon had his men finding the circular rail, and time and again their long shots counted as points, which at the end of the first half totaled fourteen. The Varsity had an equal amount, and as the second act opened the spectators were treated to an example of mid-season playing, with Manelli and Righter sharing honors at goals from the field. Dumpy Diaz however, was always where he should be and his quick movements combined with that famed twist, kept the Varsity a few points in the lead. Jim Needles found it difficult to hold himself to the smooth floor. Four personal fouls were checked against him, and he witnessed the remaining minutes of the game outside of the white lines. Up to this mo-

ment the Varsity had retained its lead, but in three short minutes Righter found himself on his old home court, and six goals were thrown from a long range, bringing victory to the boys from Stanford. The Varsity quintet: Manelli, Diaz, Fowler, forwards; Needles, Whelan, center; Ferrario, Muth, Pecarovich, guards.

Nevada 29.   **Varsity 25.**

Those who entered the gym on the evening of Friday, January twenty-third, forecasted a close game, and these expectations were certainly fulfilled.

The first half was an example of clean, fast basketball, and the guards had more than their share to do. Muth played his role in that solemn "seen but not heard" style to such perfection as to allow his man just three field goals. At half time the Varsity had registered fourteen points to the visitors' eight. In the second half a greater number of points was made by the "take a chance" variety of shooting than by the system of working the ball down to the basket. The latter

248

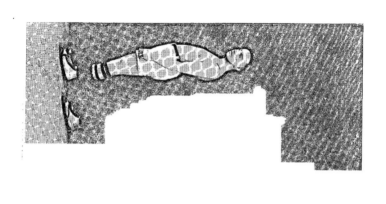

was a difficult task, due mainly to the strong defensive playing of both teams. With but twenty seconds remaining the Varsity had a lead of one point. Santa Clara had hopes of a victory, but somehow the "luck family" gave all they had to support the Nevadans, and a Varsity guard was charged with a foul. Waite perhaps had visions of a Southern Pacific depot and the schoolmates that were to meet his team at Reno, so he placed that foul through the basket causing the score to be a tie. The five minutes granted to play off the tie, resulted in three points and victory for the visitors.

Santa Clara—Manelli, Diaz, Scholz, forwards; Needles, O'Neil, centers; Muth, Ferrario, guards.

Nevada—Williams, Waite, forwards; Buckman, center; Bradshaw, Martin, guards.

Field goals—Manelli 6; Diaz 3; Muth 1; Williams 2; Waite 4; Buckman 3; Bradshaw 1.

Free throws—Manelli, five out of eleven. Waite, nine out of fifteen.

Referee—Penaluma.

Timekeepers—Cahlan, Trabucco.

Scorer—Argenti.

California 24.   Varsity 14.

On Wednesday evening, January twenty-eighth, the second league game was played in the Harmon Gym at the University of California. Dumpy Diaz and Fat Ferrario were not present, and with this handicap to contend with, it is worthy of note that during the first

half the red and white played the blue and gold "off their feet".

Caesar Manelli was the star. Although carefully guarded from the moment the game commenced, he found many chances to score, and as we glance over the pages of the purple book, he is credited with twelve of the total points scored by his team. When the first period of play had ended the Varsity possessed nine points, with California claiming eleven.

The absence of Santa Clara's regular guard and forward was keenly felt in the second half, and again Manelli was forced to play his game alone. He it was who made every point in this half despite the fact that he was "hounded" continually.

The line-ups:

Santa Clara—Manelli, Fowler, Regan, O'Neil, forwards; Needles, center; Muth, Cochrane, guards.

California—McDonald, Symes, Flooberg, forwards; Anderson, Larkey, centers; Majors, Eggleston, Green, Rowe, guards.

Referee—Glenn.

Timer—Christie.

Scorer—Argenti.

College of Pacific 14.   Varsity 17.

The lads on the wrong side of the Alameda journeyed a few miles on the evening of January thirty-first to uphold their part in the league, by offering opposition for the Varsity. We must, with all due respect, admit that the "wearers of the orange and black" possessed a basketball team, and if this fact had only been imprinted upon the minds of the members of our quintet, it is obvious that a larger score would have been made by the red and white.

Again we were handicapped by the absence of Dumpy Diaz, but Roy Fowler played his part in an efficient manner. Jim Needles and Captain Caesar Manelli both caged three baskets, and Cap's shooting of fouls was pleasing to witness, for he totaled five out of eight attempts. At half time the figures read, Varsity 10, College of Pacific 6. The close defensive playing was accountable for the small scores made.

Varsity line-up: Manelli, Fowler, Cochrane, forwards; Needles, center; Muth, Ferrario, guards.

Referee—Glenn.

Timekeepers—Kerckhoff, Corbett.

Scorer—Mollen.

St. Ignatius 31.   Varsity 27.

It has often been said that "revenge is sweet" and from the display of "Zantippy" joy which the Saints enjoyed at the conclusion of this game, we can hardly doubt the statement. To review the first half is to praise the Varsity. Seldom was the ball in the hands of the opponents, as Manelli had a fancy for converting baskets, while Paul Muth, with no fouls checked against him, played the star role, covering the floor in rare form. The half ended 17-7 for Santa Clara.

The second half found the visitors ringing baskets from wide ranges. In this period they added twenty-four

points, with the Varsity increasing its total only by ten. It was a defeat hard to take, as years have passed since St. Ignatius won over the Varsity.

The line-up: Manelli, Diaz, forwards; Needles, center; Muth, Ferrario, guards.

Referee—Glenn.

Timekeeper—Trabucco.

Scorer—Argenti.

Varsity 19.   Davis Farm 15.

The last battle of the season, a league game, was played at Sacramento on the evening of February twenty-seventh. The chief point maker was none other than Jimmy, the graceful center, although Caesar lived up to his name at forward, while Muth, his running mate, as well as Ferrario and Cochrane, at guard, deserve their part of the honors.

And so the Varsity returned to their own valley, and upon entering the club house, quietly placed their suits in the care of Manager Jim O'Connor. Two days later we saw them attired in new caps, suits, and cleats, prepared to do their utmost in finding a position on the Varsity nine.

We have told of the ways of the Varsity, but there is another collection of ambitious individuals who deserve very honorable mention, the Hooligans. It was they who, day after day, gave stiff opposition to the first team, and it was they who kept stringent training rules in order to afford our team practice that was of value in forming this year's quintet. So to give credit to whom credit is due, we write "with figures of gold" the names of Captain Zeek Coman, Mike Pecarovich, Roy Baker, Tom Bannon, Austie Enright, Ido Boyle.

TRACK.

We were not surprised when we saw the happy smile upon Coach Robert Emmett Harmon's face the first day of track practice, for it was the largest turnout that Santa Clarans have had the pleasure to witness. Quantity was there, but to speak of Volkmor, Bedolla, Rianda, Donovan, Baker, McCauley, Schall, Manelli, Needles, Pecarovich, Whelan, Kerckhoff and Dieringer, is to dwell also upon quality and with the continuance of the present diligent practice both Coaches, Roesch, and Harmon, may bring into light several "dark horses".

A few weeks ago an informal meet was held, mainly for the purpose of finding "who's who" in track, and the coaches discovered much promising material.

On April tenth, at two p. m., on the Varsity field, the annual Pentathlon will be held. This is given in honor of our esteemed President, Rev. Father Murphy, and is indeed a day of joy at Santa Clara. Twenty-five cups are to be awarded this year to those holding the greater numbers of points. These trophies are well worth trying for. To mention the Denegri Drug Company, McCabe Hat Store, Kocher Jewelry Store, Maggi's Restaurant, and the Journal office, is to speak of but a few donors.

From the prospects at present, Captain Bill Muldoon should lead a successful track team this season, which, after a few weeks of careful training and coaching, will be in a position to compete with the best in the state.

BASEBALL.

The past two weeks have been given to base running, sliding, and batting practice, but slowly the arms are limbering up, and in the box we may see Berg, Burke, Pecarovich or Elliot, with many others rapidly developing under the guidance of the coach.

At third, Geo. Haneberg looks good. He is a natural ball player, never finding fault with anyone, and covers his position without an error. At first, Hughes has been showing wonderful form, while Krutosik on short, is worthy of watching. Captain Fitzpatrick has a fancy for playing the second sack, although Garcia, who is no young one at this game, has been frequently placed in this position, as well as working at the receiving end. Bricca has of late, had the pleasure of teasing the batters, and although a small target for any pitcher, they always find him behind the plate. In the outfield there is much competition. Bedolla, Manelli, Crowe, and a few of those who have been mentioned as pitchers, may land a berth in the gardens. The schedule in baseball is the largest that has been drawn up in years, and the Varsity will meet the best teams in the west during the next two months.

As the season is young at the time of writing we can but give out the following incomplete schedule:

Sunday, March 7, Olympic Club at Santa Clara.

Saturday, March 13, California at California.

Sunday, March 14, San Francisco Elks at Santa Clara.

Tuesday, March 16, Oregon Aggies at Santa Clara.

Saturday, March 20, Sacramento at Sacramento.

Sunday, March 21, Sacramento at Sacramento.

Sunday, March 28, San Jose Club (Mission League), at Santa Clara.

Sunday, April 11, San Jose Club (Mission League), at Santa Clara.

Sunday, April 18, Olympic Club at Santa Clara.

Saturday, April 24, Stanford at Santa Clara.

Wednesday, April 28, Stanford at Santa Clara.

Thursday, May 6, Stanford at Stanford.

J. E. Neary.

Compliments of the

REX THEATER

ENNO LION, Manager   SANTA CLARA, CAL.

CONTENTS

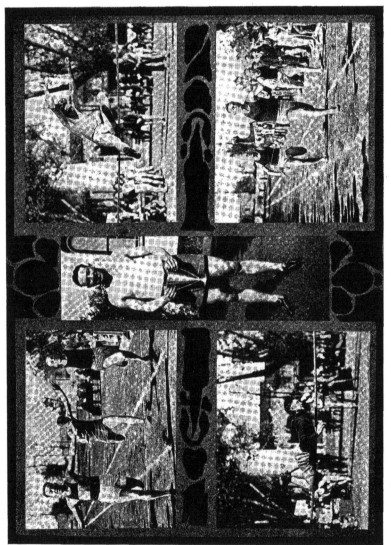

PENTATHLON. PRESIDENT'S DAY, APRIL 10, 1920

The Redwood

Entered Dec. 18, 1902, at Santa Clara, Cal., as second-class matter, under Act of Congress of March 3, 1879

VOL. XIX · SANTA CLARA, CAL., JUNE, 1920 NO. 6

Domus Aurea

 KNOW a spot in the East-land,
   Where spake the great prophets of old
And there in the sight of His angels,
   God built Him a Mansion of Gold.
And when it shone with a glory,
   That dazzled angelical eyes,
The Father, His Only-Begotten,
   Sent down to this House from the skies.
And Jesus and Joseph this roof-tree,
   Protected with fortitude rare:
And when these ascended to Star-land,
   The Spirit lingered still there,
One twilight the angels conveyed it
   In triumphant joy to the spheres,
But 'round it we were clinging our heart-strings,
   And then we had only our tears.

Solomon

Frank Maloney

DEEP hush pervaded the courtroom. That is to say a deep hush pervaded the back of the store of the Honorable Josiah Middleton of Yonkers Corners.

"This court is called to order," said the be-whiskered and venerable old Judge who sat bunched over a table near the front.

The crowd leaned forward as one man. Necks craned over necks that blocked the view; those in the rear stood up that they might better see. If one would look carefully he would notice in particular, near the window in the back of the room, neck outstretched and glaring like a beast, a little snaky bit of a man whose eyes glittered like diamonds in the sunshine.

The whole town was at the trial—the last one that old Judge Priestly would ever preside over. Yonkers Corners was waking up and in the election of the next day, Harry Weeney, a dapper young lawyer just graduated from college, was scheduled to be elected. Yonkers Corners had had enough of these old-timers who did not even know the definition of the word law.

They wanted someone who could administer justice in a modern way and they meant to get him. So all Yonkers Corners had turned out; some curious, and a few sad, to see the old Judge try his last case.

"Now, you, Joe White, can sit over here; and you, Ed Pierce, take this chair.

"Oh, we don't need to be formal," he added hastily as a titter swept over the audience. "We all know each other here, and all we want to do is get at the facts.

"Now Joe, as I understand it, you two boys both lay claim to have invented an apple peeler."

One of the "boys", a withered old man with a kindly eye, nodded his assent.

The other, a young man of twenty-one or two, jerked his head up and down with a cocksure, leering gesture, and a knowing smirk.

"You were both boarding at the same house, were you not?" considered the old Judge soberly.

Again the nod and jerks, signifying that such was the case.

"And both of you, as your landlady testifies, were working on this invention for several years."

"Yes," interrupted the young man, as the smirk disappeared, "and just as I got it down perfect this old duffer tries to steal it."

"Be quiet, now, Ed," said the Judge calmly. "We'll sift this out in a little while. Now, you claim that Joe, over here, stole your invention. Of course, you can't prove it because all his drawings and all your drawings were destroyed when your boarding house burnt down. All the evidence we have to go on is here on the desk"—and he fingered a peculiar contraption which lay on the table.

"Well, he went on, "after examining it a few minutes, "that's mightly little evidence, and I don't think even the big Judges could do much with it."

A sympathetic buzzing from his old friends in the audience interrupted him. But the little snaky bit of a man with the eyes that glittered like diamonds in the sunshine leaned forward as bitter and hostile as ever, at this admission of inadequacy.

"Anyway," added the Magistrate, when the noise had died down, "we can see how it works."

He took the object which seemed to be a sort of combination hash grinder and egg beater, and placed it before him.

"When an apple is placed in here," he explained, coolly suiting the action to the word. "And the handle turned in this way several times, the skin of the apple is cleanly removed."

In went the old wrinkled hand and out came the apple, smooth as a billiard ball, and without a trace of peal. or cut.

The audience gaped and gasped in amazement—but the little snaky bit of a man whose eyes glittered like diamonds in the sunshine, glared on in ill-feigned contempt.

"I'm not much on book learning, folks, as you probably know," the old Judge apologized. "And I guess I don't know much about the law as lots of young fellows do, but when I hadn't much else to do last winter I read a story about some chap that lived a long spell back—and I thought it was pretty good. He was a king or judge or something and his name was Solomon."

The audience smiled indulgently at the display of culture on the part of the poor old Judge—all except the little bit of a snaky man in the back of the room whose eyes glittered like diamonds in the sunshine. He remained as stolidly sour as ever.

But poor old Judge Priestly did not notice these things. With his usual composed air he beckoned to the aged man near the door, a player of the dual role of bailiff and janitor.

"Say, Pete," he whispered, "bring me the ax that's out behind the woodshed."

Pete looked a little frightened, but being a dutiful bailiff and janitor, he soon appeared lugging an old rusty ax over his shoulder.

"Now, folks," said the Judge, as he fondled the blunt edge of the instrument, "both of these boys claim this apple-peeler as their own. Well, I'm going to give each one of them a piece. That's fair, isn't it?" And he brought the clumsy tool over his head.

"Stop, stop!" shrieked the boy, whose name was Ed. "Bust that and I'll have the law on you. This ain't a regular court anyhow. And I need that peeler when I take this case to a real judge."

There the Judge stood with the ax dangerously poised in the air, with a ridiculous expression on his withered old face, looking down on the speaker. Then his gaze shifted to poor browbeaten Joe White, who had hardly said a word the whole while, but whose features were now lit up with a quiet smile.

"What do you say, Joe?" he asked. "Go ahead and bust it, Judge," the old fellow replied. "Go ahead and bust it, then I'll make another one just like it."

Then, the audience realizing the dramatic power of the situation, burst into an uproar and a shout went up from all for old Judge Priestly—the Judge incumbent, and the Judge to be for four years—that is, from all but the little snaky bit of a man with the eyes that glittered like diamonds in the sunshine. He was already tottering out on the arm of a kind friend, because he could not see through his glass eyes. He wished to avoid the rush—and he didn't have anything to do with this story anyway.

Marcello, Last of Mission Indians

(Courtesy the Columbiad.)

By Charles D. South, Litt. D.

F the twenty-one Catholic Indian Missions of California, the seventh in chronological order of establishment was that of Santa Clara de Asis, on the Arroyo Guadalupe, near the southern extremity of San Francisco Bay; and of the thousands of red men who were fed, clothed and educated there by the self-sacrificing sons of St. Francis, and who labored to upbuild and maintain this heroic Christian settlement in the territory of the Olhone, or Constano, tribes, the name of Marcello alone has survived, and his personality stands dimly outlined in solitary hugeness against the hazy background of California's pastoral age.

Most famous of all the Mission Indians, Marcello, last of his race, joined the innumerable caravan only after his life had spanned, it is claimed, a full century and a quarter—a century and a quarter which more than ''tinges the sober twilight of the present with color of romance.''

To the tribes which occupied the heart of the valley of Santa Clara at the advent of the Franciscans, accord-

ing to local tradition, Marcello came a stranger, speaking a strange dialect. His heroic size and princely bearing seem to have lent credence to his boast that through his veins coursed the blood of kings. His ancestors are supposed to have been royal Yumans of the valley of the Colorado River, and this reputed scion of a great aboriginal family was instinctively hailed as a chief by the tawny sunworshipers whose wigwams cast their shadow in the fretful Guadalupe. He was hailed instinctively as chief, perhaps, because his very figure was commanding, since he is said to have loomed above the squat Indians of Santa Clara as the Sequoia looms above the dwarf pines of the Sierra.

An inscription in the San Jose public library informs the reader that Marcello's measure of life was 125 years; that he opened his eyes on the world in 1750, and was gathered to his fathers in 1875. The longevity of his existence may be better appreciated by reference to characters and incidents of the history which civilization was inditing the while Marcello rose to manhood and stalked, an imposing figure, through the romantic Mission age, through the

257

revolutionary Mexican period, through the epochal era of maddening gold strikes, and on down through the still greater era of American progress—an era in which not the mineral gold but the richer vegetable gold becomes the stable basis of prosperity.

This Indian celebrity, who is said to have assisted Padre Thomas de la Pena to raise the storied Mission Cross near the laurelwood on the banks of the Guadalupe, January 12, 1777, and who is quoted as having averred that he had seen Lieutenant Jose de Moraga raise the royal emblem of Spain at the founding of the Pueblo de San Jose, was supposedly toying with wampum and feathers in the wigwam of his father when young George Washington, leading a band of colonials, accompanied the British General Braddock and his veterans on the disastrous march against Fort Duquesne. Assuming that 1750 was the date of Marcello's nativity, he was five years of age when Wolfe's intrepid redcoats stormed the Heights of Abraham and when Montcalm heroically welcomed the death that shut from his vision the surrender of Quebec. He was fifteen when the British Parliament passed the Stamp Act which precipitated the American Revolution; and when the Liberty Bell rang out the glad tidings of the Declaration of Independence in 1776 he was enlisting in the service of Padre Junipero Serra for a peaceful invasion of the valleys of Alta California. The chief, as Marcello was called, had pass-

ed his thirty-ninth year-post when Washington was elected President of the United States, and had he survived one year longer he might have participated in the first centennial of American liberty.

Following out the natal-day hypothesis, Chief Marcello was nineteen years old when Napoleon Bonaparte was born, and when the French Revolution burst into throne-consuming flame this Indian was marching into a wilderness of the unknown west with the cowled Grey Friars of St. Francis. He was fifty-four when Napoleon, at the age of thirty-five, was crowned Emperor of the French; fifty-six when Bonaparte reached the zenith of his career at Austerlitz, and sixty-five when the star of the Corsican genius went down in blood at Waterloo; and, moreover, it may not prove uninteresting to note that this towering aboriginal was still conspicuous in the ranks of the living, having reached his hundred and twentieth year, when the third Napoleon, after overthrowing the French Republic, was himself overthrown at Sedan.

George II was on the throne of England while Marcello was yet a whimpering pappoose, and during the chief's lifetime George III blundered out his long, inglorious reign and William IV served a brief term at wielding the British scepter. The gentle Victoria was pretty well along in age and queenship when Marcello (who had beheld California in its tribal stage and then successively under Spain, Mexico and the United States) ultimately surrendered to the inevitable; and, finally, before this super-Indian looked his last upon the sun there was already reigning on the Austrian throne that ill-starred monarch of the House of Hapsburg, the late Emperor Francis Joseph, whose edict in 1914 set Europe ablaze and plunged the world into a war so colossal as to render small in comparison the sum total of destruction in all the wars of Alexander, Caesar and Napoleon.

According to trustworthy authority, Chief Marcello was a veritable walking encyclopedia of Mission history; yet nobody in his time saw fit to make a transcript of his story and that possible source of infinitude of details of the early annals of Santa Clara is now shut off forever.

Nobody living knows exactly where the first Santa Clara Mission stood. Marcello knew the location; but, odd as it may seem, little interest appears to have been taken in the subject until after Marcello's demise. When the book was eternally closed, the people became eager to read.

This copper-skinned giant, in his prime, stood six feet two inches in his bare feet, weighed 250 pounds, was rawboned and possessed of prodigious strength. There is no evidence other than the unauthenticated stories handed down by the old Spanish families that he had assisted in the erection of the wooden frames of the original Mis-

sion on the banks of the Guadalupe, and it is not certain that he witnessed the destruction of the settlement by flood in 1779; but there is plenty of corroboration for his story that he aided Padre Jose Antonio Murguia to build the adobe Mission on the second site, now marked by a simple white cross which stands some two hundred paces west of the Southern Pacific Railroad depot at Santa Clara.

Anterior to the coming of the Friars —long before Marcello had set eyes on this fair scene—the Spanish Sergeant Ortega, at the behest of the renowned Captain Gaspar de Portola, in 1769, had led a band of scouts along the southern borders of San Francisco Bay and had described the future Santa Santa Clara valley as "The Plain of Oaks." Subsequently, for a number of years, the region was designated as the "Meadow of San Bernardino," and the beautiful name, Santa Clara, after the holy nun of Assisium, was the happy selection of the illustrious Junipero Serra.

While the honor of founding this Mission is shared conjointly by Padre Pena and Lieutenant Moraga, the famous Colonel d'Anza, who had led from Mexico two hundred colonists to form the village of San Francisco and the civilian nucleus of the Mission of Santa Clara, was regrettably deprived of the historical prominence due him through a military exigency which impelled his sudden return to San Diego. Thus was his lieutenant left to celebrate the crowning of labors which owed their successful fruition to the masterful preliminary achievements of his brilliant superior officer.

Marcello saw the natives raised from a low state of savagery to the enjoyment of the condition of civilization; for the valley Indians when the Padres came, shunned clothing and strode about in ablutionless epidermal simplicity. Like animals of the lower order, they subsisted on roots and acorns, having little ambition to bend the bow in pursuit of noble game. He saw them in after years decently clad and abundantly fed; he saw them tilling the soil and reaping its harvests; he saw the erstwhile lazy Olhones become proficient at many trades, blacksmithing, carpentering, tanning, weaving, shoemaking, and the manufacture of bricks and tiles. He saw them trained not only in the manual arts, but in letters and music and painting. Orchards and vineyards soon dotted the land; herds and flocks increased until, at the close of the eighteenth century, cattle and sheep each numbered five thousand head, while the annual harvest of grain approximated ten thousand bushels.

In this day of frequent disputes over the hours of labor, it may be interesting to note that the work-day of the Missions was only five hours long, and that the remainder of the day was devoted to study, games and pastimes. In 1827 the population of Santa Clara included 1,500 Indians, and the common property was 15,000 cattle, as many sheep, and

2,800 horses. The lands reserved for the native converts who accepted a settled life extended from the Guadalupe to the summit of the mountain range on the west, a domain of eighty thousand acres, exempt from taxation during Spanish rule. Under Mexican authority, the Missions were secularized and plundered, and there soon remained only a vestige of their once prosperous communities. In our time admiring and sympathetic Americans are devoting money and energy to the restoration of the unique buildings which still stand as landmarks of the Franciscan era, and a great university, at Palo Alto, California, has adopted and preserved in its general design the style of architecture which was characteristic of the Missions and which owes its origin to the genius of the Padres.

The Alameda, the palm-bordered avenue of patrician homes which links the sister cities of San Jose and Santa Clara in the heart of the rich valley at the southern extremity of the San Francisco peninsula, is still "The Beautiful Way," but Marcello knew the Alameda when it was far more lovely and enchanting than it appears in the splendors lavished on it by modern wealth and artistry. He had acted as foreman of native laborers who constructed the Alameda under the direction of Padre Jose Viader, the assistant of the venerable Padre Magin Catala, at the dawn of the nineteenth century.

When his years had told a hundred,

the aged chief found pleasure in traversing the foliage-canopied league which separates San Jose from Santa Clara, and delighted in entertaining fellow pedestrians with tales of the days when the great willow trees, which in summer afforded impenetrable shade along the winding road, had in their infancy been tenderly nursed by him and his companions after the slips had been borne to the Camino Real in bundles on the backs of tawny laborers. He described how the trees had been planted in three rows extending all the way from the second Mission site to the second site of the Pueblo de San Jose, and pointed out with his staff the courses of long zanjas or ditches which carried water from the Guadalupe to the nursling willows.

The destruction of the second Mission by an earthquake in 1818 led to the selection of the third site, on which recently the imposing structures of the University of Santa Clara have been reared. Of the third Mission buildings, the old church alone remains, and of this church Marcello—still vigorous at the age of seventy, straight as a poplar, like some tall tower defying the assaults of time—Marcello was the overseer of construction. The Mission church had undergone many changes and alterations, but it still retains the original altar, the unique Indian paintings and the impressive wooden crucifix celebrated in Charles Warren Stoddard's miracle story of the sainted Magin Catala—El Padrecito Santo;

and from its majestic towers, the historic bells, presented to Santa Clara by King Carlos V—bells, with music voices that have never faltered—still summon the faithful to devotion, still charm the air morning, noon and evening with their silvery prelude to the aspirations of the Angelus.

In the old Mission, always as the nocturnal shadows fell, the spirits of the dead seemed calling, calling to the living in the mournful notes that issued from the weird owl belfry, and at that pious summons every head was bowed in silent orison. Now, when the day fire is extinguished and meditative night has drawn her sable curtain over the world, solemnly they ring, even as of yore, to bid the Christian breathe De Profundis for departed souls; for these bells, let it be said, were given by the Spanish monarch under the single condition that nightly they should be tolled as an appeal to the faithful to lift heart and voice in the prayer: "Out of the depths have I cried unto Thee, O Lord! Lord, hear my voice! Eternal rest grant unto them, O, Lord! And let perpetual light shine upon them!"

Marcello loved these bells, and doubtless they recalled to his memory many a face and many a voice and many a scene of a vanished age. At their ropes his stout arms had toiled full many a time. They knelled his passage from the house of clay; and, if spirits of the dead are conscious of the things done in the abode of the quick, the soul of the chief must find joy in the prayers that rise to heaven at the nightly bell-call to De Profundis.

With the sequestration of the Missions, the large majority of the Indians, deprived of the paternal care and protection of their Franciscan benefactors, dispersed to the surrounding hills and again became wedded to the savage life. Marcello was more fortunate for a period, but he, too, fell from his high estate. He was ninety-six years old when, in 1846, Governor Pio Pico granted him a veritable principality known as the Ulistac rancho, situated between Santa Clara and San Francisco Bay. It was a landed estate worthy of a chief, and Marcello became exceedingly vain of his reputed royal descent.

The shadow of war fell on the country and, when the shadow passed, a new flag—the Stars and Stripes—floated over California. Then Marcello, in his ignorance of law and in his blind eagerness to obtain the wherewithal to satisfy his cravings for the worldly pleasures introduced by reckless newcomers, for a few paltry pieces of sordid gold, signed away to a land-grabber all his vast domain. It was then divided into small farms, and years afterward, Marcello was accustomed to plod from house to house in the sovereignity he had lost, to request and to receive food and raiment from his successors, whimsically regarding such favors not as charity but as a right.

The Caucasian, represented in the Mission Padres, had raised Marcello and his brethren from savagery to a degree of civilization; had taught them the arts of peace and equipped them with the rudiments of science; and the Caucasian of another type, actuated by conscienceless greed and avarice, destroyed the Missions and reduced to pauperism and helpless misery such of the natives as were left behind when the bolder spirits of their tribes fled to the wilderness to lapse into the bestial life of their ancestors.

That Marcello became an easy victim to the duplicity of a certain species of white man may be logically attributable to his education by the Grey Friars of the Mission; for the Padres, like Goldsmith's pedagogue, had "lured to brighter worlds and led the way." Deservedly they had won the confidence of the Indian, whose filial trust in the Franciscans had never been betrayed. Marcello's loss of the Ulistac grant was, therefore, conceivably due to a childlike belief that those Caucasians who swarmed the lands on which lay the crumbling Mission ruins were as free from guile as their cowled predecessors. It was his misfortune to discover too late that a white face may not be an index to virtue and honor.

At the age of a hundred the chief was forced to content himself with a humble cabin donated by a generous farmer in a remote section of Pio Pico's grant. In gratitude for Marcello's early services to the Padres, and eager to make comfortable the old chief's declining days, the Jesuit Fathers of Santa Clara, apprised of his hardship, invited him to abide permanently under their roof. The big chief, however, had discovered an aversion for any suggestion of celibacy. He had heard the call of the wild, as it were, and his aboriginal nature was again dominant. He was no longer Marcello, the neophyte of the Missionite. He was Marcello, the Indian; Marcello, the slave of passion; Marcello, the free rover of valley and hill—until at last a reawakening conscience urged him totteringly back to the humility of repentance.

When the third church was altered in compliance with modern necessity—when the adobe walls, six feet thick, were razed to be replaced by the more sanitary redwood frame, a steel track was laid from the interior of the edifice to a nearby field, and flat cars were operated for weeks removing the historic debris till the recipient sod, in contrast with the surrounding surface, resembled a tableland. Then, moistened by the rain of winter and quickened by the benificent beams of the sun, the life that was latent in the adobe sprang forth anew and burgeoned, blossomed and bloomed in a splendor of golden poppies, which were strangers to the adjacent soil.

Far back in the idyllic Mission days, seeds of Christian virtue had been planted in the soul of Marcello. In the half-century since the destruction of the Mission, that seed had been sealed up in the dark breast of the Indian, dry and unnurtured, like the seed in the old church wall. For half a century

the chief had pursued the way of the world in flagrant disregard of Mission precept and example. But the seed of Christian virtue is never sown in vain, and it never fails to bear good fruit, although the harvest may sometimes be early and sometimes very late. At length, in extreme old age, the spiritual seed, dormant for fifty years in this son of the wilderness, responded to the nurturing years of repentance and flowered under the smile of Divine mercy, and Marcello passed away with the comforting hope that, in a better sphere, he would rejoin the holy Padres in immortal life.

Ninety-eight years in the Santa Clara valley must have confused Marcello's memory with their procession of changing scenes and characters: First, the savage gives way before the conquering Caucasian; next, the Mission rises where the wigwam stood; then, the forests fade, and spire and dome appear, as in a dream, and, by what Ruskin terms the "art of kings and king of arts," civilization conjures fabulous riches from earth's hidden cells.

"Where stalked the bronze-skinned brave
In savage pride of power,
The paleface treads the Indian's grave."

Marcello came, in 1777, a stranger to a strange land, and again, at the last, in 1875, still more of a stranger in a land stranger than of old, he crosses life's divide, hopeful of rest after a strenuous day. The red man disappears from view. The paleface garners the earth and, with his monuments of trade, usurps the upper spaces of the air; and where, for nearly a century, this Indian colossus flourished, like a mighty oak, pitting its knotty bulk against the ravages of time and the elements—where, for ages, his striking figure was as familiar as the gray adobes and the Spanish tiles—the people of today, save for a few literary pilgrims groping among the dustheaps of California history, know not that there ever existed such a being as Marcello, super-Indian of the Santa Clara Mission.

In Honorem Sancti Aloysii

Seculi fallacis opes refugit,
  Gentis et sceptra et patrios honores
Agminis Christi Lodoix decora
  Signa seeutus.

Ut solet saepe altivolans videri
  Negligens terras volucris supremos
Nubium campos petere, et secare
  Aethera pennis:

Ipse sic fortis Lodoix fugaces
  Respuit gazas celeremque famam;
Respuit quae offert peregrina tellus,
  Sidera spectans.

Te decent sedes Superumque regna,
  Nulla quae sternent peritura secla,
Nam tui semper placuere gesta,
  Usque placebunt.

Nunc juvat frontem redimire myrto
  Sempiterna, purpureisque gemmis,
Quas per exactae bene comparasti
  Tempora vitae.

Occulent umbrae generosa facta
  Regios actus simul et fugacem
Gloriam partam populis domandis
  Ense cruento.

Sed nihil magnum sinit interire
  Nil mori virtus patitur, reservans
Posteris sanctae monumenta vitae
  Condita fastis.

Te lyra sumit celebrare vates
  Teque per gentes imitatur arte
Sculptor, et cives tibi jam verenda
  Templa dicarunt.

Te cupit doctis tabulis sacrare
  Pictor, et gaudet numerare laudes
Pontifex templis pueris decoras
  Atque puellis.

Tum per Europae spatiosa regna
  Tum per ardentis Libyae latebras
Et per Indorum penetravit arva
  Gloria Divi.

Hic manet corda intaminata splendor:
  Hi viros justos decorant honores,
Quos quidem nullum reticebit unquam
  Temporis aevum.

Ille nunc civis rutilantis aulae
  Annuat votis populi rogantis,
Sorte mutata, ut redeant in aurum
  Tempora priscum.

J. C. S. S. J.

265

The Christmas Goose

A. J. Steiss, Jr.

T HE Stag Head Inn, Sudbury, London, is one of the pleasantest of taverns. I first stumbled upon it one Christmas Eve, wandering about the frosty streets, a stranger in a strange city. Every window beamed with benevolence and the hearty good-will of the times; merrymaking was going on in every dwelling; few were in the streets, save belated shoppers, for Christmas Eve is a time spent in the home. But alas! no lighted windows welcomed me, nor music cheered me, for I was alone and homeless on Christmas Eve, of all the days in the year. As I passed rapidly over the crisp snow on a quiet by-way I noticed opposite a small edifice, with cherry red curtains, and a sign that read Stag Head Inn, over the door. The shadows cast by the fire danced weirdly on the windows. It seemed to be a quiet hostelry, and suited to one of my sedentary pursuits. Forthwith I crossed, and shoved open the door, and was greeted by a blast of warmth. From the kitchen I could hear the pleasant sound of sizzling and broiling, and the clattering of dishes, and at times merry laughter.

There were only three in the public room,—the coachman from Dover, a crumpled-up little book dealer and an old clerk with enormous spectacles perched on the end of his nose. They invited me to join them at the table, and were soon chatting with me, and discussing affairs in general. After dinner we were silent for a while, save the coachman, who was whistling softly to himself. The book dealer had closed his eyes, the clerk was looking into the fire, and I, watching the shadows leap upon the low, holly-hung ceiling, was lost in pleasant reminiscence.

"My friends," said the clerk, his hands deep in his pockets, his eyes fixed on the red embers on the hearth, "the goose we have just disposed of put me in mind of one I enjoyed a year ago."

"Nothing notable in that," said the book dealer, without opening his eyes. "This goose reminds me of about fifty of 'em."

The clerk removed the spectacles from his nose. "Ah," he answered, "but thereby hangs a tale."

The coachman stopped his whistling. "See here," he said, "be sure it isn't the one you told last year. We heard that three times in succession."

"Thomas," answered the old clerk, "you mustn't scoff at my forgetfulness; you should respect it; it took fifty years to develop it. Anyway, this ain't the one ye've heard; it's a new tale completely."

"Proceed," says the coachman, "as long as it ain't that old one."

The clerk mopped his forehead with an enormous red handkerchief.

"I had a friend once—"

"Very remarkable circumstance," mused the book dealer aloud; "very."

"If you interrupt again, Michael, I'll start on that story ye've heard three times already."

The book dealer seemed asleep.

"I had a friend once, who lived with his wife and three children in St. Bernard's Court, near King George's Market in Clerkenwell. If you know the place, you know that it's black with soot, and blacker with shadows, and when the wind blows, those old houses shake like they'd got the ague.

"However, my friend could afford no better, for he was not blest with an abundance either of the luxuries or of the necessaries of the world. In fact, he had a deal of labor to hold his home together, and often had barely enough with which to meet the landlord on his visits."

"Ah me!" sighed the book dealer.

"Didn't that goose agree with ye?" queried the coachman.

"I was only thinking how similar that story is to my own sad tale."

"You can tell that afterward," said the clerk.

The book dealer chuckled.

"But to come down to the point, they both loved their children a great deal better than themselves, and they would hold their noses to the grindstone year in and year out, to make their children happy at Christmas Tide. And being wise parents, they knew that the principal cause of a child's delight is the expansion of his stomach, and he must therefore have a tender goose for Christmas.

"Well, on this particular Christmas Eve, the holiday bustle had delayed the husband's homecoming till the supper hour, and he had not yet had time to fetch it. As night came on a cold wind had arisen and the drizzle had turned to a storm. But he had his eye on a goose at a certain market, and if he did not make his purchase that evening, perhaps it might be sold when he went next morning.

"Like the whole clan of timid widows, his mistress prayed that he should wait till tomorrow, for in the snow he might catch his death of cold and so forth. But the husband was firm in his purpose—"

"Like the whole clan of husbands," added the coachman.

"Exactly, Thomas. And so the husband bade her good-by, assuring her that he would return as fast as his legs could carry him, for these cold nights were not to his liking anyway. Through the blackness of the court, the old dwellings loomed like elderly gentlemen in cocked hats, with their teeth chattering in the wind. Walking was dangerous, and more than once my friend contemplated returning to his home, but the thought of his sleeping children urged him onward. Now he was clear of the Court, now walking down C—— Lane, and now he had arrived at the bridge, with its stream of water rushing madly in eddies beneath."

The clerk's audience was watching the coals, apparently inattentive.

The clerk stretched his feet out toward the fire, his elbows on the arms of his great chair.

"Perhaps the roar of the river had made him dizzy, or his foot may have slipped upon the ice (I don't believe he knows to this day), but in the middle of the bridge he fell, his head striking the pavement; under the railing he rolled and into the torrent. About fifty yards below he was cast up on a bit of rock, and here he awoke just as the Christmas dawn was breaking over the city."

The clerk sipped his steaming ale and mopped his brow.

"And now, Michael," he continued, "if you will wake up, you can listen to the curious part of my story."

"Go ahead," said the book dealer; "I've been awake since you started, but so far I ain't heard much."

"Well, you'll hear something directly. It may have been the blow he received in falling that caused it; or the shock of the immersion into the icy water of the stream, or the exposure through the long night, but on regaining his consciousness, he had lost his memory; his past was darkened; and though otherwise normal, he remembered neither family, home, nor name."

"Well, that was curious," broke in the book dealer. And he stooped for a coal for his pipe. "In fact, such a happening is quite out of the ordinary."

"If you will wait, you will hear something more remarkable than that. My friend climbed from the rock whereon the current had tossed him and made his way into the city dazedly. And shortly after his bedraggled figure had disappeared into the fog, his wife in sore distress came upon the scene of his adventure, and on the bridge she saw a hat—her husband's. Surely, she thought, if he had fallen into the river, no human power could have saved him from drowning. And she sadly made her way homeward to her children.

"From that time on, the unfortunate mother considered herself a widow. There were few things she might do to earn her daily bread, but as she was handy with the needle, and naturally industrious, she at first was able to make out fairly well. But as time went on, and sorrow had made its inroads upon her fresh countenance, and her unwonted labor had exhausted her, she sank slowly, month by month.

"In the meantime, however, her husband had been enjoying circumstances far different from her own. In a fever, he had thrown himself down on a door-step that Christmas morning, and a jovial-hearted banker, stepping out to Church, found him there, and being moved by deep pity, and for the sake of the holy tide,, revived him and gave him a good position; and being of an intelligent turn of mind he had risen with speed, and was soon comfortably placed.

"But as the months passed, he reasoned that others might have suffered from his misadventure. He had a vague feeling that he should share his money with someone; and so ever he gave, and ever he made the warmest friends in the world. Two years passed in this manner, and again the Christmas Tide was at hand.

"In St. Bernard's Court, the wife had waited and waited, but she could not wait for long now. Her strength was failing, and when the landlord should next come to the Court, there would be no money to give him. In the next room the children were asleep, but she had lain sleepless for many nights, and she was not going to bed. She sat by the window in the darkness, looking out at the court, all covered with white snow, and at the fog, and at the dim black ghosts of houses over the way.

"But the husband, seized by a curious whim, had turned his footsteps to the bridge, whence he had fallen two years since. And it was only a whim; he did not know why he was there; but

nevertheless it was with some degree of interest that he gazed about him, as he stood, his elbows on the railing, the seething river dashing beneath him. Suddenly he felt himself sway, he threw up his hands, and striking his head against the opposite railing, fell limp upon the pavement. He stirred soon, and before long, arose—and it was a stormy night, two years ago, and he had merely fallen upon the stones and had been dazed!"

The old clerk tips the tumbler of ale to his lips, and as he sets it down, sneezes. "But I am not finished yet," he said. "His wife was still sitting by the window, when a dark figure pressed on toward the unlighted dwelling. She saw it scrape the snow from its feet, and climb the stairs, and a loud knock resounded through the still house. The poor woman flew to the door, and flung it open; and her husband entered the room. His wife felt his cheeks, as if believing he was a ghost, and then flung her arms about his neck, sobbing hysterically.

"Of course, the husband was very bewildered. Handing her a parcel, he said, 'Mary, my dear, here is the Christmas goose.'"

The clerk laughed. "Well," he said, "that is all."

The coachman seemed pondering. "Lor'" he said, "it took him a long time to get the goose, didn't it?"

"Yes," laughed the crumpled-up

book dealer, "it did. But I would like to know where our friend found the goose that put him in mind of such a story."

"Bless me!" exclaimed the cl "the goose was the one that the band carried home, and I can as you it was juicy as the rarest."

MICHAEL J. PECAROVICH, AS MATHIAS IN "THE BELLS"

"The Bells"

Henry C. Veit.

OR a period of some eight years one of Santa Clara's most famous organizations, the Senior Dramatic Society lay dormant for want of an annual stage production to keep alive the ideals and high aspirations that had become so thoroughly identified with the time honored institution.

Not since 1912 has the thespian organization essayed a production of repute. That year will be remembered by Santa Clarans in particular, and the old University's friends in general, as the year of the unparalleled success Martin V. Merle's Mission Play enjoyed. Others will be reminded of the fact that not since that time has any production been able to compare with the recent play, "The Bells". The three-night run of the production came up to almost every expectation entertained for it prior to its staging.

"The Bells" marked the revival of Santa Clara's old-time dramatics and opened the door to a future pregnant with possibilities that bids fair to outshine anything that past years have witnessed within these hallowed walls.

So thorough was our enjoyment after leaving the famous old auditorium when the last show was over and so purely pleasant was the taste that Henry Irving's classic left with us that we delved deep into Santa Clara's dramatic past in quest of her many sons who long since have reflected credit upon their Alma Mater in the Thespian Art.

The first to reward us in our search was John T. Malone, one of the many renowned interpreters of Shakespeare's plays. Mr. Malone's rise to fame behind the footlights was meteoric. From Santa Clara he went direct to Broadway, where he continued his success in Shakespearean roles. His fame even rippled to the distant shores of the Bard of Avon's homeland.

Actors and playwrights alike were revealed to us. We learned of Clay M. Greene's Passion Play and the fact that Mr. Greene's prolific pen was responsible for many of the best productions Broadway has ever known.

There were John A. Waddell, John J. Barrett, James Bacigalupi, Edmund Lowe, Martin V. Merle and a host of others too numerous to mention that passed with all the wealth of their abilities before our mind's eye.

271

The Senior Dramatic Society of old was Santa Clara's polishing school. From it her pupils graduated possessed of poise and grace so essential to almost every walk of present day life, political, professional or commercial, and more particularly to him who would seek fame in the oratorical world. It produced a Delmas, that prince of eloquence, and a John J. Barrett, recognized today as one of California's leading orators. It has sent matinee idols behind the footlights and stars to the silver sheet.

"The Bells" blazed the trail for repetition in the future of all that the past could boast. For Santa Clara it carried a deep significance.

Henry Irving made "The Bells" a classic and played in the leading role for the greater part of his career. In Michael Pecarovich as Mathias, the Burgomaster, Santa Clara has one of whom she can be justly proud. His deep resonant voice, his masterful stage presence, and highly emotional ability never once failed to enthrall his audience or drive home with telling effect the pointed moral, "murder will out" and the "wages of sin is death."

The scene of the play is laid in a village of Alsace. The story is of a Polish Jew mysteriously murdered and robbed of his gold. In the opening scene a raging snow storm prevails which recalls to the village folk gathered in the Burgomaster's inn the strange disappearance of the Jew fifteen years before. A haunting sound of jangling

bells keeps Mathias in constant remembrance of his foul deed. The act closes with an apparition of the Jew driving by in a sleigh over the identical spot where he had been murdered fifteen years before by Mathias. Here Mr. Pecarovich's portrayal of the part was superb. One could sense the horror and hear the sigh of relief that passed through the audience as the act ended.

The second act revealed the coming marriage between Annette, the Burgomaster's daughter, and Christian, a young officer in whom Mathias had placed his hope—the only refuge he could fly to when conscience overpowered him.

The dream of Mathias wherein he is dragged to the assizes and charged with the murder of the Polish Jew has become a vital part of the whole play and is actually reproduced. In an hypnotic slumber produced by the summoned mesmerist, Mathias reveals all the horrible details of his crime. The death penalty then inflicted is the final blow to the Burgomaster. A guilty conscience gnaws away the last spark of life within him. He dies as his friends summon him to participate in the merriment attendant upon the marriage of Annette to Christian.

Responsible in great part for the success of "The Bells" was the clever scene painting done by Mr. Michael O'Sullivan of San Francisco. He will be remembered for his exceptional work in The Mission Play and

The Passion Play of past years. In "The Bells" he outdid his past efforts a hundred fold.

The 1920 production by the Senior Dramatic Society of "The Bells" on the nights of May 6th, 7th, and 8th, marked the time of triumph for Santa Clara. Had it only served to pave the way for future dramatic triumphs, "The Bells" would have been a success. But coupled with this fact is the financial increment the Student Body realized for its Athletic fund.

Santa Clara, we are proud of you because of "The Bells". And we love you more, for days to come will dawn upon the grand spectacles of the Mission and Passion plays that so materially aided Santa Clara in years gone by.

RESOLUTIONS.

Whereas, The Senior Dramatic Society of the University of Santa Clara enjoyed an unprecedented success in its revival of dramatics, by the recent presentation of "The Bells", a classic production, which reflected great glory upon the University, and

Whereas, this great glory was made possible only through the untiring and disinterested efforts of Father Joseph A. Sullivan, S. J., who directed the play, and Mr. Louis B. Egan, S. J., who staged it,

Be it Resolved, that we, the Associated Students of the University of Santa Clara, extend to both Father Sullivan and Mr. Egan our sincerest thanks in warm appreciation of the great part they have contributed toward the success of "The Bells".

THE ASSOCIATED STUDENTS.

HENRY C. VEIT,
President.

LOUIS F. BUTY,
Secretary.

EDMUND Z. COMAN,
Treasurer.

JAMES R. NEEDLES,
Sergeant-At-Arms.

JAMES B. O'CONNOR,
Student Manager.

Frenzied Finance

Frank Maloney

JOE SMITH drove up to the front gate, climbed down from his lofty seat on the wagon and hitched his thin, morbid-looking team to a careening fence post. Then, in a leisurely way that characterized all his movements, he began unloading a motley collection of tools, which gave evidence of being near the junk-pile stage of their career. Apparently he was deeply absorbed in his work, at least he did not so much as glance up from it when Jack Crowe's loud voice burst on him.

"Hello, Joe," said Crowe, "pow'ful hot this evenin'."

"Good evening," Joe grumbled.

"Heard you'uz going to dig a well for Jim Thurman."

Joe grunted noncommitally.

"Dad blamed hard up for a job, ain't you? Now, I promised to help you from now on, but I wuzn't countin' on us a-workin' for that old crook. He beat me out of a month's wages, onc't."

The person spoken to threw a heavy monkey wrench on the ground, then turned and looked at his companion sourly.

"Who's a-hirin' you, me or him?" he demanded in guttural tones.

"Why, you o' course. But s'posen he don't pay you for the well we dig; where do I come in at?"

"He'll pay me, all right."

"If we don't strike water on that there land—and 'tain't recorded that we will; you know all them dry holes 'round there—if we don't, I say, we'll never get a cent for the work. I got no time to throw away, neither have I any money to do the same thing with."

"I tell you I'm good for this money."

Jack glanced dubiously at Joe, a tall, stooped figure in ragged overalls, then at the emaciated team.

"You can't pay me," he snorted, "if Thurman don't pay you."

"He'll pay me, all right," persisted the other doggedly.

"You mark my words, we'll get stung. That old boy, he's tricky. Jest when you think he's your best friend, he quits you cold."

By this time they were seated on the rickety bench, in front of the gate. Joe was filling his much-used, blackened pipe, and Jack was cramming his mouth with tobacco. Both turned at the sound of a timid voice behind them. A slim, brown-eyed girl, about fourteen years old, came and stood by Smith's elbow.

"Pa, give me a quarter. Ma said so."

"What for?" he demanded, roughly.

"Can o' tomatoes for supper. I'm going after it."

He fished in his overalls pocket and brought out the required amount.

She took the money and started down the road.

"Yep," continued Crowe. He don't mind skinning nobody. That's the way he done Tom Coleman who 'uz one of these trustin' kind. Tom gets Thurman to hold down a section he 'uz homesteading out, and what does Jim do? He ups and steals it."

But Joe was not listening; instead, he was watching a bit of byplay with lowering brows and angry eyes. A short distance away from where the men sat, Jane, Joe's daughter, had caught up with a girl of about her own age. She spoke shyly. The girl swept her with a cold stare that took in her faded cap, equally faded dress and rusty, ill-shaped shoes. Then, without a word, she went on. As Jane dropped behind in evident embarrassment, the two were overtaken by a costly automobile. In the tonneau were several young girls. With a loud honking the car came to a stop.

"Get in here, Gerty Jones," one of the girls said. "WE are going to Kate's to help her fix up for the party. We need you, too."

Laughing gaily, Gerty scrambled in among the chattering friends. The machine shot ahead, and Jane, a forlorn little creature, was left staring after it wistfully. Then, blinking the tears from her eyes, she started dejectedly toward town.

"Whose car 'uz that?" Joe demanded with an oath.

"Whose? Why, that's Jim Thurman's," replied Jack.

He leaned back in order to replace a piece of tobacco in his pocket.

"As I 'uz sayin'" he continued, "Jim he——"

"Aw, shut up! Everybody knows what he done," snarled Joe, taking his anger out on an inoffensive tin can nearby. "I didn't hire you to talk about Jim Thurman from mornin' till night. Guess he works, at least, which is more than I——"

"Say, what's catin' you, anyway?" demanded his companion.

But Smith was half way down the path, which, hedged in by wild millet and sickly hollyhocks, led a wandering way to the house.

Jack stood and stared at the retreating figure with a puzzled look.

Joe strode into his ramshackle dwelling and stormed through the front room and on into the kitchen.

His wife, a slight, dreary-looking woman, who sat darning an old sock, glanced up listlessly, when he banged his fist down upon the rickety table and thundered:

"I want you to go to town this very day an' buy Janie a satin dress. Satin, get me? Don't want no other kind!"

"What in the world's come over you?" she demanded in a tired voice. He glared at her. "You get that dress, I say. Janie's got to have some decent cloes."

"How're you goin' to buy any satin dress? Huh? Joe Smith, you're crazy."

"We can," he returned, doggedly, subsiding a bit. "Snaggs will charge it."

His wife laughed shrilly.

"I see myself tryin' to get him to charge a satin dress. He knows you can't even pay for gingham, much less a satin 'un."

Joe seated him on a rickety chair and began slowly to dust the ashes from his blackened pipe.

"He'll charge it, I think——" he began, his bluster subsiding.

"Stop droppin' them ashes on the floor," snapped his wife. "I jest swept."

He reached over and deposited what remained in the stove.

"He knows I'm goin' to start drillin' for Jim Thurman."

Mrs. Smith's lips set in a thin straight line.

"You ain't a-goin' to start that till you have to," she replied scornfully.

At that moment Jane entered the house, bearing her late purchase. There were tear stains on her cheeks that enhanced the wistfulness of her big eyes. She stood irresolute, glancing first at her father, then at her mother.

"I tell you, I'm goin' to start that

well in the morning," he said. "An' this kid's goin' to be as dressed up as any other kid."

Jane dropped her can of tomatoes. A look of incredulous joy filled her eyes.

"I don't believe you'll do any such thing," remarked his disillusioned mate.

"Oh, Ma, maybe he means it," cried Jane, a new hope in her voice.

Joe turned toward his daughter.

"You b'lieve me, don't you?" He spoke gently, in a tone she had seldom heard. "Me an' you'll git that dress, if she won't."

"You bet we will. Let's go an' git it right now, Pa."

They left the house. Mrs. Smith looked after them with puzzled eyes.

"I wonder if he'll get that there dress," she said, half aloud. "I can't believe it of him—still it does look sorter——" her words trailed off into silence.

II

The next morning he got up at four o'clock. He went across the street, yanked Jack Crowe out of bed, then came home and cooked breakfast for the two of them. The amazed Jack took no pains to conceal his resentment over having been deprived of his morning's peaceful slumbers. His remarks regarding Joe's business-like preparations for the day's work were stinging and profuse. But, Joe, his lips set determinedly, his shoulders straightened from their habitual stoop, ignored alike his remarks and look of astonishment. He gave the old grays an extra portion of feed, hitched them to the wagon carrying his drilling equipment, and set forth, accompanied by the still sarcastic Jack.

An hour later they pulled up at the Thurman ranch. Jim Thurman himself met them at the gate.

"So it's you, Joe," he sneered. "Didn't expect you inside a month."

"I'm here, though," was the short return.

"Ready to start work?"

"Jest as soon as you come through with a couple of hundred as part pay," was the reply.

Thurman was very much surprised.

"Look here, Smith," he said craftily, "what do you think you're tryin' to do?"

"Nothin', only I want some of my money before I start in."

Thurman finally sat down and wrote out the check when he saw there was no other way out of the difficulty.

Smith went at the Thurman well like the professional he was. He worked with a precision and steadiness of which no one had dreamed him capable. Scarcely a word during the long days did he speak to Jack Crowe, except to order him around. Jack sweated and swore at the man's astonishing energy. Jack's chief reason for hiring himself to Joe had been to get an easy job. Thurman made frequent visits to the scene of action, watching with keenest interest the progress of the well. Once he brought his daughter. She stayed around a few minutes, asked a few inconsequential questions, and then left.

After that, Joe's grouchiness increased to such an extent that Jack took to watching him out of the corner of one eye and even ceased to mumble, except under his breath, over the long hours and heat.

"Well, Joe," remarked Thurman one morning, in a very satisfied tone, as he strode pompously about the well machine, "you're doing a darn good job here. Had no idea you could work like this. When we strike water, this land is as good as sold for forty dollars an acre."

"You got it cheap enough," commented Jack, maliciously.

"Only paid five for it," grinned the other. "I don't pay any more'n I have to for anything. That's my style. Boys, if there's sich a thing as best to a game, I jest naturally git it."

The mud-spattered Smith emptied his "slush bucket"; then without looking at his employer, spoke in his usual tone.

"Should 'a had that there—Coleman here. Like as not he'd 'a give it to you."

"Wish some kind, good fellow like that would set me up in business. Say, Jim, where do them kind grow now?" inquired the unabashed Jack.

"Perhaps if you had sense enough to know a good thing when you see it, you'd be somebody, too," returned Thurman. "It's jest feeble-mindedness that knocks most people out o' success. That section I got hold of twenty years ago was a square enough deal. I was holding it for Coleman. He had to go home to look after his father. He fixed my wages so that I'd get them when the place was his. Well, when the time came, I refunded him the wages and kept the land. This property we're drillin' on now came cheap because I had a mortgage on it and closed the feller out.

"Say," said Jack. "Johnson's no fool. He could have paid the mortgage if he'd a wanted to. There's a bug under the chip some place."

"What do you mean?" demanded the "business man," sobering instantly.

"Why, there's no water here!"

"Joe, do you think——" began Jim, apprehensively.

"Can't say," replied Smith.

"How deep are you now?"

"'Bout two hundred and thirty feet."

"This well and the one I sank last year cost me over six hundred dollars. If we don't have luck this time, I'm a sick man," said Thurman, with conviction.

"I dug five holes for Johnson. We never struck water."

"I know that, but that's no reason why I shouldn't get any."

"No. Still, I think we're headed for another dry hole," was the reply.

"How deep did you go for Johnson?"

"Three hundred. Nobody ever went below that in this country. But it's a pretty safe bet that if you're goin' to strike a stream at all, it'll be around two hundred."

"Well, go as deep as four hundred. As I said, this land'll be worth forty— or even more—an acre."

"But if you don't get it, you can't give this land away," was Jack's consoling reply.

III

Almost the only catastrophe that could wring the heart of Jim Thurman was a money catastrophe. He deplored the smallest loss as the greatest tragedy that could befall him. In view of this fact, it was not surprising that the days that followed were tense ones for him. He spent nearly all the time he had with the drillers, waiting, hoping for the signs which his employees told him were not. And every foot that was drilled meant seventy cents out of his pocket.

"We're down four hundred feet now," said Joe to him one day just after he had arrived at the drill. "Shall we go any farther?"

"I should say not! Shut her down! It's cost me too much already!" bawled Thurman.

Joe made no comment, but his sullen black eyes held a look of unholy pleasure.

"Seems to me that a man of your

experience would 'a known about this. I should think you'd 'a——"

"That's enough from you" cut in Joe. "I told you I didn't think we'd have any luck with this well."

Thurman was the picture of despair. "All that money gone for nothing," he mourned.

Jack snickered; Joe prepared to gather up his tools.

"You need a feller like Coleman to give you another start," sneered Joe.

Thurman ignored this thrust.

"Joe," he said, "I have to have water on this land. I want you to dig me another well—that is, if you'll cut your price in half."

Jack put up his hands in protest. "Don't you be countin' on me to help Joe Smith any more. Here's where I go one way an' him the other. He needs a human steam engine, that'll—"

Thurman shut him up with a glance.

"Will you do it, Joe?"

"Nothin' doin'."

"Very well," replied his employer. "Maybe you'll guarantee me water for full price on another well."

But Joe would do nothing of the kind.

"Well, then, what's the fairest proposition you can make me?"

Joe's only response was an unholy grin.

"Come, come. I can't wait around here all day. Let's hear your proposition. What have you got to say?"

"Oh nothing much, only I'll buy the land for what you paid for it."

Thurman seemed stunned. Finally he regained his powers of speech.

"Say, do you think I'm crazy? Where'd you ever get that notion?"

"Nowheres. Only if I wuz you, I'd sell quick. With all holes in this property you can't get any more for it than you paid—unless you strike water. You know that hasn't been done."

Thurman thought a while. He took out a notebook and began to figure. Finally he looked up, a crafty smile on his lips.

"Think I'll take you up on that."

"All right. But remember, I'm just doing it to please you."

They got into Thurman's machine and hurried to town. A couple of hours later, they were back again, the deed to the place safely in Smith's pocket. As they were about to pass the drill, he insisted that they ought to look it over.

Thurman didn't mind particularly.

A puzzled expression came over his face when he saw Joe crank up the engine and start the "slush bucket" once more on its downward journey. When presently it was drawn up, and a stream of clear, cold, sparkling water flowed from it, his features became ashen, his lips moved but emitted no sound.

"Seems as though I'd found something," said Smith, not over startled.

"You knew whether water'd been found or not!" shouted Thurman in a rage.

"Mebbe I did, and mebbe I didn't," was the reply.

"But you told me——"

"Yes, I told you we wuz down four hundred feet," cut in Smith, "but if you'd a remembered right well, I didn't say anything about striking any- thing. Remember how you got 1 section from Coleman?"

"Yes, well, what's that got to with this?"

"Nothing so very much, except his brother-in-law that's all," rep Joe Smith with a grin.

The Redwoo

PUBLISHED BY THE STUDENTS OF THE UNIVERSITY OF

The object of The Redwood is to gather together what is best in the literary work doings and to knit closely the hearts of the boys of the prese

EDITORIAL STAFF

EDITOR-IN-CHIEF - - - - - -
BUSINESS MANAGER - - - - -
ASSISTANT BUSINESS MANAGER - - - - -
CIRCULATION MANAGER - - - •

ASSOCIATE EDITORS
EXCHANGES - - - • - -
ALUMNI - - - - - - - -
UNIVERSITY NOTES - - - - - -
ATHLETICS - - - - - - -

EXECUTIVE BOARD
EDITOR   BUSINESS MANAGER   EDIT(

Address all communications to THE REDWOOD, University of Santa Cla:
Terms of subscription, $1.50 a year; single copies 2

EDITORIAL

Of What Value

It frequently happens that services rendered by our dearest friends can never be adequately compensated for in mere dollars and cents. There is the case of one who has saved our life; or again some truly noble comrade who has given his all that one he holds dear in closest friendship might not taste of death. Such men you properly style heroes. Such can-

not be adequa great service th Here in our r nor fully rea blessed by twc Fathers Sulliva sacrificing and duction of "T] success it righ them "The Bel nothing.

281

Hard work, sacrifice and valuable time was what they gave that the play might succeed. Of what value are these? We cannot begin to measure their priceless worth. At best we can show our deep appreciation to them by living up to what is to be expected of us to the best of our ability. Anything less would be the basest ingratitude. Let us begin to realize that "our pleasures with some pain are fraught". We are the recipients of pleasures and joy; they and the rest of the good Fathers typify the "pain" and sacrifice necessarily attendant upon our pleasures.

To Fathers Sullivan, Egan and to all the other members of the Faculty we offer our sincerest thanks in fullest appreciation for their numerous kindnesses.

***

Finis

Too completely filled with the grieving thought of having to leave these hallowed walls after years of intimate association, we reluctantly pen a farewell to our Alma Mater. For some it means but a short three months of vacation, then a return to the books and scenes they have grown to love so well. For others it means a commencement in life without the protecting, guiding sway of old Santa Clara. Blessed with the full knowledge of those principles making for right, justice and true Catholicity the departing graduate can turn to them for his solace when the way of the world grows weary and the uphill fight of life becomes too steep.

Whether here or elsewhere what is so exhilarating as the memory of days well spent in close communion with College fellows? Although separated in body, the close union must ever remain in spirit. Armed with the principles of honor and truth and with his Catholic Faith deeply planted in his heart, the true Santa Claran must succeed in the one all-important aim of life.

To you who linger a while longer by the side of Alma Mater we extend our deepest wishes, while for ourselves we can only reiterate the beautiful words of the poet:

"There is a word, of grief the sounding token;
There is a word bejeweled with bright tears,
The saddest word fond lips have ever spoken;
A little word that breaks the chain of years;
Its utterance must ever bring emotion,
The memories it crystals cannot die,
'Tis known in every land, on every ocean—
'Tis called 'Good-bye' ''.

University Notes

President's Day

The field events of the day are enumerated in another column of the Redwood, while it falls to our lot to extol the vaudeville show in the Auditorium, given in honor of Father Murphy. At 7:45 o'clock the curtain rose before a large, appreciative audience that witnessed two hours of well dispensed comedy. The minstrel show, which concluded the performance, was by far the best number on the programme. The four end-men with their full quota of sunburn, rendered catchy songs and snappy jokes in the genuine "darktown" way. They included Joe Barnard, Ed Hamilton, "Hard" Boyle, and "Fat" Ferrario. The quartette of "Toffs", Emmet Daly, Ray Schall, Dewey Elliot and Fred Moran, blended a few chords individually and collectively. Henry Veit, as interlocutor, aided materially in making the show a success. The "Jazz" Band, with Turk Bedolla at the piano, Williamson on the violin, Elbert with the moaning trombone, Harris as banjoist, and Jones at the drums, put the necessary spice in the act.

The other acts were: "Romeo and Juliet," by Joe Barnard and Ed Hamilton, "nuff sed"; "The Last Drop," by "Fat" Ferrario and Fred Moran; "The Hawaiian Maid," Jimmy Glynn; "Walking Delegates of the Giddy Family," a gloom chaser of the first order, by Zeek Coman and Tul Argenti. As was fitting and proper there were five acts in all at the close of a five-event Field Day.

House of Philhistorians

Since the Ryland Debate there have been no meetings of the House that called for a debate. Twice, however, the members convened to determine whether or not there would be any gathering around the festive board to fittingly close the term. The question of photographs was discussed and it was decided by unanimous vote to adorn the Sophomore Classroom, along with the Representatives of previous years, in the manner adopted by the society. Since this decision Rep. Rudolph, chairman of the committee, has had difficulty in persuading the bashful debaters to sit before the camera.

Although an atmosphere of victory and pride, caused by the recent honors won in the Ryland Debate, has permeated the assembly hall of the house, nevertheless, it was deemed best to abandon the idea of a banquet. A majority of the members are concerned in similar class activities, not to mention the proximity of the "finals," so the step taken regarding this matter was considered a wise one. With laurels a-plenty, Clerk Neary closed the minute book, concluding this year's doings, to the satisfaction of all.

Ryland Debate

This year the two factions of the Literary Congress brought forth well planned arguments on the question: Resolved, "That one of the great reconstructive measures to meet the present condition of social unrest in the United States, would be the enactment by Congress of more stringent and comprehensive immigration laws." For the second time within the last twelve years the House of Philhistorians defeated the Senate. The House argued against the question and was represented by Messrs. Raymond Copeland, Emmett Daly and Frank Damrell, the latter being awarded the first prize. Mr. Capelle Damrell, winner of the second prize, Mr. Edwin Heafy, winner of the third prize, and Mr. Eugene Jaeger were the Senators who opposed the House. The question of debate itself being one of interest and importance at the present time, commanded the attention of every one in the packed Auditorium. The debaters are to be congratulated on the manner in which they labored for success, and on the convincing statements produced on the night of April thirteenth, the date of the contest.

Redwood Picnic

In corduroys and sweaters the staff drove quietly from the gates of Santa Clara one bright May morning to seek complete diversion from all that hints of books and things. With Big Basin as the goal we bounced over some of the roughest roads in these parts and through valleys of rare beauty that brought us to a cool spot in the Basin. There under the big trees we annihilated steaks, sandwiches, fruits and all the other favorites of a picnic lunch. Not least among the consumers was "Tul" Argenti, who, together with Heine Veit, cast off his bashfulness for the day. We returned by Santa Cruz, taking in every concession at the Casino, where all got a huge "recoil"; especially when a Madame Zuzu told "Tul," via a penny machine, that he should study art for art's sake. We then lost no time until we were again within the sacred walls, happy for a day well spent.

Junior Letters

Weird signs and strange gestures savoring of the mystic have been observed the last few weeks among the Junior Letters men. They foretell great events for the Senior year of the class of '21· Class meetings are held frequently, and at the last meeting on May 11, President "Zeek" Coman stirred up great pep with a snappy talk on "Unity and Co-operation", which has been adopted as the motto of the class. Though small, by thus acting as a unit, '21 will leave a prominent mark in the annals of Santa Clara.

'20 Final arrangements for the graduating functions have been made, and present indications are that Class '20 will close their pilgrimage in a most successful manner. · The committee in charge, consisting of Mr. Savage, chairman; Mr. Bricca, and Mr. Sullivan, have announced that the Graduation Ball will be held at the Country Club, on the evening of June 8th. Invitations have been sent the Alumni, and the affair is likely to be an impressive one.

In accordance with the custom of the University, the Seniors have procured their graduation rings, which are now being worn by the members of the Class. The ring is very similar to last year's and it is intended that the design be made permanent for all graduating classes in the future.

"The Bells" After eight years of inactivity, the Senior Dramatic Society has once more reorganized to bring back the histrionic past, and to show that it has done so, and at the same time won new glory along these lines, we need but point to the wonderful success which has crowned the latest production, "The Bells".

Under the able supervision of Father Sullivan, aided by Mr. Egan, S. J., to both of whom in particular the Student Body attributes the success of "The Bells", the cast, after three weeks of training and rehearsals was enabled to present the drama in a manner never before equaled on the Santa Clara stage.

In attempting to analyze the success of the play, as a whole, we must not overlook the efficient work of the stage crew, whose handling and setting of the scenery contributed in no small degree to the effect which the play produced. To the orchestra, too, the Student Body is indebted, especially to Prof. Mustol, who arranged the various selections.

There is one more angle from which "The Bells' is considered a success. and that is from a financial point of view. The four performances netted close to $3000, which will be applied to the removal of the $7000 debt, under which the Student Body is now laboring. For this the Financial Secretary, and his staff of assistants are to be given due credit.

In criticism of the play itself, we can best quote from the San Jose Mercury Herald of May 7th: ·

" 'The Bells', presented by the Senior

Dramatic Society of the University of Santa Clara in the University Auditorium last night, was greeted by a very enthusiastic and apppreciative audience, and that old melodrama of a bygone day, with its pointed moral that 'murder will out' and 'the wages of sin is death', was well presented by the young actors. Even as dignified a melo-drama as 'The Bells' can very easily be overdone, and the fact that last night's performance did not smack of 'mellerdramer' is a compliment both to the directing of Rev. Jos. A. Sullivan, S. J., and to the intelligent work of the actors.

"Michael Pecarovich, as Mathias, the old inn-keeper, who has for years been remorselessly hounded by the tortures of a guilty conscience, is an actor who could well take his place on the professional stage. His conception of the character, and his interpretation of that character were excellent. Both in the second act, and again in the court scene in the third act, he held his audience spell-bound ten minutes or more— an accomplishment very few professional actors have to their credit. In fact, the work of this young man in the court scene, where old Mathias first vigorously denies his guilt, and later, under the influence, describes the terrible deed in detail, would in itself provide a no mean act in vaudeville or on the chautauqua circuit.

"The comedy vein of the play was very creditably presented by A. Ferrario as 'Father Walter' and M. Boyle

as 'Hans'. Both young men did very good work. Frederick J. Moran as Christian, presented a very creditable Swiss officer of the gendarmes. Adolph Vergara as the mesmerist, portrayed well a character which might have easily been overdone.

"The scenery or 'sets' which were painted by Michael O'Sullivan, a former University of Santa Clara student, now in the scenic painting profession in San Francisco, were very good, particularly the rapid shift effect in the first act, and the court scene in the third act.

"The University Orchestra, under the leadership of its director, S. J. Mustol, gradually warmed up. Too, the music was rather liberal in volume, especially in the more tense moments, but that will doubtless be corrected at tonight's performance. The tones of the sleigh-bells which haunt the conscience-stricken burgomaster, could be well softened, but that, too, will doubtless be corrected tonight.

"Withal, 'The Bells' is a very interesting and well-played melodrama and will no doubt deserve the capacity houses which are already sold for Friday and Saturday night."

The cast: ,
Mathias, the Burgomaster............
............Michael J. Percarovich, '22
Christian, Officer of the Guards......
............Frederick J. Moran, '22
Wilhelm, Brother of Mathias............
............Arnold R. Beezer, '23

Hans, Land Owner...Merrill C. Boyle, '23
Walter, Wealthy Farmer.............:.....
.....................Alfredo A. Ferrario, '22
Supreme Judge ....
.... Thomas J. Moroney, Jr., '20
Clerk of the Court ....
......................Louis F. Buty, '20
The Notary ....James M. Connors, '23
Mesmerist ....Adolfo Vergara, '21
Doctor Zimmer.....Tobias J. Bricca, '20
Lorenze ....James R. Needles, '23
The Polish Jew.....Raymond Schall, '23
Franz, Servant of Mathias.............
......................John McDonald, Prep.
Gendarme ....:......Edward Hamilton
Barristers..................
Joseph Barnard, Dewey Elliot,
Ernest Bedolla, Jay Hughes.
The Senior Dramatic Society:
President...Rev. Joseph A. Sullivan, S.J.
Financial Secretary ....
.....................Frank Camarillo, '20
Stage Manager......James E. Neary, '23
Electrician ....Jean P. Reddy, '22
Assistant Electrician ....
......................Louis Lettunich, '24
Property Manager.....Thomas Crowe, '24
Assistant Stage Manager ....
.....................Thomas J. Bannon, '23
Assistant Stage Manager................
.....................Emmet W. Gleason, '23
Assistant Stage Manager................
.....................Francis O'Shea, '22
Assistant Stage Manager................
.....................Robert A. Duff, '24
Assistant Stage Manager................
.....................Carl F. Williams, '23
Assistant Stage Manager................
.....................George Ryan, '24

Costumer ....Robert E. Shields, '24
Head Usher ....William de Koch, '21
Publicity Manager.....Henry C. Veit, '20
Assistant Business Manager ....
.....................Fred Florimont, '23

Student Body Officers

As is customary, the final meeting of the scholastic year concluded with the election of officers for the coming year. Seldom, in the past, has the honor and office of Student Body President been conferred on a non-resident student. This year, however, popular choice fell upon Roy Fowler for the position, notwithstanding the fact that Roy is now classified in the records as a non-resident student.

Roy's popularity extends back to 1916, when he starred on the Varsity which administered a 28-5 defeat to Stanford, and became known as the best first-five ever turned out on the Pacific Coast. During the war, he was commissioned an Ensign, and served in the Navy in that capacity until the close of hostilities, when he returned to continue his course. His record during the war, his experience in intercollegiate circles and his popularity on the campus, mark him as a man eminently fitted to lead in student activities, and it is certain that, under his guidance, the course of the Student Body during the coming year will be well-directed.

The position of Secretary was hotly contested by the two nominees, Fred

Moran and Jim Neary. Both men enjoy no small degree of popularity on the campus, and both are their respective class Presidents. However, the final count of the ballots gave Moran a majority of two over his opponent. The office of Treasurer was unanimously bestowed upon Tom Moroney. "Zeek" Coman, the present Treasurer, was nominated for re-election, but withdrew from the race.

Jimmy Needles was elected Sergeant-at-Arms by a comfortable majority over Porter Kerchkoff.

Coming with the election of officers was the announcement by the Faculty Board of Control, of the appointment of James B. O'Connor to the position of Graduate Manager for the coming year, and Tullio "Tuts" Argenti as Student Manager.

Under the administration of the newly elected officers, the Student Body can look forward to a most successful year.

Oratorial Contest

On the evening of April 27th, the Auditorium was filled with an appreciative audience, which had assembled for the annual oratorical and elocution contest for the Owl and Junior prizes. The program was quite interesting and the selections very well rendered.

The following gentlemen acted as judges: Rev. Father Richard Collins, pastor of St. Patrick's Church of San

Jose; Dr. Tully Knowles, President of the College of the Pacific; Mr. George Nicholson, Mr. David M. Burnett, and Mr. Faber Johnson.

The program:

American Patrol ....Meacham
University Orchestra.

Introduction ....Henry C. Veit

JUNIOR PRIZES

High School Classes

The Angels of Buena Vista...(Whittier)
Francis Edward Cotter.

The Soul of the Violin.............(Merrill)
William Lawrence Crutchett.

The Death Penalty ....(Hugo)
William Carey Callaghan.

Pancratius ....(Wiseman)
Albert Donald Halloran.

The Love of Spring............(Rolfe)
University Orchestra.

The Maniac ....(Anon)
Lloyd Benedict Nolan.

The Shipwreck ....(Dickens)
Henry Beaumont Martin, Jr.

America and Ireland ....(Anon)
Henry Moise Robidoux.

Sunnyland Waltzes ....(Rosner)
University Orchestra.

THE OWL PRIZE.

Social Unrest ....
...............Arnold Roswell Beezer, '22

Arbitration and Solution ....
...............Louis James Trabucco, '22

A Defence at the Tribunal of Bolshevism ....Thomas A. Sperry, '22

Golden Sunshine ....E. Smith
    University Orchestra.
Our Present Constitution............................
    ....Peter Francis Morettini, '20
Angelici Diaboli ....
    ....Randall Oswald O'Neill, '20
Yankee Grit ....(Cooke)
    University Orchestra.
    At the termination of the contest
the judges announced that first prize
in the Junior Contest had been awarded to Lloyd Benedict Nolan, and the
second prize to Albert Donald Halloran. The Owl Prize was awarded to
Randall Oswald O'Neill.

**May
Devotions**
The coming of May,
the month of flowers
and Nature's beauty,
brings with it the revival of a custom
inaugurated some years ago, of nightly
devotion to Mary, the Queen of Heaven.
Each evening a member of the upper
classes addresses the students in chapel,
taking as a subject some title of the
Blessed Virgin of the Litany, after
which Benediction is given. ·
    The program of talks · given during
the month, follows:
    May 1. Henry Veit, Holy Mary.
    May 2. Louis Buty, Holy Mother of
God.
    May 5. Tobias Bricca, Mother, Most
Pure.
    May 6. H. Dieringer, Mother of Our
Saviour.
    May 7. P. Morettini, Virgin Most
Powerful.

May 8. W. Heaney, Help of Chris-
tians.
    May 10. E. Jensen, Virgin Most Mer-
ciful.
    May 11. T. Moroney, Seat of Wis-
dom.
    May 12. A. Prothero, Cause of Our
Joy.
    May 13. F. Camarillo, Mystic Rose.
    May 14. H. Flannery, Morning Star.
    May 15. W. Sullivan, Health of the
Weak.
    May 16. J. O'Connor, ·Refuge of
Sinners.
    May. 18. L. DiFiore, Comfortress of
the Afflicted.
    May 19· H. Nulk, Queen of Angels.
    May 20. R. Scholtz, Queen of Peace.
    May 21. H. Veit, Our Queen Immac-
ulate.
    May 22. W. Muldoon, Mary Our
Life.
    May 24. R. O'Neill, Mary Our
Sweetness.
    May 25. William DeKoch, Mary Our
Hope.
    May 26. J. Savage, Santa Clara's
Queen.
    May 27. J. Henderson, Our Queen
Triumphant.
    May 28. E. Jaeger, Under Mary's
Mantle for All Eternity.
    May 31. Father President, Gate of
Heaven.

    The devotion to the Blessed Virgin
Mary is a beautiful practice, continued
from the early days of the University's
existence, and looked forward to and

back upon with yearning by those who love and honor the Blessed Virgin.

Student Body

The adoption of American football, which necessitated the amending of the articles of the Constitution relating to the awarding of football blocks, has brought with it far-reaching effects. The more stringent and exacting requirements adopted for football, have resulted in correspondingly strict amendments for basketball and baseball.

When, in former years, the Stanford-Santa Clara game was considered the "Big Game", and blocks were awarded in football for participation in the one game, the relations between Stanford and Santa Clara were such that basketball and baseball blocks were awarded according to the Stanford games. With the coming of the new game, however, and a schedule calling for at least four intercollegiate football games per season, the tendency is to develop athletic relations with colleges, and the awarding of blocks on a different basis than that followed, was found necessary.

To draft amendments to the Constitution which would meet the new conditions, President Veit appointed a committee consisting of Mr. Moroney, chairman, Mr. Trabucco, and Mr. Koch. At the March meeting of the Student Body, the proposed amendments were submitted, approved, and posted in the manner prescribed by the Constitution, and adopted at a special meeting held for the purpose, on April 12th. The provisions of the new amendments, which are now incorporated in the Constitution, read as follows:

"Amendment to Section 4—

Participation in basketball: One must play in the whole or any fraction thereof, of three-fourths of the entire number of games scheduled, comprising the basketball season.

(a) Those games deemed by the Executive Committee as being practice games, are not to be considered as scheduled games.

Participation in baseball: (1) One must play in two-thirds of the entire number of innings played in intercollegiate games, and in three-fourths of the total number of innings played against any clubs other than college teams.

(a) Special provision for pitchers: Anyone pitching a full intercollegiate game, or in one-third of the total number of innings played, including both college, and clubs other than college teams, shall be awarded a block S.-C.."

For the purpose of determining who would be entitled to blocks under the provisions of these amendments during the past season, President Veit put the matter in charge of a committee consisting of Mr. Koch, chairman, Mr. Argenti, and Mr. Rudolph.

At the final meeting of the semester, held on May 15th, the committee reported that the following men had

fulfilled the requirements for basketball: Muth, Needles, Ferrario, and
Manelli. In baseball, the requirements
were fulfilled by: Berg, Burke, Fitzpatrick, Manelli, Hughes, Bedolla,
Hanneberg, and Garcia.
They were formally awarded their
blocks by a vote of the Student Body.

St. Joseph's Day Sunday evening, April
25th, the Student Body
and Faculty of the Uni-
versity observed the beautiful devotion
to St. Joseph, held each year in honor
of that great Saint, patron of Study.
The Student Body marched to the
shrine of St. Joseph in military formation, being led by the Band.

After a brief speech by Father President, a poem in honor of St. Joseph,
was read by Jack Lipman. President
Veit then addressed the Student Body,
after which they marched to the Chapel,
where solemn Benediction was given.

Louis F. Buty.

Fred J. Moran.

ENGINEERING NOTES

"The dance is on!" On the night of
)ril seventeenth at the Hotel Ven-
me, this was the thought voiced
th a tinge of eagerness, as the music
gan. The Engineering Society was
ring its first dance.

In the ball room of the hotel young
uples danced to the syncopated
ythm of the orchestra. A spirit
good fellowship and wholesome fun
emed to permeate the gathering; and
e felt good to hear the cheery greet-
g of old friends, as the active, honor-
y, old, and new members met one an-
her. A few of the old graduates were
esent to keep up the spirit of bygone
ys. The room itself was well deco-
ted with greens, pennants, and Santa
ara plaques, placed where the mellow
ht of the tall lamps could play to
st advantage upon them. As Father
irphy, president of the University
d an honorary member of the Soci-
', was to leave early in the evening,
e third dance was made the "Engi-
ering Special". As the slow strains
the waltz began, the lamps were
nmed to bring out the effect of the
ecial lighting system. The room
ked oriental in coloring. Suddenly
e Society's insignia blazed forth in
electrical design above the fireplace.
The proud Santa Clara block, surrounded by the words, Engineering Society,
formed a fitting setting for the dance.
The members are especially grateful to
the following men of the Entertainment
Committee for their work in completing
every detail of the dance: Mr. Leo
DiFiore, chairman; Mr. Dan Minahan,
secretary; Mr. Ken Berg, art director;
and Mr. Tom Bannan, treasurer. We
also thank the electrical engineers, who
so generously rendered their assistance
to the Entertainment Committee. Finally, we earnestly express our gratitude to those who acted as our patrons:
Professor and Mrs. G. L. Sullivan;
Professor and Mrs. W. D. Lotz; Professor and Mrs. A. O. Evans; Mr. and
Mrs. Robert A. Fatjo; Commander and
Mrs. Paul Fretz; Mr. and Mrs. David
M. Burnett; Mr. and Mrs. William
Pabst; and Mr. and Mrs. Frank Reidy.

It was the expressed opinion of
everyone present that the affair was
a huge success, and that it should be
repeated next year. However, in the
light of one accomplishment, we must
not forget that much more lies before
us. Constantly keep in view the real
aim of our Society, and double your

efforts toward that aim, even though: "The dance is over."

The Annual Banquet of the Society will be held on Tuesday, May 25th, too late for an account to be written before this edition has gone to press. Hence, we will anticipate the happenings of that evening. As was the case last year, the scene of the event will be the Hotel Montgomery, San Jose. There the guests and members of the Society will assemble promptly at 7:30 p. m., and proceed to the banquet hall, where an enjoyable meal along with surprises of novelty, is promised by the Entertainment Committee. The menu is one capable of tickling the palate of the most exacting epicurean. For the different items and courses, engineering terms have been substituted,—but we are permitted to know that an abundance of fried chicken on toast forms the "main dish" of the evening. Of course the hall will be decorated; and in a manner suitable to the Engineers. For those who depend upon the melodious symphony of music, or the crash and din of the weird instruments of "Jazz", to stimulate their appetites or to increase their digestive capacity, the committee has provided an orchestra from the University. Last year the music furnished an important part of the evening's entertainment. Then we are sure to have some of those interesting speeches which are a part of every feast, but whose "pep" is characteristic of our Engineering Banquet. The honorary members invited are: Mr.

R. C. Behan of San Francisco, guest of honor; Rev. Father Timothy L. Murphy, President of Santa Clara University; Rev. Father Joseph A. Sullivan, Vice-President of the University; Father L. B. Egan, Professor of Chemistry; Mr. William O'Shaughnessey, City Engineer of San Francisco; Colonel J. Donovan, former professor of engineering at the University; Mr. Irving Ryder, County Engineer of Santa Clara. We cannot but look forward with anticipation to the night of the twenty-fifth: though we must needs regret that time when the Engineering Banquet of 1920 shall have hurried by and become one of the events of the past.

Vacation is again upon us. Therefore the publicity editor should straighten out his accounts, and clean up the remaining business of the year. First of all, we must offer a word of congratulation to one of our esteemed members, Mr. Roy Fowler. His election to the office of Student Body President was welcomed with joy by the Engineers. In Roy Fowler, the members of the Society have always recognized a man of character, reputation, true efficiency, and honest worth. Santa Clara must realize this already: and hence it is that the Engineers heartily greet Roy to his new office, and wish him all success in Student Body affairs.

Year after year has witnessed our leave taking of the sacred walls of Alma Mater. And, while the sad and earnest words of the valedictorian are more expressive of our thoughts on the subject of farewell, we feel it our duty to wish God-speed to those Seniors who are leaving this, their University home. The disputes and tussles of the past have served but to endear these men to us; and it is with true sorrow that we bid them go to find the difficulties of life, and conquer them. We admonish them to live always loyal to the teaching of Santa Clara,—to be ever true to the principles of our own organization. And let them, too, bear in mind that, however far they travel from here, whatever be their dignity or social standing, whatsoever they may do in the puzzling stretches of the future; —they can never venture beyond the friendly circle of the Engineering Society while remaining steadfast to the commands of God, of country, of home, and of Alma Mater.

Next in order, we must thank the speakers who have addressed us during the past year. It is far beyond our power to adequately thank our Dean of Engineering, Professor George L. Sullivan, for all he has done for us. His explanation, at the beginning of the year, of the workings of a large ore mill in Arizona, was instructive and beneficial. Then, too, we are tempted to recall a pleasant evening spent last semester at Professor Sullivan's home. In all our activities the hand of Professor Sullivan has played a guiding part, and it is with these few words that we wish to convey some inkling to him of our heartfelt appreciation. Last

semester, Fr. Timothy L. Murphy greatly pleased his friends, the Engineers, by a real "live" talk, "straight-from-the-shoulder", as is Fr. President's custom. Likewise Fr. Joseph A. Sullivan benefited the Society greatly by an animated lecture on Parliamentary Rules of Order. Next came the speech of Fr. L. B. Egan, who exemplified for our benefit the various processes employed in the manufacture of paper. Fr. Egan is one whom we cannot easily forget. His willing and hard work has often helped us while in difficulty: and the more we say of him, the harder it becomes to express our real gratitude. We were then privileged to hear an address by Colonel Joseph Donovan. The Colonel has proved himself in every instance a true friend of the Society, ever solicitous for its welfare. At this point, we recall that we have never thanked the Colonel for keeping score of the forty-one runs of the Junior-Senior baseball game at the last picnic. Perhaps the victorious Juniors should attend to that. Mr. Joseph Fretz was the next speaker to address the Society. He told us of his experiences in contracting work while building docks and highways in Houston, Texas. The talk was of great value to the members. At the next program meeting we listened to Mr. William Crawford, who had recently returned from Mexico. He outlined the workings of a large mine there, and gave us valuable information of working conditions in that country. Following this talk came the speech of Professor Alvin O. Evans, who interestingly described some of his experiences in electrical power plant work in South Dakota. Only last month Mr. Irving Ryder gave us a lecture on cost of accounting as applied to construction work. The last speaker of the year will be Professor Charles B. Wing, Dean of the College of Engineering at Stanford University. He will speak to the Society on the twenty-fifth of May. We wish to thank all of the above gentlemen for their talks. By hearing them we have gained some experience, as well as a more intimate knowledge of the qualities of each speaker. And we trust that the words of each shall be remembered, and shall not have been said in vain.

The rest is easily finished. Too much praise cannot be heaped upon the Entertainment Committee, which we have spoken of above. The Program Committee has been exceptionally good this year. Mr. Harold Flannery is to be congratulated, as are his assistants, Mr. Tom Ford and Mr. Paul Reddy. Modesty forbids us to do more than mention the Publicity Committee, Mr. Al Abrahamsen, chairman, aided by three efficient men, Mr. Dave Tuttle, Mr. Bill Osterle, and Mr. Bill Koch. The Society was fortunate in having this list of officers during the past year: Mr. John Savage, President; Mr. Leopold DiFiore, Vice-President; Mr. David Tuttle Jr., Secretary; Mr. Herman Dieringer, Treasurer; Mr. Alfred Abrahamsen, Reporter; Mr. Clarence Sullivan, Librarian; and Mr. Adolfo Vergara, Sergeant-at-Arms. The members are grateful for the individual efforts of each man, and now await the arrival of next meeting, when new officers will be elected to carry on the work of the Society. Till next year, then, we must say: Goodbye!

Alfred J. Abrahamsen.

Mr. James P. Sex, President of the Alumni Association, has issued the following letter:

"My Dear Brother Alumnus:

Of late years many of the old boys have hoped to see the Alumni Banquet brought back to the old College. This year the faculty has made the thing possible by inviting us most cordially to assemble on the campus on Saturday evening, June 5th, at six thirty o'clock. The faculty is providing the time and the place, the committee on Arrangements will provide everything else that goes to make a real old time Santa Clara Banquet. We all want to see the old place again; so here's our chance to see it in company with the fellows with whom we learned "to be boys." We ought, all of us, to second the wish of the faculty to see us come home again. 1 know, too, the Student Body is taking advantage of the occasion to give us a rousing welcome; they want to know the old S. C. men—and perhaps, after all, 'twill be well for us to see our-

selves in these boys as we were years ago.

Please forward your acceptance card to our Secretary—immediately; his success with the caterer is absolutely dependent on your promptness in replying—$4.00 per plate."

As an encouragement to the faithful as well as a prod to those in whom sleeps the spirit exemplified below, we are happy to have received just at going to press, the following response to the above general invitation:

Stockton, California, May 26, 1920.

"George A. Nicholson,

First National Bank Bldg.,

San Jose, California.

Dear brother Alumnus:

The thought of wandering back, just for a while, to feast again upon what still remains of the quaint old settings, and to transfix through the new of this day, the comely ones adored but of yesterday, and there to rove amid the grandeur of it all, and to recall the benefits that have flowed therefrom, and to contemplate its future destiny and

296

greatness has proven the controlling force in causing me to attend the banquet.

I may look in vain for some of the old boys of '79, but while there I will gambol and live over again with them the old days in the old "home" and thus in my solace be comforted with my lot.

I shall, nevertheless, be cheered with the youth there of today, and with the many others by our presence add to the sum of the whole in the encouragement thereby given them, reflecting as it will our faith and confidence in ours, and their seat of learning.

Accordingly as an evidence of my devotion, I enclose herewith my personal check with the required banquet card.

Sincerely yours,

Cecil Paul Rendon."

That the banquet will be a huge success this year goes without saying, and that our guests will receive a "rousing welcome" from the Student Body is almost superfluous. Come on fellows, let's show the "old boys" that there is still a lot of spirit left in Santa Clara.

'86 Judge Ferry is at present visiting in California after several years duty on the bench in the Islands. The Judge is protracting his stay in order to be present at the banquet.

'87 The Alumni of Santa Clara showed their loyalty to Alma Mater in a very generous manner during the recent staging of "The Bells". One of the most loyal of these was John W. Somavia. Mr. Somavia expressed himself as delighted at the way Santa Clara "came back" in dramatics.

'87 Peter Dunne of the same class occupied a box during the last performance. Mr. Dunne was an exceptionally fine actor in his college days and played many important parts in the plays staged in the early eighties. He was brought back after his graduation to play the part of St. Peter in the "Passion Play."

'89 Dr. Fred Gerlach was also among those present on Alumni Night. The doctor was enthusiastic and stated that it was one of the most satisfying performances he had ever witnessed in the Santa Clara stage.

'90 On the evening of April 27 we were honored by the presence of Hon. Joseph J. Trabucco, who came down from Mariposa to witness the elocution contest and incidentally to hear Louie, our silver-tongued young spellbinder deliver an oration. The Judge was much pleased with the showing made by the contestants.

'92 John J. Barrett will be remembered as one of the greatest of Santa Clara's tragedians and a star in all the big dramatic enterprises of early days. He, too, was very enthusiastic over the wonderful acting he witnessed at the last performance of "The Bells".

Comm. '03 William Whealen, brother of Nick, the husky star of old football days, has accepted a remunerative position with the Standard Oil Company in South America. After leaving Santa Clara Bill traveled to Canada, where he remained until the world war broke out in 1914. He then enlisted for foreign service and saw action for three years with the Canadian forces in France, being wounded several times before his discharge. The South American appointment found him in San Jose, where he has been visiting his family for several months past. The "Redwood" wishes him every success in his new venture.

'02 Harold Hogan and James Bacigalupi were present at the same performance and shared the sentiments of their older college fellows. James Bacigalupi is considered by many as the finest actor Alma Mater has ever produced.

'06 Martin V. Merle telegraphed his felicitations from the south in the earlier part of the month on the attempt of Santa Clara to re-establish her old reputation in dramatics. Mr. Merle became prominent on the stage before his graduation and it was he who wrote the famous Mission Play which was so successfully produced here in '14. He has since become famous through the successful presentation of many of his own plays, and in the last few years has devoted himself to scenario writing.

'07 James F. Twohy, '07, though unable to be present, sent his congratulations on the success of "The Bells", besides remembering the students in a very substantial way.

'12 Dr. Adolph Baiocchi is fast becoming prominent in the medical profession in San Jose. He materially aided the cause of the Student Body by bringing a host of friends to the auditorium on Knights of Columbus evening.

'13 The class of '13 was ably represented at "The Bells" by Percy O'Connor and Ervin Best, who declared themselves surprised at the talent displayed.

'14 William Shipsey is associated with the law firm of Shipsey and Shipsey in San Luis Obispo. Bill was very popular on the campus and held several offices in the

Student Body during his four year stay here.

Ivor Wallis, a classmate of Bill's, is chief deputy in the County Recorder's office of Santa Clara County.

'16   When Cupid shoots, it is said, he always Mrs. In the early part of last month one of his shafts pierced Miss Marie Irillarry, sister of Jack, a former Santa Clara man, and she became Mrs. George Nicholson. To enumerate all the bridegroom's achievements as an undergraduate would require a separate issue of the Redwood. Suffice it to say that he was Student Body president, winner of the Ryland Debate, Graduate Manager of Athletics, and one of the ablest and most popular fellows on the campus. The "Redwood" extends its heartiest felicitations and best wishes for a long and prosperous wedded life.

'17   Ted Ryan has entered into a law partnership with Mr. McGee of Oakland and is now practicing in that city. Ted was very popular on the campus, having held several offices in the Student Body and Debating societies.

'18   Cyril Coyle was down from Sacramento for the dinner dance given at the Country Club by the Knights of Columbus.

Cyril is meeting with much success in the practice of law in the Capitol City.

Ex'18   Bob Tremaine recently became the father of a bouncing eight pound son. We offer congratulations and venture to state that it will not be long before Bob Jr. is upholding the family name at the University.

Ex '18   The class of '18 is scattered over almost the whole globe. "Silent Bill" Bensburg, star football and track man in his undergraduate days, is connected with the Bretcht Company, dealers in farm machinery in the wilds of darkest Africa.

Ex '19   We were pleased to see George Ench on the campus a few weeks ago. He reports that he is a prosperous business man in Oakland.

Ex '19   Word has reached us that George Todd has passed the examination for dentistry and has opened an office in Santa Cruz. George was a member of the famous "Bearcats", the peppery prep. class, which graduated in 1915.

Ex '19 Alex A. Gardner was on the campus a few days ago visiting his friends among the Engineers. After leaving school he enlisted in the navy and succeeded in winning a commission as ensign. At present he is attending the University of California.

The following clipping was taken from the San Jose Mercury Herald: Vic Larrey, better known as "Pooch," and Miss Emma Laveroni of this city, were married in San Jose Saturday. Vic attended Santa Clara University for several years. He is playing third base for the Hollister Alpines this season. Both he and his wife have a large circle of friends here who join in congratulating the happy couple.

Comm. Ex' 19 Fred Mitchell, manager of the Chicago Cubs, recently offered $10,000 and two players for Jim O'Connell, our former star outfielder. That Jim-O made an unqualified success in baseball is witnessed by the following statement from Charley Graham, manager of the Seals: "San Francisco needs O'Connell as badly as Chicago does. That kid is the greatest natural hitter I have seen in many years. He can play with my ball club any time for my money." Jim has many friends at Santa Clara, who are watching his rise to stardom with eager interest.

Ex '22 James F. Mackey and family motored down from the city during the month to see the Varsity in action. Jimmy is a dignified business man at present, but his college pranks, among them his management of an embryo "Charley Chaplin" are still well remembered among the older students at Santa Clara.

EXCHANGES

The "Bay Leaf" The third number of the "Bay Leaf", coming to us in an artistic cover of green, is indicative of no mean attempt to establish an enviable reputation for the land of William Penn. Of the verse, "Christmas Night" stands first in all respects, and its praise, therefore, is well merited. "To One in Cloister" is a bit of verse that is quite unusual and quite good. The short stories are uniformly excellent, making it difficult for the Ex-man, in his attempts to be impartial, to single out any particular one for special mention. Perhaps the only unfavorable comment that can be offered is that some of the stories are just a bit too brief, as, for instance, "The Dropping Shots of Dan." In "The Game and the Girl," the action of the blonde lady seems just a little unnatural. Essays like "The Idealism of Fiction", and "John Ayscough" are good examples of literary criticism. To us it savored a bit of impropriety to insert between the crispy covers of this magazine a tedious debate; moreover, the custom is not so widespread

as to justify such an insertion even in a girls' literary medium. As a final suggestion may we not remark that a periodical of as high a standard as the "Bay Leaf" should be accorded the privilege of a more frequent appearance?

The Xaverian From the shores of Nova Scotia, lapped by the icy waters of the Atlantic, comes the Xaverian. Distance and a lack of common interest do not prevent us from enjoying the well-written contents of this magazine. We could not but appreciate the excellent thought of the opening poem, "Christmas Eve"; while "Moriri non Potest" arrested our attention. Of the short stories, "Dread Waters" is a good example of a well arranged incident, culminating in a breathless suspense that is not relieved until the last line. "In Sights of Other Days" character study is a very pleasing feature. We appreciated the scholarly exposition of the talents of two Canadian poets. The essay was the more noteworthy in that

301

its constructive and impartial criticism gave evidence of an unbiased mind. Needless to say the editorials were well written, containing as they did an able defense of the cause of Ireland.

The Dial

Since the time of De Maupassant, "The Necklace" has been the fertile source of many stories, good or otherwise, for aspiring young authors. "Lady Cataret's Necklace" which apparently was removed from the sight of the lady's husband for the purpose of breaking the ice of characteristic English snobbishness, of which a talented American beauty was the unfortunate victim, shows traces of the French author's influence. "The Fourteen Jewels," with its simple language and pointed application to present circumstances, is a fable well-nigh worthy of Aesop. Among the essays, "The Hidden King", and "Golden Jubilee Sermon" by their thorough development and interesting style, merit close and attentive reading. The editorials comprise a variety of subjects both timely and well presented.

The Canisius Monthly

"I saw her standing robed in blue and gold,
Her visionary eyes were fixed afar,
As one who muses on a distant star,
And in the silence hears Time's changes told."

Thus begins the dedicatory poem in the February number of this sprightly magazine. Quite an improvement over last year, Canisius! However, for a college boasting an enrollment of more than six hundred, the contents of your magazine are rather meagre. Just one poem and one story! A football story, too, with a plot too common to be interesting. The last two paragraphs, insignificant as they are, might well have been omitted, since the action closes with the words "with the ball two inches over the line." For one fond of Horace, "A Letter to the Sabine Farm" makes very pleasant reading, something that sets us back a couple of years to unsophisticated youth and laborious decipherings of the language of the Roman poet.

The Prospector

From the shadows of Montana's mighty Rockies comes the Prospector to the Valley of sweet-scented blossoms. What most attracted us was the fine discernment of the editorials—indicative as they were of the high literary standard of the North-western quarterly. Almost equal excellence, of a different order, is shown in the quality of the verse, particularly in the "Angelus." But we could find no excuse for "November", away back in the local news. It might appear to better advantage among the more favored literary productions. Among the short stories, "The Withered Hand" sets a pointed moral; while the "Last Big Job" appealed to us because of the surprising turn of events, culminating in a good object lesson. Greatest praise, however, is probably due to "The Sleeping Indian", on account of its picturesqueness of setting and noble, self-sacrificing action. The essays on Newman and the Oxford Movement of today bring back the memory of that great religious struggle which gave to the Church one of its most zealous champions.

Duquense Monthly

Some few weeks ago we had occasion to peruse a review of this interesting monthly from the pen of an ex-man of a college in our immediate vicinity. Forthwith we decided to add our mite of praise or blame. In the February number, we were unable to avoid noticing the imperfect meter and rhythm of "Visions of Lincoln," and we reluctantly came to the conclusion that it had left the borders of the poetical and veered into the prosaic. The struggle for the proper application of the theme to Ireland was only partially successful. In vain did we look elsewhere for another sacrificial offering to the Muse of Poetry. We were compensated somewhat, though, on reading "Bulls, Chiefly Irish." The monotonous "The Morgan Murder Case," though somewhat Victorian in its lengthy enumeration of details, was nevertheless plausible and forceful enough to hold our interest to the end. A word, Pennsylvania. The name of the City of the Golden Gate, written as it should be, in full, is San Francisco.

Peter F. Morettini.

When Coach Bob Harmon placed his first call for baseball candidates upon his favorite bulletin board, he was indeed surprised at the turnout. But nature was against him, for no coach can defeat cold weather, rain and wind.

The following are the games played this season:

California 4. Varsity 3.

This score is an indication of a close game, but from the spectator's point of view the story has no climax. Ken Berg was in his old form, backed up with wonderful support, while the display of enthusiasm from the bleachers as well as the diamond brought back memories of last year's contest. Fog may have its good qualities, but here it was worthless. Of the third inning until the ninth little can be written. In the first inning California scored two runs, due to the three-base hit of Hudson. This failed to dampen the

spirit of the Varsity, and Manelli was leading from third as Bedolla drove the sphere through short, scoring him. Bricca reached home on a sacrifice by Captain Fitzpatrick, while George Hanaberg's single put Bedolla over. This ended the first inning, with a three-two score, but California netted one run in the third and its last in the fourth, due to an error by the Varsity's second baseman.

Ernie Bedolla can remember that his first Varsity game was played on California field, March thirteenth, and that that date had no terrors for him, for out of his four trips to the place, he connected with three hits.

The box score:

	AB	R	H	PO	A	E
Fitzpatrick, 2b	4	0	0	2	2	2
Hanaberg, 3b	5	0	1	0	0	0
Burke, rf.	3	0	1	0	0	0
Krutosik, ss.	4	0	2	2	3	2
Bricca, c.	3	1	1	5	1	0

	AB	R	H	PO	A	E
Manelli, cf.	4	1	0	1	0	0
Hughes, 1b.	4	0	0	8	1	0
Bedolla, lf.	4	1	3	2	0	0
Berg, p.	2	0	0	0	1	0
Garcia, c., 7th	2	0	0	4	0	0
	35	3	8	24	8	4

Umpire—Baumgartner.

Oregon Aggies 2.   Varsity 9.

On the afternoon of March 1 , the Aggies played the first game of their Southern tour on the Varsity field. Father Ricard's sun spots were rather large that day, while an Oregon wind was running the bases, and occasionally sprinting into the bleachers, offering Prof. Mustol and his harmonians stiff competition.

Ken Berg was again in rare form. His heaving from the port side sent the first three web-footers to the bench via the strikeout route, and during the entire game he was master of his position, allowing but one man to reach first on balls, fanning nine, and giving but six easy scattered hits.

The Oregonians are credited with one inning, the second. In this frame they held two bases, given by an error and a walk. It was a two base hit by Hartman that scored these men, and here ended their only opportunity to increase their tally.

The Varsity's runs were well earned by the safest method, hitting the ball. The third inning found the score a tie, with the Aggies warming up every pitcher on the bench. Babb was sent out on the mound to stop the Red and White track practice. He failed, although we must admit that he gave his best. Captain Fitzpatrick started the sixth with a perfect hit over short. Manelli drove into left, while Fitz walked across the plate. When the eighth opened a new pitcher faced Manelli, who reached first on a fielder's choice. Garcia walked, Hughes then scoring Caesar on a hit over second. Herbie stole home from third.

It has been many moons since we have faced such a trim, peppy, and husky baseball team as the Oregon Aggies. Their playing was not that of a College nine, however, and the long trip, with the sudden change of altitude, may have been at fault. The Varsity showed the result of careful coaching since their last game, and the few changes in the lineup were for the better. The box score:

OREGON AGGIES

	AB	R	H	PO	A	E
Hubbard, 3b	4	0	0	1	1	0
Seibert, 2b	2	0	1	0	2	1
Palfrey, 1b	4	0	1	6	0	1
Kramien, rf	2	0	0	0	0	0
Kasberger, ss	4	0	0	2	2	3
Gill, c	4	1	1	12	1	0
Summers, lf	2	1	0	0	0	0
Hartman, cf	4	0	1	2	0	0
Hughes, p	1	0	0	0	1	0
Baker, rf	1	0	0	0	1	0
Keene, lf	2	0	2	0	0	0
Babb, p	1	0	0	1	0	0
Miller, p	2	0	0	0	1	0
Total	33	2	6	24	8	4

SANTA CLARA

	AB	R	H	PO	A	E
Fitzpatrick, 2d	4	2	3	2	2	1
Hanaberg, 3b	3	2	2	2	2	1
Schall, rf	5	1	1	0	1	0
Krutosik, ss	4	0	0	3	2	1
Manelli, cf	5	1	2	1	0	0
Garcia, c	3	1	1	11	0	0
Bedolla, lf	4	1	1	1	1	0
Hughes, 1b	5	1	2	8	0	0
Berg, p	4	0	0	0	3	0
Total	37	9	12	27	11	3

Umpire, O'Mara. Scorer, Argenti

Sacramento 6.   **Varsity 2.**

On March 20, Coach Harmon took his aggregation of ball tossers up to the Capitol city, and here a hard fought game was held with the "Solons", of the Coast league. Rodgers, the skipper of the "Solons" placed his premier port sider, Walter Mails, on the mound and he held the Varsity hitless for the first four innings. Kuntz was the next pitcher in order, and our team found it less difficult to locate the sphere, securing three scattered hits that tallied them two runs. Pecarovich, Bedolla, Krutosik, receiving the credit for the hits that placed Schall and Krutosik across the plate. Mike Pecarovich performed the twirling for the Varsity, and, considering the batting ability of his opponents, he pitched a good game. Coach Bob Harmon was holding Ken Berg in reserve for the second game, but due to the inclemency of the weath-

er, Berg was unable to demonstrate his skill against the Sacramento pennant aspirants.

	1	2	3	4	5	6	7	8	9	R	H	E
Sacramento	2	0	0	1	0	2	1	0	x	6	14	1
Santa Clara	0	0	0	0	0	0	0	2	2	3	2	

Batteries: Sacramento: Mails, Kuntz, Cook. Santa Clara: Pecarovich, Garcia. Umpires: Ludeman, Bacon.

San Jose, Mission League 0. Varsity 4.

The crowd that entered the Varsity field on the afternoon of March 28, was treated to an exciting display of the National pastime. This marked the first of a two game series, and the San Jose nine brought with them a loud support.

Don Burke, the modest young man from the Northwest, took the mound for the Red and White, and, though he pitched to men that for years have played the game, he allowed but six hits, walked none, and was seldom in warm water. Not content with his pitching alone, he secured two long hits and registered one run. His teammates were in good form.

The Varsity placed a deuce upon the scoreboard in the seventh. Although two were down, Burke hit to deep center, reaching second. Capt. Fitz heard a voice in the grandstand and placed a long drive over third. On this hit Burke and Fitzpatrick scored. In the following inning Krutosik and Bedolla scored runs by the clever work of the Varsity in bunting.

```
          1 2 3 4 5 6 7 8 9 R H E
San Jose   0 0 0 0 0 0 0 0 0 6 3
Varsity    0 0 0 0 0 2 2 x 4 9 0
```
Batteries: Cantua and Martinelli; Burke and Garcia.

Time of game: One hour and forty minutes.

Umpire: O'Mara.

San Jose, Mission League 4. Varsity 5.

On April 11, the San Jose aggregation again attempted to even up the series with the Varsity. Elliott started the game, but his arm, which had been slightly injured in sliding, failed to stage a come-back, and the Mission leaguers found opportunity to run up four runs in the first three innings. Ken Berg came to the rescue and gave but four hits in the last six innings.

In the third frame Santa Clara found no trouble in making three runs, but the bulk of the credit must be given to George Haneberg and Dumpy Diaz, whose hits were badly needed.

Both teams then settled down to steady playing and as a result no runs crossed the plate until the eighth inning when the Varsity rallied and led the score, which then remained unchanged. Berg and Diaz brought in the two needed tallies, aided by the hitting of Schall and Manelli.

```
            1 2 3 4 5 6 7 8 9 R H E
San Jose    0 1 3 0 0 0 0 0 4 6 1
Santa Clara 0 0 3 0 0 0 2 0 5 7 4
```
Batteries: Cantua, Flaherty, and Coleman; Elliott, Berg and Garcia.

Umpire: O'Mara.

Olympic Club 4. Varsity 3.

On April 18, the Olympic club came down from San Francisco and nosed the Varsity out in a hard fought game. Throughout the contest, close plays were in order, with heavy hitting the feature of both teams. Capt. Fitz started the fray with a clean single and was scored by Garcia's timely hit. Santa Clara failed to tally again until the fifth when Haneberg and Herbie Garcia made the circuit. The winged O men added three runs to their credit in the fourth frame, and one in the fifth.

The remainder of the game was scoreless. The Varsity attempted to even matters in the seventh with a squeeze play, but Haneberg was tagged at home. Little Herbie Garcia was the star of the game; behind the bat he is ever alert, and his throws to second have nailed many an opponent. His work at bat was good, securing four hits out of five trips to the plate.

The box score:

OLYMPIC CLUB

	AB	R	H	PO	A	E
Maggini, lf	4	1	2	2	1	0
Myers, rf	3	0	1	0	0	0
Perasso, 2b	4	1	1	4	0	0
Varney, ss	4	1	1	1	2	1
Morrissey, 1b	4	1	1	9	0	0
Maloney, 3b	4	0	0	1	4	0
Kennedy, cf	3	0	0	3	0	1
Riordan, c	4	0	1	7	2	0
Madcraft, p	4	0	0	0	4	0
Total	34	4	7	27	13	2

VARSITY

	AB	R	H	PO	A	E
Fitzpatrick, 2b	5	1	1	1	1	1
Haneberg, 3b	4	1	2	0	4	1
Garcia, c	5	1	4	8	0	0
Cochran, rf	4	0	2	0	0	0
Krutosik, ss	4	0	1	4	4	0
Bedolla, rf	3	0	1	2	0	0
Manelli, cf	3	0	0	2	0	0
Hughes, 1b	3	0	0	10	0	0
Pecarovich, p	0	0	0	0	1	0
Burke, p	3	0	0	0	0	0
Total	34	3	11	27	10	2

Umpire: O'Mara. Scorer: Argenti.

Stanford 6	Varsity 2.
Stanford 3.	Varsity 12.
Stanford 2.	Varsity 3.

And thus we have the result of our series with the Cardinal team. Of the two games played on the Stanford diamond we won the second but lost the first. The contest staged on the Varsity field was batting practice to the wearers of the Red and White, as every pitcher on the Stanford list was used in an attempt to stem the tide of runs. They failed however, and two of the homers, made by Haneberg and Manelli shall long be remembered as the longest drives ever seen upon our field. The results of the careful coaching in bunting was seen throughout these contests, while the track practice that was partaken in by every member of the team, greatly assisted the bunters in reaching the keystone sack.

The first game at Stanford on April 24 was pitched by Don Burke, and had good support been given him, the score might have been different, but Spring was bursting forth with all its glory, and a fever was in the veins of the players, while the spectators dozed in the bleachers.

The second contest was thrilling to witness from our viewpoint, but a sad example of the National game on the part of the Cardinal men. Burke again attempted to uphold his reputation as a pitcher, and the score indicated that he knows how to perform on the mound as well as with the bat.

The third battle was played at Stanford. A crowd turned out to witness the last and deciding game of the series, and they were given a good brand of baseball, with but two errors checked against each team. Stanford made two runs in the sixth, while the Varsity tallied one in the fifth, sixth and eighth.

The following are the official baseball averages for this season.

Name.	Games	AB	R	H	Pct.
Garcia	10	32	4	13	407
Fitzpatrick	9	32	8	11	344
Bedolla	11	36	3	10	278
Cochran	6	18	5	5	278
Haneberg	11	40	6	11	271
Pecarovich	3	4	0	1	250
Hughes	10	34	2	8	236
Manelli	10	38	4	8	211
Burke	8	19	4	4	211
Schall	8	28	3	5	179
Diaz	3	12	1	2	167
Berg	6	14	1	0	000
Elliott	4	4	0	0	000
Krutosik	5	19	2	4	212

FIELDING AVERAGES

Name	Chances	Errors	Pct
Bedolla	26	0	1000
Burke	10	0	1000
Pecarovich	7	0	1000
Elliott	4	0	1000
Garcia	66	1	985
Hughes	102	3	971
Diaz	17	1	942
Manelli	27	2	927
Schall	15	2	867
Berg	6	1	834
Fitzpatrick	51	9	824
Krutosik	32	9	844
Cochran	11	2	811
Haneberg	28	7	750

HANDBALL.

When the Rev. Father Murphy offered large cash prizes to the winners of a handball tournament, Jim Needles was swamped with entries, both in the Junior and Senior divisions. The old Gaelic game has its thrills, but few realize this for the obvious reason that they have never enjoyed a close match. The past tournament was played on the elimination basis, and of the sixty teams that entered for the Senior prize, the semi-finals found the Ferrario-Moroney and Abrahamsen-Heaney teams still in the running. Three games were to be played between them, and while the former pair won the first, the latter won the second. The third, and deciding game was one of the most exciting that has ever been witnessed upon the courts of this institution. Fer-rario and Moroney were off to a good start, and at one time had their opponents 16-3. Abrahamsen and Heaney heard someone on the lines shout, "Come on you Engineers!" and they did, winning by a score of 21-19.

In the Junior department thirty teams were entered, and feeling ran high among the various classes. After three weeks of playing, the semi-finals drifted down to Haviside-Hamilton, against Marine-Nolan. The former were in perfect condition, and gained the victory in a few moments after play had commenced. They won their game and the championship of the Junior department, by the score of 21-18.

The success of this tournament was due to the kindness of our esteemed President, Rev. Father Murphy, S. J., and to the labors of one Jim Needles, combined with the willingness of the aspirants to follow the schedule.

TRACK.

The fifth annual Pentathlon was held on Saturday afternoon, April tenth, an ideal day for the runners as well as the spectators.

The track was perfect. Days had been spent by members of the Prep department, under the guidance of Coach Harmon, in putting the cinders in a paramount condition, while the Sophomore engineers demonstrated their skill in shop work, by placing before us a new set of standards, that, from all appearance, will stand the test of time.

Before the clock in the town hall had disturbed the atmosphere with two lonesome rings, the newly erected bleachers were filled with spectators from all parts of Northern California. High up in the thin ether, on the east side of the Scientific building, were Prof. Mustol and his collection of well-known musicians, while upon the track were the various athletes coaxing the stiffness out of their forms.

And then the husky voice of one Alfredo Ferrario announced that the first event was in order. With one parting glance at the display of magnificent cups, amid the strains of the band, the fifty-six track men strolled to the start of the hundred. At the pop of the starter's gun the men were off, and from then until the sun had dropped below the line of the stately "ship", the guests were ever busy watching the track and field events.

To Raymond Schall were given the highest honors of the day. There were many "dark horses" in suits, but Ray was the leader of all. His work in the high jump, the shot-put, and the half mile merited much praise.

100 yards—Bedolla, 10 2-5; Baker, 10 3-5; Palomares, 10 3-5.

High jump—Schall, 5.6; Baker, 5.2; Cochran, 5.2.

Shot put—Schall, 37.8; Manelli, 37.6; Kerchkoff, 37.2.

Broad jump—Baker, 20.4; Bedolla, 19.8; Kerchkoff, 19.3.

Half mile—Muldoon, 2.15; Cochran, 2.19; Rianda, 2.19.

The committee of the day was composed of Coach Harmon, Captain Muldoon, Manager O'Connor, Rev. Father Sullivan, S. J.

The trophy winners and the points made by them:

Schall, 4720.
Baker, 4540.
Bedolla, 4170.
Kerchkoff, 3985.
Cochran, 3950.
Muldoon, 3715.
Rianda, 3500.
Pecarovich, 3425.
Manelli, 2980.
Heaney, 2870.
Needles, 2850.
Halloran, 2845.

SPRING FOOTBALL.

When one stops to think over the past year in Athletics he will doubtless conclude that it was a genuine success. In football we had many obstacles to overcome. We were new at the game, and Rugby had found a home at Santa Clara. But a week after the arrival of Coach Harmon, Rugby was buried with all due respects. Then came the training; a training that was difficult to settle down to, for Rugby ways had never been forgotten. Meeting the best teams in the state is not the wisest policy for an eleven new at the game, but the Red and White has never backed from any aggregation, and its opponents were often surprised that the score stood against them.

Then came basketball. The coach had but few veterans from whom to build his quintet, yet their victories showed what a good coach can accomplish. Track, swimming, handball, tennis, and boxing have all been successful. Spring football was completed but one week ago, and when handshakes are again in vogue, and cork tips are carried in the pockets, when the classroom doors swing open on their rested hinges, the Varsity that is to represent Santa Clara will return from training at Manresa, in perfect physical condition, with an amount of football knowledge and practice that will be sufficient to defeat every team next fall.

Manager O'Connor has at present an incomplete schedule, but with the possible addition of Notre Dame on New Year's day, and a battle with the University of Oregon, the season will be the greatest in the history of the institution.

Sept. 9—Olympic Club, at San Francisco.

Oct. 2—California, at Berkeley.

Oct. 23—Stanford, at Stanford.

Nov. 13—U. S. C., at Los Angeles. (Tent).

Nov. 25—Nevada, at San Francisco.

J. E. Neary.

PREP NOTES.

The preps were handicapped by a lack of games this season, probably because other high school nines did not want to suffer defeat. The only contests staged were with Tamaplais Military Academy and with San Jose High, the former being won by a score of 15 to 5, while the latter went to the visitors, 8 to 6, in seven innings.

Turner, Koch, Florimont, and Regan were the batting stars for our lowly preps, while Kinnison and Lambrosa held undisputed sway in the fielding line. "Hoppy" Mollen did some very fine hurling, striking out fifteen men in two games. Then, too, Captain Carl Koch got a homer off the Tamalpais pitcher; while Carson repeated the performance against the Garden City representatives.

Next year, we hope to see more doing along the prep line of athletics, although the untiring efforts of Father Sullivan and Coach Roesch worked wonders with the high school boys this season in baseball, basketball, and track. As we have often heard coaches say, "The preps are the makings of future Santa Clara Varsities," from the looks of things this year, the Varsity will be a world beater in two or three seasons.

Frank Maloney.

Compliments of **REX THEATER**
ENNO LION, Manager   SANTA CLARA, CAL.

Here is Something That You Should Read ...

And let it make an impression on you. Ready for your inspection are the latest models in this season's suits — suits that accentuate the verile spirit of the day. Dash, vim and vigor are personified in these clothes of quality and merit. . Spend 15 minutes looking over these clever styles. We make a specialty of young men's wearing apparel.

POMEROY BROS.

First Street, corner Post   San Jose, Cal.

...WILLSON'S...

Operating Three Dining Rooms

Cafeteria   Quick Service Grill   Hotel Dining Room

Special Attention to Parties and Banquets

Hotel Montgomery Building
32-34-36 West San Antonio Street

Telephone San Jose 840   SAN JOSE, CAL.

Oberdeener's Pharmacy THE KODAK STORE

College Boys' Headquarters for
Stationery, Fountain Pens, Soaps and Shaving Necessities